CW00969858

HOT CHERRY

The Best of Marcus Armytage

HOT CHERRY

The Best of Marcus Armytage

Illustrated by Peter Curling

Published in 2005 by Highdown,
an imprint of Raceform Ltd
Compton, Newbury, Berkshire, RG20 6NL

Raceform Ltd is a wholly-owned subsidiary of Trinity Mirror plc

Reprinted in 2006

A CIP catalogue record for this book is available from the British Library.

ISBN 1-905156-13-8

Cover designed by Tracey Scarlett
Interiors designed by Fiona Pike

Printed in Great Britain by William Clowes Ltd, Beccles, Suffolk

CONTENTS

ACKNOWLEDGEMENTS

This book would not have been possible without the help, some of it unwitting, of several people. Firstly, the two sports editors during my 12 years at the *Daily Telegraph*, David Welch who was brave enough to take me on in the first place, and Keith Perry who continues David's good work. I would also like to thank Lucy Higginson, editor of the *Horse & Hound*.

The job of sub-editors, it seems to me, is usually to 'sub' out all the good bits. That emphatically hasn't been the case on the *Telegraph*'s racing desk. Knocking my words into intelligible sentences, correcting the spelling and checking the facts for longer than they care to remember have been Adrian Hunt, the racing editor, Kevin Perry, Michael Roberts, Stephen Dillon and Danny Coupland. Likewise, Catherine Austen at the *Horse & Hound*.

As I haven't ever been the best secretary to myself, I relied heavily on Lucy Stanford to take various cuttings, yellowed bits of old newspaper and scrap books of old articles to type them up and save them electronically. It is somewhat surprising she hasn't turned to drink during this time.

Last, but not least, a big thank-you to the many subjects themselves, often for telling stories against themselves and for allowing us to have a bit of fun at their expense. Maybe it is something to do with working with and around horses but I'm not sure any other sport or industry has the capacity to do this in quite the same way.

INTRODUCTION

I once read in an obituary that the recently deceased had a great sense of humour 'but never at anyone else's expense'. They won't, alas, write that of me when I'm gone.

For most of the 12 years that I have been employed as a racing correspondent for the *Daily Telegraph* I have written a weekly column, variously called 'On Saturday" or, when it hasn't appeared on a Saturday (for obvious reasons), the 'Racing Diary'. Latterly I have written once fortnightly for the *Horse & Hound*.

In these columns we have tried to come up with amusing anecdotes from the extremely colourful sport of horseracing. Many of the characters we've come across have not been champions or multiple winners but people who have lived off their wits and, thankfully, their bottomless pit of humour.

If it is stuff on racing's most successful you're looking for then in *Hot Cherry* you're probably looking in the wrong place. Often the stories involve hideous misfortune of which there seems an unending source where horses are concerned and, equally often, it has been politically incorrect … for which we make absolutely no apology. In fact if you're at all sensitive or a crusader for political correctness then I'd advise you to put this book down at once.

The idea behind the *Daily Telegraph* column has always been to lighten up racing for people who might not necessarily be experts or fanatical punters, though hopefully they might have been tickled occasionally. Instead we've tried to draw in people from outside racing and those with just a passing interest so we hope this collection has a wider appeal than your average 100 per cent-proof racing book.

Equally, not everyone (sadly) reads the *Daily Telegraph* and some who do don't get as far as the sports pages, hence the reason for putting together the best (make that least worst) items under one roof for those who may be unfamiliar with them.

Undoubtedly the best things about *Hot Cherry* are the illustrations by Peter Curling, Ireland's foremost equine artist and raconteur. His serious stuff, I might add, is even better than his sketches for this book. We were lucky to get him on board before one of his commissions was sold at a charity auction for two million euros and he got any high-faluting ideas about payment.

Marcus Armytage
July 2005

CHAPTER ONE

HOT CHERRY – BLOWN OUT OF ALL PROPORTION

Anticipating the start

TRAINERS MAY BE SWANNING OFF TO SANTA ANITA and Melbourne with their older horses at this time of year but back at home it is anything but glory. It is business as usual, or in many cases more business than usual. All those yearlings bought at the autumn sales are now coming in to be broken, and across the land brave test pilots are being fired into orbit.

It doesn't need me to tell you that some horses are little dollies to break and others are very difficult, depending on their character, their breeding, how they've been brought up and how well fed they've been for the sales. For last weekend's Champions' day card at Newmarket I stayed with Ed Peate who runs a 'spelling' yard in Dullingham. The bulk of his work at this time of year is breaking yearlings for some of Newmarket's biggest yards.

In the case of the Peates it is like father, like son. Jeffrey Peate, Ed's father, is now retired but used to break in jumpers for people like Toby Balding and Kim Bailey as well as train pointers with great success on the southern circuit. Obviously, as they're older and stronger, jumpers can be worse than yearlings if they want to be difficult. Jeffrey was once sent a horse to break that was proving impossible. Someone else had already had a go at it and failed, and though he had some tough staff at the time, this horse was beginning to damage them. As soon as he'd bucked them off he would have a crack at them on the ground. In short, it was the worst horse Jeffrey had ever been sent. What was really taxing Jeffrey was how he could get this brute used to having a jockey on his back without expending any more staff. Then he had a brainwave: he'd send off for one of those blow-up dolls – which, I'm told, are advertised in the back of gentlemen's magazines – strap her to the back of the horse and, hey presto, job done.

There was great excitement at breakfast in the Peates' Sussex household a few days later when a brown paper parcel arrived containing a neatly folded, completely deflated Hot Cherry complete with round face, wild, expectant eyes and a gaping mouth. Before he could finish his toast and marmalade old Jeffrey was out in the garage searching for the foot pump, and in no time at all Hot Cherry, in all her naked glory, had been enrolled as the newest member of staff.

Penny Peate, Jeffrey's ex-supermodel wife, was slightly ashamed at the sight that arose, phoenix-like, off the floor as her husband furiously pumped his foot up and down, all the while chuckling to himself. It was time, Penny thought, for a little decorum, and before she let Jeffrey take his new lass out to work she dressed her up in jeans and a jumper.

The horse was produced in the lunging ring and Hot Cherry was attached with string, by her knees, to the saddle. That was a great success, and all went well until the horse was encouraged to trot. At this stage, Hot Cherry, legs and arms akimbo, started to lurch back and forth in the breeze. The horse took one look over its shoulder and, horrified – let this be a lesson to any of you girls who go riding eyelashed up to the hilt – jumped out of the lunging ring, galloped through two sets of posts and rails, and headed for the village of Frant. His emotionless jockey, meanwhile, swayed from one impossible angle to another but nonetheless stuck tenaciously to her mount. If she'd been expecting a ride, by God she was getting one.

Which brings us neatly to the local vicar. He was quietly tending his pansies in his front garden when horse and jockey clattered past in the direction of Tunbridge Wells. A doer of good deeds, he thought he should ring his local stable. Penny answered. 'I've just seen one of your horses running away with one of your girls,' said the vicar. 'She looked rather distressed and appeared to be screaming.' If only he'd known.

Of course Hot Cherry, who suffered a couple of unfortunately terminal puncture wounds, was a huge success. After he'd been caught the unscathed horse was completely pooped. His spirit broken, he was ridden around for the rest of the morning like a child's first pony. I'd like to tell you that the horse in question turned out to be Morley Street, but Jeffrey doesn't recall its name and to the best of his knowledge it never made the racecourse.

So, if a million-dollar yearling is proving a bit of a handful, would Ed Peate ever consider employing similar tactics? 'Not for the horses,' he says.

MICK EASTERBY, HORSE DEALER, farmer and racehorse trainer, is enjoying one of his best seasons for years with 40 winners so far. It's training with no frills but lots of thrills.

Easterby, 66, has won over 2,000 races. He trained his first twenty winners in a neighbour's field before the neighbour ever found out, and bought his three most successful Flat horses, Lochnager, Mrs McArdy and Polly Peachum, for £600, £500 and £400 and a saddle respectively. But however much Mick Easterby likes winning races, he prefers a good horse trade. Only the late Arthur Stephenson ever managed to get one over on him. 'He got me tight one day and sold me a blind horse,' recalls Easterby. 'Another time the deal with Arthur was a horse for 50 bicycles – unseen. I thought I couldn't go wrong because the horse was a bad bugger but they were troop bikes with no handlebars, no saddles and no wheels.'

Easterby is a legend. Once, after a few drinks, some farmers bet him a fiver he wouldn't spend the night in a local haunted house. He got there, settled down in his sleeping bag with owls a-hooting and the wind a-howling, and was quietly terrified. He thought he had better see it out though. Then he heard a voice: 'It's only me and thee.' It sent a shudder down his spine. Five minutes later the voice returned: 'It's only me and thee.' This time a horror-struck Easterby replied to the 'ghost', 'As soon as I get my boots on it'll only be thee.'

When Lady Sheriff won the Peugeot 406 Coupe Handicap at Goodwood in July, Easterby was presented with a sponsored car for a year. The bad news for the sponsors is the Sheriff Hutton trainer's record with cars. It took Easterby six years to pass his driving test, and he still isn't the best. He once nearly lost his arm to a lorry while executing a hand-signal which resulted in a large black cross going down on the examiner's clipboard.

For one of his many tests he went to York with a little old Ford in which the passenger seat wasn't bolted to the floor. A surefire way to fail, his sister had told him, was to let the car roll backwards at traffic lights. So as soon as they turned amber he was off like a rocket. But because the passenger seat wasn't bolted down, the examiner ended upside down on the back seat. During the three-point turn, he found himself in Easterby's lap. The examiner, by this time pale and shaking, ordered him back to the test centre.

'Has he passed?' asked another examiner on their return.

'Passed?' said Easterby's examiner. 'The man's a bloody lunatic.'

Another time he was lent a taxi for a month by a local while his own car was being repaired. During that time a neighbour wanted to borrow his boar pig. As Easterby had no other means of transporting the pig, he put him in the back of the taxi. However, after a couple of sharp bends, the pig found his way on to the front seat and sat there for the rest of the trip, beside our trainer. The pig, of course, stunk the car out. Easterby tried to clear the muck out with grass but the smell would not go away. A few days later he returned the car to its rather simple owner.

'Cor, what a stink,' said the taxi driver, whose first passenger, a frail old lady, subsequently asked to get out after two miles.

'Anyone would think you'd had a pig in here,' she said.

THIS IS A BUSY WEEK FOR GAY KINDERSLEY. Tomorrow he will give an address at Fred Winter's memorial service – a daunting task to do the great man justice if ever there was one – and on Thursday he will oversee a big charity lunch at Newbury in aid of Spinal Research. The day culminates in a charity Flat race in which Catherine Dettori, Frankie's better half, will have her first ride in public.

Last week, an extraordinary thing happened to Gay, 74, in Wantage. He had just popped into Waitrose to buy some food and was in the process of paying for it when the little girl at the check-out desk asked him if he'd like some cash back.

'That's really awfully sweet of you. How kind,' said Gay – not a regular in the shops, I think it's fair to say – musing about the benefits of modern shopping and the ability to win cash prizes.

'How much would you like?' she asked.

By this time Gay was in a state of wonderment. Not only was he being asked if he wanted cash, but how much! If he asked for too much they'd think him greedy; too little and it wouldn't really be capitalising on his good fortune. So he hedged his bets.

'Fifty pounds, please,' he replied. 'You know, it really is awfully kind of you.'

With the shopping under one arm and £50 in his pocket he proceeded, as is his wont when in possession of loose change, across the road to Ladbrokes to invest his new-found wealth on the first 10–1 shot he set his eyes upon. It duly romped home.

On leaving the bookie, the state of play was thus: having arrived at Waitrose ostensibly empty-pocketed other than a piece of plastic, he was, just five minutes later, cash liquid to the tune of £500. It really was his lucky day.

Gay, I needn't tell you, is a gentleman of the old school and his first thought was to reward the little girl who had made it all possible, so he went back to Waitrose to seek her out. But there had been a shift change. Gay's memory not being quite what it once was, and with check-out girls all looking pretty much alike, the manager was called and an identity parade was arranged. Eventually the girl responsible was brought down from her tea break to gratefully accept the tip of a tenner. 'Really has been my lucky day,' thought Gay. 'I'll give everyone else on the check-outs a fiver each because I'm sure they'd have done the same.'

End of story? Well, not quite. Yesterday, Gay's credit card statement arrived. His groceries (a pasta meal for two and a punnet of strawberries), he noted, came to £57.35. He's now somewhat clearer about the term 'cash-back'. ▣

ANOTHER JOCKEY – AND I USE THE WORD IN ITS LOOSEST SENSE – joined the long list of those to have ridden a winner for the Queen Mother last week. To Dick Francis, Bill Rees, Dave Dick, David Mould, Terry Biddlecombe, Mick Fitzgerald, Kevin Mooney and numerous other greats, add the name Bobby McEwen.

Bobby who?

Lambourn-based Bobby, 47, is racecourse vet at Royal Ascot, and though his skills with a stethoscope may well have been by royal appointment, it is safe to assume that none of his previous four rides, spanning several decades, was. Last Saturday he steered the Queen Mother's Braes of Mar, a horse he has hunted all season, to success in the VWH Members race at Siddington, near Cirencester. No mean feat for a rider whose only previous win came in a walk-over and who once hit the deck four times in the same race. If that needs some explanation, let's just say the horse refused four times at a fence going away from the horseboxes at Larkhill, each time firing his rider over his head.

Anyway, fortified by a swig of 'jumping mixture', the vet, contrary to starter Peter Walwyn's instructions that he should 'be in front over the first', got there last and, showing all the tactical patience of Paul Carberry, remained tail-end-Charlie for a circuit. This was the perfect waiting race. That is to say, Braes of Mar was just waiting for Bobby's legs and arms to give way. This they did after one circuit, whereupon the sprightly eleven-year-old took off. The Austrian Cavalry (various assorted relations of Barbury Castle owner Konrad Goess-Saurau) tipped up at the fourth-last and, apologising profusely as he passed people – the sort of gentlemanly conduct that disappeared when Siegfried Sassoon hung up his boots – Bobby and Braes of Mar went on to a famous victory at 12–1.

The Queen Mother, we have it on very good authority, was delighted. But she still can't believe that Bobby was the jockey. ■

LAST SUMMER we recorded that the Lambourn trainer Peter Walwyn had his leg trodden on by his hack. An occupational hazard, and nothing particularly outstanding about that – except for the fact that when the wound failed to heal his doctors called up a brace of hungry maggots and, hey presto, the healing process was back on course. In that article, I wrote: 'Walwyn is not accident prone, but when he does injure himself, he does not do it in half measures.' After recent events I feel the first half of that statement is up for review.

Following a bravura pro-hunting performance on *Channel 4 Racing*, and the success of the Countryside Rally, Big Pete returned to the more mundane job of chairing the AGM of his local hunt, the Vine and Craven, in a barn decorated with antique agricultural machinery. At the end of the meeting, Walwyn caught his foot on a chair, fell forward and impaled himself on the handle of an ancient clay-pigeon trap. A case of fox's revenge has scarcely been worse. The trap handle was unscrewed and Walwyn was rushed to Basingstoke General Hospital, where it was removed from his stomach under local anaesthetic. Then, under a general anaesthetic in an operation to gauge the full extent of the damage, his gall bladder was whipped out. He is now recovering in a ward and hopes to be out early next week.

You will know by now that whatever the trail of destruction left in Walwyn's wake, among it there is always some humour to be found. You will also be aware that mobile phones are not allowed in petrol filling stations because, apparently, they can trigger explosions. Well, mobile phones are also banned in hospitals because they can do funny things to the computers that control vital equipment – and I don't mean that trivially, I mean 'vital' as in 'necessary for sustaining life'. Big Pete's first visitor was his wife 'Bonk'. She did not bring flowers or grapes. Oh no. Like any dutiful trainer's wife, she brought a mobile phone and his entry book so that her husband, who was still hooked up to drips and oxygen, could establish contact with the outside world again and continue the smooth running of his training operation (seventeen winners this season to date).

No sooner had he pressed the 'green' button than sirens went off in the hospital, the oxygen supply was cut off to the intensive care department, heart defibrillators started working of their own accord, the lights went out in the operating theatre where a lobotomy had just reached a delicate point, and the elderly patient in the next bed, who had not moved for a week, sat bolt upright in bed as if a miracle had just been wrought. The mobile phone has been confiscated, but until 'early next week' these remain exciting times for Basingstoke General. And you do not have to be Gypsy Rose Lee to see an early discharge on the horizon. Get well soon. ▪

A BACHELOR FRIEND WHOSE MAIN HOBBIES ARE HUNTING AND RACING has two questions he asks when 'interviewing' a female to test potential compatibility. The first is 'What time do hounds meet?', and the second is 'Can you explain a handicap chase?'

In Paris for the Prix de L'Arc de Triomphe, his friends primed a delightful but completely incompatible Texan girl with the answers. Having shown no interest in her all weekend he dropped the hound question into conversation at dinner on Sunday night after the race. 'The hounds usually meet at eleven,' she replied on cue. Well, his pupils turned heart-shaped, his ticker picked up a couple of gears, and the rubber-suctioned tip of Cupid's arrow was firmly planted on his forehead.

However, you try explaining the intricacies of handicap chasing to anyone, let alone a Texan. It's a bit like explaining Iraq to George Bush. Regarding the girl in a completely different light now, and on the cusp of true love, he turned the subject to steeplechasing and delivered the question. Given the right reply it would probably have been followed by a proposal of marriage, but after fumbling around with the word 'weight' for a while, the object of his new-found love delivered her reply. 'It's a race,' she said, 'for disabled horses.'

His search for a wife continues. ▪

IT IS NOT EVERY DAY you can say you've scooped *Which?* magazine, but, my goodness, they love this sort of thing.

It is a long but extraordinary story so bear with me while we go back to last January, when Jim Wordsworth, boss of Anglo Hibernian – a leading bloodstock insurance service – and all-round good egg, was invited by Mary Philipson, along with several other Newmarket worthies, to to go shooting at Lofts Hall Stud. A productive bag and enjoyable day was had by all, until it came to the last drive, which was a duck flight. In the gathering gloom as the duck began to fly off the pond where the guns were stood at the ready, Jim, a deadly shot, plucked from the skies what for all the world looked like a run-of-the-mill common or garden mallard but on retrieval turned out to have snow-white plumage. Much to his embarrassment, it was the prize pet duck belonging to his hostess.

Afterwards there was a lot of leg-pulling, and Jim was forgiven. He thought nothing more of the incident, but Andrew Bedford's loader, a practical joker, carefully placed the dead white duck under the bonnet of Jim's car. The idea was that the duck would slowly cook there, then gradually go off before causing a bit of a smell, at which point Jim would notice, open the bonnet and the joke would become apparent. The duck would have come back to haunt him, as it were. For one reason or another, probably the cold weather, the duck never did go off. It just sort of petrified there on the engine.

Now fast forward ten months to this October. The same guests reconvene at Lofts Hall and they recall the pet white duck incident. 'Notice any funny smells in your car this summer, Jim?' they enquire with wide grins. 'Find any ducks under the bonnet?'

'Er, no,' Jim replies, thinking they were two damn odd questions. Then they tell him of their prank.

I should point out at this stage that Jim is one of those people for whom cars don't do it. They are purely the most practical means of getting from A to B. Oil? Where's that go? He's one of those for whom knowledge of where to put the fuel, a simple choice of petrol or diesel, is all you need.

On opening the bonnet, there, to collective astonishment, spread out in all its glory, is the white, now crispy, duck, feathers unruffled and still attached to the skeleton. You could not miss it.

But it was not the duck that bothered Jim. A week before he had taken the car for its annual service, and sitting on his desk was a bill for said service for £620. It was beyond his comprehension how his car could be serviced with a 'mature white duck sitting on top of the engine' and for it not to be noticed. Is Jim alone in being interested to know how a reputable garage can do a full service without lifting the bonnet? A Christmas Day truce between client and garage looks unlikely. ■

A LITTLE BIT OF RACING HISTORY, a local legend and a man with all the attributes of one of this column's heroes – and more – retires at the end of this month. John Bosley, great amateur rider of his era and long-time small trainer in Oxfordshire, hands over his yard to his son, the about-to-be-retired jockey Martin, on 1 February 1997.

Bosley, 66, had his first ride, for Bruce Hobbs, as a fifteen-year-old in 1945 when Lingfield was an overnight journey from his home near Didcot and when paper-thin, chin-strapless cork helmets saved only your hair from getting ruffled when you fell.

He trained his first winner as a permit-holder at Hereford in 1966 when David Elsworth, riding the runner-up, unsuccessfully objected. Bosley achieved the notable double-double of not only breeding and training the winning horse but also the jockey – on more than one occasion. Among other things, he also taught Richard Dunwoody how to use a dandy-brush (an art the jockey has now long forgotten) by giving him his first job in racing.

A generous party-giver, Bosley once (within the last decade) as a form of entertainment jumped his hunter over the wall into the garden where all the guests were, and at Christmas he would take his young lads carol-singing round the pubs of Bampton – on horseback – which was one of the most alcoholically productive first lots ever to have taken place. For some time he also held the course record at Liverpool's Adelphi Hotel for a descent of the stairs on a silver tray – a popular eve-of-Grand National entertainment for jockeys in the old days.

And as a civilian, Bosley succeeded where the Russians failed. At the height of the Cold War he put an end to noisy military manoeuvres one night at Brize Norton (his farm used to back on to the runway) by taking his shotgun and shooting the bulb out of a searchlight so that he and his horses, two of whom were running the next day, could go back to sleep. Instead of getting a medal for accuracy, he narrowly escaped a 'stretch of porridge'. 'I could see the cells from where I was sitting at court,' recalls the man who became something of a *cause célèbre* at the time.

As an amateur, though, Bosley, whose father was a butcher, farmer and bookmaker (as opposed to butcher, baker and candlestick maker), was in his time second only to the great Lord Mildmay. The highlight of his 97 winners was victory in the 1954 Aintree Foxhunters' over the original National course (when there were no aprons on the fences and you could go white-water rafting in the brook under Becher's) on Dark Stranger, whom he had been asked to ride only the night before. 'I said I couldn't ride it because I had just started farming at Bampton,' recalls Bosley, 'and I was due to start drilling spring barley for the very first time on my own land that day. It was an important day in the farming career of John Bosley. When I told this to Len Colville, the trainer, he told me I'd got my priorities wrong.'

Bosley had never sat on Dark Stranger, who the week before had turned over in a point-to-point, but the rider knew he was in the habit of getting left at the start so he asked the assistant starter to give him a couple of cracks round the hocks with a 'Long Tom' when they set off. That he did. Dark Stranger was first out of the gate (for a change) and went on to win by four lengths.

Aintree was also the scene of two of his training highlights, although he was a permit-holder at the time. Eyecatcher was sent to him to qualify for point-to-points but he liked her so much he bought her. She won seven races and finished third in two Grand Nationals, behind Rag Trade and Red Rum. Eyecatcher's legs weren't great and Bosley used to take her (and a large cigar) down to stand in a stream as a form of therapy. He reckoned by the time he had smoked the cigar she had been standing there long enough. When he couldn't go, so the story goes, he'd send Martin, then aged nine, to the same stream with the same-sized cigar.

In the breeding department, Bosley was successful with a mare called Diamond Talk, who bred Corn Street (winner of twelve races), Pusey Street (nine) and Bridge Street Lady (three). All the 'Streets' were named after garages run by their owner. On one occasion, Corn Street and Pusey Street won on consecutive days at Ascot.

Two years ago, Bosley sold his farm and moved the yard to Kingston Lisle, which is where Martin and his wife Sarah, one of our better lady amateurs on the Flat, will take over. Martin, who will inherit the training of two of Eyecatcher's grandchildren, will retire from the saddle some time in mid-January. 'I'll go to the races and I won't necessarily have to go out on a winner,' he says, wisely, otherwise his riding career might overlap his training career by a year or two. 'If I come home having enjoyed a good day, that'll be it.' ▣

IN BRITISH RACING there's only one father prouder of his son's exploits than Peader McCoy and that is Gay Kindersley, former amateur rider and trainer, a steward at Newbury and a legendary singer of ballads.

His son Rory is clearly a chip off the old block. Earlier this week he took to the field at St John's, Antigua, for the final Test match – with the England cricket team, but without his clothes. He was last seen, via satellite television, running naked across the outfield pursued by a posse of burly policemen.

Gay wasn't watching at the time but was telephoned with the good news. 'We haven't spoken to Rory since,' he said yesterday, 'but we only hope it's true.' ■

TOM JENKS RETURNS TO THE SADDLE ON MONDAY after falling foul of the Jockey Club's 'totting up' procedure for his collection of whip bans.

'What are you going to do about your whip problem?' asked the Disciplinary Committee, expecting the reply to contain at least two mentions of the 'air-cushioned whip' and one of correcting his over-arm action. Knowing he was facing a three-week 'holiday', Jenks replied, 'Go skiing, sir.'

He did as well, but he is now having tutorials on whip use from Peter Scudamore, which should do the trick. He'll be able to hit them harder and more often but without getting caught. ■

IT HAS BEEN A WEEK OF RETIREMENTS. David Bridgwater and Francis Woods, Cheltenham specialists from either side of the Irish Sea, have both accepted medical advice telling them to hang up their boots when both might have reckoned that but for injury they had a good few years left.

Bridgwater's elbow problem stems from a complicated fracture, the result of the opposite of what he's having to do now – being hung up by his boots – after being brought down on Time Won't Wait at Aintree on Grand National day last year. If only the IRA had issued their bomb warning about half an hour earlier, he would still be riding. However, time did refuse to wait, and despite a couple of returns to the saddle, the problem remains.

Almost teetotal, except for the day in 1994 when he rode Earth Summit to win the Scottish National and Corrouge to win the Scottish Champion Hurdle for Nigel Twiston-Davies – it is one of the trainer's rules that his jockey celebrate victory and commiserate with the losers with a drink – Bridgy seems, three days into it, to have taken to retirement well. His wife Lucy told me not to ring before 8.30 because he would still be in bed. His idea of a good night out, much to the regret of his colleagues, is chasing rabbits with his two whippets and a torch. When they used to come in to work tired and hung over, Bridgy would come in just tired, having been out most of the night.

After leaving school he worked for Lester Piggott before joining the 'brat pack' at David Nicholson's yard. You'll remember from a previous column how a few jockeys, when driving to the races with the Duke, used to ring the great man from the back of the car on the mobile before hanging up. They would do it so often that eventually the Duke would order a new phone. When Bridgy was driving, the Duke would invariably nod off. The joke was to keep waking him by braking extra hard at every available opportunity so that the Duke ended up not only awake, but on the floor.

Bridgy came to prominence when he won the 1991 County Hurdle at Cheltenham on Winnie the Witch. Last year, he rode his fifth Festival winner on Flyer's Nap in the National Hunt Handicap Chase. In between he spent a season with Martin Pipe, where the trainer's obsession with a stopwatch – 'to the extent that he would time how long it took for the kettle to boil' – was a constant source of amusement. What appeared a marriage made in heaven, though, ended in a quickie divorce and Bridgy's career never really got going again.

Francis Woods' injured shoulder is the result of clearing a hedge – something he's done all his life on a horse but never, before last summer, in his car. As he found out, cars don't land quite as well as horses. Winner of the Queen Mother Champion Chase on Klairon Davis, Woods also won two Irish Nationals. Unlike Bridgy he has no intention of training and it would be a great surprise if he didn't end up with a decent job within racing. ■

AT WORCESTER LAST SATURDAY a jockey returned unplaced having completely disregarded his trainer's advice. He had made the running and ground to a halt turning into the straight. The jockey, however, showed that rare quality among his breed by putting his hands up and instead of coming out with some long-winded excuse admitted that he had made an error.

'I suppose,' he said to the trainer, putting things into perspective, 'with Nato mistaking the Chinese embassy in Kabul for an arms dump my ride wasn't quite the biggest tactical disaster of the day.'

'Clearly,' replied his disgruntled trainer, 'you and Nato both suffer from a lack of intelligence.' ■

PHONSIE O'BRIEN WAS ONCE IN AMERICA looking at a horse to buy on behalf of his brother Vincent. The horse in question was trained by the great Woody Stephens, who was an equally adept salesman. After firing every question in the book at the trainer, Phonsie wanted to know if the colt was a good doer.

'Does he eat?' he asked.

'Eat?' said Stephens. 'He's the eatenest horse I ever had.' ■

STATEMENTS ON RACECOURSE PUBLIC ADDRESS SYSTEMS tend to be a bit limited. These days we're pretty much restricted to 'Could a trainer or his representative come to the weighing room' (if, soon afterwards, you see the trainer dodging his way to the car park then you know he's required for an inquiry of the non-triers variety) or occasionally 'Could the parents of a lost child please collect it' (usually intoned as 'do anything with the little brat providing you get it out of our office'). But as the runners circled the paddock before the first at Newmarket on Wednesday we were treated to the following novel request: 'Could the pilot of the plane that's been left in the car park please remove it.' ■

PERTH MAY HAVE LOST ITS THREE-DAY SPRING FESTIVAL to the waterlogged state of the ground but it has not lost its sense of humour – quite.

The racecourse has been inundated all week with people wishing to know about the prospects of racing, so much so that even its chairman, David Whitaker (whose wife Fiona owned the National winner

Lucius), was roped in to man the phones.

'Hello, Perth sub-aqua club,' he answered to one enquiry.

'Oh, I'm terribly sorry, I thought it was the racecourse,' said one polite caller before putting the phone down. ■

ROGER CHARLTON HAS ENDURED A QUIET SPELL WITH HIS HORSES, but the week's evidence suggests they are back in form just in the nick of time for Royal Ascot. Not so with other aspects of the trainer's life. Between first and second lot on Tuesday, Charlton's car was stolen from outside his front door at Beckhampton by a particularly benevolent thief.

Unlike most members of his trade, this thief left a replacement, albeit a somewhat downmarket one, in the shape of a white pick-up van. Our thief really went beyond the call of duty though by also leaving a cheque for £1,000, an address book full of women's telephone numbers and a load of sand in the back.

In case you see Charlton's car parked through the window of your local jeweller's, it's a blue Subaru Legacy, registration R263XKM, and it has a sticker on the back advertising Kevin Williams – Newmarket's 'Mr Fixit' for cars. The white pick-up was nicked from Wiltshire the day before so, alas, we won't be seeing the royal trainer and his wife Clare arriving at Ascot in it.

Car theft, the Charltons may like to know, is not just restricted to trainers in the vicinity of Swindon. Bloodstock agent Anthony Stroud experienced an even more audacious theft when his BMW was stolen from under his nose at an Essex petrol station. It was just a couple of days after he had ceased to be Sheikh Mohammed's racing manager. Talk about your luck being out …

Unsure of what to do next, he rang his old office.

'It's Anthony here,' he said.

'Sorry,' said a receptionist who had slightly misheard him, 'Anthony doesn't work here any more.' And with that she put down the phone.

Next he rang his ex-girlfriend to explain. 'Anthony,' she said before putting the phone down, 'you're wearing long trousers now. Sort it out yourself.'

The car was found three months later by an eagle-eyed policeman. Although the registration plates had been altered and the CDs changed from 'easy listening' to 'gangsta rap', this particular thief had made a schoolboy error by leaving the fox mascot on the bonnet. 'Ah,' the policeman had thought, his suspicion suitably aroused, 'a foxhunting Rastafarian. Now that's just too good to be true.'

I WAS RECENTLY BEST MAN AT THE DORSET WEDDING OF A FRIEND who had met and courted his bride in the hunting field – always a good test to see how the potential spouse goes when mounted. As the country where this great romance took place was the Duke of Buccleuch's in the Borders the newly weds could probably claim to be the last couple to meet and get hitched as a direct result of foxhunting in Scotland.

The hunting field is a great meeting place for like-minded people – Dateline on horseback, as it were. As the bride's stepfather John

Rawlins, who has just taken on the onerous role of joint-master with the Blackmore and Sparkford Vale, pointed out in his speech, it is criminal for the government to be contemplating banning hunting. 'How would decent and right-minded people find their twin souls?' he asked. 'And, for that matter, how are the less decent and wrong-minded going to find their mistresses?'

Having taught the groom, James Denne, to ride horses in his early twenties while we studied at the Royal Agricultural College in Cirencester, and having, in the opinion of some noted judges, completely failed in this task, I thought I'd be up there among the favourites for the position of worst man and, at best, a seat in the back pew. In the early days James's learning concerned being 'trotted off' with and once he was run away with, only coming to a halt when the snowdrift he had aimed for proved deeper than his horse.

But it was out of my hands when he began his brief but incident-packed race-riding career. During that time he became a titan of the tartan turf and single-handedly reduced the jockeys' average ratio of one fall in every thirteen rides to one in two. Never had such a short career – four rides – been so eventful, and the regularity of his visits to Kelso Infirmary was such that they issued him with their first loyalty card. He was regularly seen out hunting wearing a leather harness to keep his shoulder from dislocating – a device last used by Siegfried Sassoon on his return from the Great War. The only trouble with the harness is that it reduces your ability to balance on top of a horse, and when you have precious little of that commodity anyway . . .

Even his finest hour wasn't totally straightforward. His mount, Cruise Home, had trailed in a distant second of two finishers – that's last in my book – in the Buccleuch Members race at Friars Haugh. The first past the post, however, weighed in 5lb light, and in controversial circumstances and amid scenes of near-riot, the clerk of the scales objected to the winner and James was awarded the race.

Off the course he improved enough to ride out for some of the greats of British racing, though they've all – with the exception of Clive Storey, which doesn't bode well for him – either retired or died since.

Without question – and this is where you might recognise the name and face – his greatest moment was the thunder-stealing interview of all time at the 1997 Bomb Scare Grand National which was won by Lord Gyllene. He upstaged not only the horse, but also the horse's owner Sir Stanley Clarke, his trainer Steve Brookshaw, the jockey Tony Dobbin and even the IRA who'd delayed the race by two days.

On the Saturday when the race had to be postponed because of the bomb scare, James had been staying at the Brookshaws' dog-sitting. On the Monday when the race was re-run they had given him a lift in the lorry to the races. As Lord Gyllene strode clear up the run-in, a BBC TV camera picking up connections in the owners' and trainers' stand picked out James as he yelled the horse home. James was invited into the winner's enclosure afterwards by Mrs Brookshaw, and a sharp-eyed producer saw that he was the very man whose contorted expressions they'd caught so well in close up on camera. Sir Stanley Clarke had barely begun his interview with Des Lynam when he was rudely shoved to one side and Des, receiving instructions in his earpiece from his producer, thrust the microphone under James's chin.

'Who are you?' he asked, expecting an answer along the line of owner's son, trainer or even a hastily changed jockey.

'I'm an estate agent from Shrewsbury who should be at work,' said James, who then went on at considerable length to Des and ten million viewers about his crucial role as dog-sitter to the Brookshaws and how, when it came to Grand Nationals, he'd been there, done it and got the T-shirt, having been involved with the Mr Frisk team of 1990.

The next day the tabloid press, unable to get to grips with the name Denne, reported on the antics of, variously, a Mr Henne, a Mr Dean and 'the mad punter without a penny on'.

The consequences of this interview were far-reaching. Soon afterwards James was recognised in Marks & Spencer in Shrewsbury. Unable to handle his new-found fame, he returned to Scotland to take up a job with Knight Frank. Des Lynam, interestingly, moved to ITV, who had no sport at the time; his career is only now back in recovery mode thanks to the current World Cup. At one stage it looked like his only regular employment would be on *Blankety Blank*. Lord Gyllene was eventually taken away from Steve Brookshaw – the first National winner I've ever known to be removed from the winning trainer – and the IRA immediately handed in their weapons and started embracing the 'love not war' hippy ideals of the sixties.

Long live hunting in Scotland to keep James Denne out of trouble elsewhere. ▣

YOU HAVE TO HAND IT TO THOSE AUSSIES. They beat us at almost everything, and if they don't play it then they know how to watch it. Bank holidays here mark saints' days, resurrections and, every 25 years, a jubilee. Down Under, a two-mile staying handicap, the Melbourne Cup, warrants a day off for the whole nation, except its barmen. What would they do if they ran a half-decent race in Australia? Run out of beer, presumably.

Apart from the big occasions, Australia is also famous for its little country meetings, and last week 5,000 racegoers soberly celebrated the tenth anniversary of the 'new-look' Bong Bong Picnic Races at Bowral. 'So?' I hear you saying. Well, it also marked the anniversary of the last 'old-look' Bong Bong Races, when 35,000 turned up and, in the words of the local MP, made 'a Roman orgy look like a Sunday picnic'.

Tales of the 1885 Bong Bong Picnic are not something you'll find in *Ascot: The History* and are now the stuff of legend. Open fornication, urinating through car windows, the pelting of the race commentator (is that why Jim McGrath came to Britain?) and the sort of practical joke they used to play at the agricultural college I attended – putting a girl in a Portaloo and rolling it down a hill. Imagine a Borgia family reunion coinciding with a St Trinian's outing at Cartmel races on August Bank Holiday and you start to get the picture.

It was too much even for the Australian Jockey Club, which revoked Bong Bong's once-yearly race licence until 1992, when it limited the crowd to 5,000 members and their guests. Typical of the new-style racegoer, according to the *Sydney Morning Herald*, is a clearly sensitive Sydney lawyer. 'Quality is not the right word for the racing here,' he said. 'Horses are either winners at country tracks years ago or young horses who are at the crossroads of making it or going to the glue factory.'

Last week, the only reminder of the occasion's great sporting past came when the $15,000 Bong Bong Cup went to a filly called Shagney Miss.

CHAPTER TWO

BEFORE THEY WERE INFLATED

Bumping and boring

NEWMARKET'S NEWEST TRAINER IS CALIFORNIA DREAMIN'. Well, he is and he isn't. Robert Cowell, much like Newmarket's other prodigal son Jeremy Noseda, is back after training for a couple of years on the west coast of America – and glad to be here. He officially started the latest phase of his career at his father's Bottisham Heath Stud when a combined trainer's licence plopped through the letterbox on Thursday.

Cowell, 28, is that rare thing according to my sister – a good-looking trainer. That, apparently, is good news for Britain's female racegoers whose fantasies only ever seem to be stirred at Christmas when François Doumen arrives from France for the King George VI Chase. Unlike most other British trainers, Cowell has appeared on *Baywatch* (for a full three seconds) and annoyingly looks a little like Tom Cruise, a sometime Hollywood actor. At school he was also selected to run for the national cross-country team. So he has, as it were, the tracksuit.

Cowell first came to this column's attention when he got up on stage at a dance and gave 350 people, including me, a mean rendition of the hit 'California Dreamin''. 'All the leaves are brown, and the sky is grey/I've been on a walk, on a winter's day.' The opening lines were probably written by a Californian visiting Newmarket at this time of year. His curriculum vitae for training is as impressive as you can get, though that, of course, is no guarantee of success. He had school holiday stints with David Nicholson, learnt how to use a pitchfork and dandy-brush with Gavin Pritchard-Gordon and how to graft during a year with Jack Berry, and spent another two years in France with John Hammond, where he rode out Suave Dancer as a two-year-old. 'As soon as the horse showed a sign of life, my backside was removed from his back,' recalls Cowell. From Hammond he went to Neil Drysdale, at Hollywood Park, where A. P. Indy was one of two Breeders' Cup winners in the trainer's care. After two years – believing, by his own admission, that he knew it all – he started to train and did well with a small number of horses. To get his business on a sounder commercial footing he has now returned home, where he knows more people and therefore more potential owners. He is, according to Gavin, as hard-working as he is charming.

So you've got the background. He'll have about a dozen horses, a few of which will run on the all-weather this winter, but it was in France as an amateur rider that he excelled as far as this column is concerned. He was nicknamed 'Stopper' by Hammond because no matter how in-the-purple a horse was bred, no matter how small the track and no matter how short-priced a certainty his mount was, he usually returned home to Chantilly beaten.

One day at Montier-en-Der he was due to ride a good thing. 'Stopper, not even you can get this beat,' were Hammond's last words. Victory was, he insisted, obligatory.

The track, by a river (presumably the Der), was so rural that the race was to be started by flag. As the starter raised it, there was a huge splash behind the lined-up field, and into the Der slipped the odds-on favourite and our hero. The horse, owned by Cheveley Park Stud, climbed up the vertical bank and Stopper, drifting rapidly downstream, had to be rescued by dinghy (cue David Hasselhoff). After a suitable delay, while Stopper was turned upside down to rid his boots of water before being remounted, they set off. Stopper, whose mount could, as it turned out, swim faster than the opposition could gallop, duly hacked up by six lengths despite his weighing in 10kg heavier than he had weighed out. Apart from there being no killer jellyfish in the Der, like all *Baywatch* plots it had a satisfactory ending.

ONE OF THE SUCCESS STORIES OF THE FLAT SEASON IS GARY MOORE. As we go into Royal Ascot – where he runs No Extras, Chewit and Supply and Demand – his 29 winners stand him in fifth place, numerically, in the trainers' table.

Success on this scale had been brewing for some time before he went home to Brighton to take over from his dad, Charlie, back in January after a four-year training stint in Epsom. This is the welcome fruit of hard work, a great, grafting family and 4.30 mornings. Moore, 40, rode 150 winners as a jump jockey. He was one of the few who ever rode longer than Luke Harvey and was to Fontwell what Ray Goldstein was to Plumpton. Remember Amrullah, the twelve-year-old novice chaser and perennial loser? Well, Gary was the other half of the Amrullah partnership. 'I rode him about 300 times,' he recalls before qualifying the statement: 'Without success.'

Moore's arrival in racecourse car parks was usually accompanied by a screech of brakes and a flustered run for the weighing room. Late again, he once took what he describes as 'a few liberties' (driving up the pavement) on the way to Fontwell one day. When he came to weigh out, he was greeted not only by the clerk of the scales but by a policeman. On another trip to Fontwell, when he was struggling with his weight, he persuaded his father to drop him in Arundel and he ran the rest of the way. 'I was so knackered I had to walk the last half-mile, but the filly won.'

On another occasion, his tardiness and weight problem combined to produce a suitably nasty outcome. Roger Rowell was giving him a lift in his Porsche to Stratford. At the outset of the journey, Moore had taken a 'pee pill', but they were so late for their race that they could not afford to stop. The car lacked a watertight container, and after he had tried putting his head out of the sun-roof and doing it out of the window (a manoeuvre Rowell eventually persuaded him not to persist with), Moore found an empty cigar container which, as you can imagine, held about a fifth of his bladder capacity. This is a family column so I'm not going to go into details, but have you ever tried stopping mid-flow? What a character-building trip that must have been.

Moore retired no more battered than your average jump jockey, he says. However, at Plumpton one day he had his face rearranged by a flying hoof and lost five of his front teeth. That evening, his mum and dad came to see him in hospital. Lorna Moore, who had come straight from feeding the horses (she still does the feeding), was in her wellingtons and waited outside the room. When Charlie emerged, she wasn't there.

'Have you seen someone in wellingtons?' he asked a nurse.

'Yes,' she replied. 'She's on the operating table.'

'Why's that?' asked Charlie.

'She passed out and is having her ear stitched,' said the nurse.

Those teeth played merry hell with Gary for the rest of his riding career. He had five sets of dentures before finding some that fitted, and without them post-race discussions always involved a certain amount of dribble. One of the great weighing-room practical jokes of all time involved the swapping of his denture wash, in which he placed his teeth while riding, for Colman's English mustard.

It isn't just numerically that Moore is proving a success now. The horses he trains are considerably better than the ones he rode day in, day out. Ray Goldstein recalls a foggy day at Folkestone when they were both riding big, half-fit 'boats' that had never run. Keen to know what sort of rides they were in for, Goldstein suggested that as the fog was so bad they pop a hurdle going to the start. Moore's refused and Goldstein's ran out. ■

IF THE REPORTS ARE TO BE BELIEVED, there is only one thing more stressful than being an Exmoor stag with a pack of hounds at your heels, and that's training racehorses. On Tuesday, one of the latest recruits to the profession, Hughie Morrison, saddles the first big runner of his career when his 1,000 Guineas hope Dame Laura lines up for the Nell Gwyn Stakes at Newmarket.

Outwardly, rookie trainers look pretty chilled out, but my goodness they can sweat up under their rugs. If you take a blood test and measure Hughie's stress hormones on Tuesday afternoon, then the National Trust will have to ban the trainers of racehorses from their land. Too cruel to put people under such pressure, they will say. When you have had as few runners has Hughie has (four), you get stressed out about little things, such as arriving at the races on time and the saddle staying on. It even prompted some wise advice this week from Derby-winning trainer William Haggas. 'The trouble with you young trainers,' said Haggas, who at 36 is the same age as Morrison, 'is that you get to the races two hours too early.'

Most of us know more about the filly than the trainer, who true to form arrived at Nottingham at 12.30 yesterday – just in the nick of time to saddle Bellow in the 4.10. Dame Laura was trained by Paul Cole last season, and Morrison, who assisted him at the time, is a part-owner. She was second in the Queen Mary at Royal Ascot but went on to finish two lengths second to Reams of Verse, who is now third-favourite for the first Classic. *Raceform* describes Dame Laura as 'a real trier'.

The Honourable Hughie – his grandfather was given the title of Lord Margadale in 1964 after serving as MP for Salisbury for twenty years – says, 'Though he won't remember telling me this, I once asked Henry Cecil how I should go about becoming a trainer. He said I should do something else first.' Morrison, who has a degree in business management, took that advice by the scruff of the neck. For more than a decade he worked in the manufacturing industry. 'Anyone who has run a lighting business in Manchester in the depths of the recession can cope with stress,' he says of his grounding. The Morrison rise to the ranks of trainer looks something like this: nearly rusticated from Eton for being caught at Windsor races; arrested, aged seventeen, for being drunk in charge of a bicycle in London (the bike was on its side but he was still pedalling furiously); and point-to-point jockey who fell off with alarming regularity in between riding five winners. Later, presumably on the strength of the above (a keen interest in racing and drinking), he was made a local steward at Newbury.

Morrison got more serious about the actual training side of the business when he joined Paul Cole as an amateur assistant last season. At the end of it he swapped his house in Lambourn for Summerdown, the yard Simon Sherwood built in East Ilsley, and press-ganged most of his relations, even the godparents of his children, into ownership. He started the season with fourteen horses. Morrison's first runner, Tayovullin – named after a beach on Islay where his family have an estate – recorded his first success last week, on the sand at Southwell (which slightly takes the gloss off the occasion). So, apart from the stable's hack having a heart attack the moment it heard Morrison had been granted a licence to train, things have got off to a flying start.

As for Dame Laura, 'She's well enough,' says Morrison. 'She carries very little weight and doesn't eat a lot so we have to tread carefully. She's working all right rather than spectacularly.' ■

NORMALLY, THE NAMES OF HORSES, not riders, provide commentators with a headache. We are a fairly simple sort whose main players are no more exotically Christian-named than Mark, Richard, Mick or Adrian. Or so it seemed until conditional jockey Xavier Aizpuru rode his first winner back in December. Since then, 'Whatsisname' has rather swiftly ridden nine more and is looking forward to his first Festival ride, in the Coral Cup, on Linton Rocks.

Having one unpronounceable name is one thing; having two is another. In that respect, late-developing Xavier, 22, has scored a double whammy over the commentators' box. 'Both my parents are Spanish,' he says, 'but have lived here forty years.' His father, from San Sebastian, is landlord of the Horse and Groom at Bourton-on-the-Hill, near Cheltenham, and it was through David Nicholson's bringing owners to the pub that Xavier was introduced to the sport. He started riding out for the 'Duke' at the age of nine, joined him full-time on leaving school and had his first (unsuccessful) rides for him last year. In the summer, Xavier joined Robin Dickin in the hope that it would give him more chances. It clearly has.

So, is Aizpuru jump racing's first bilingual (other than Gaelic and English, and not many people understand their English) jockey? 'Sorry to disappoint you,' he says, again without a hint of pidgin.

According to Warren Marston – who last week lost his job (with Jenny Pitman) and his three front teeth (to a hoof sandwich) but this week gained another job (with Mark Pitman) and three replica teeth on a plate – Xav, pronounced in the Cotswolds as 'Shav', has attitude and a touch of the Jeff Kings about him. 'We were riding out in a blizzard at the Duke's one day,' recalls Marston, 'the coldest day in history, and we were all balaclava'd up. The Duke was standing by the gate of Jackdaw's Castle asking each member of the string if their horse was all right after their two canters. "All right?" he'd ask. "Yup" was the reply all down the line until he got to Shav. "All right?" he asked. "Yes," said Xav. "Fan-f***ing-tastic. Why don't we canter up again?"' The Duke's response, so the story goes, made the blizzard seem like a summer breeze. ■

LAST WINTER, WHEN JOHNNY PORTMAN, who had just been granted his trainer's licence, emerged from the Jockey Club into the London square named after him, he was greeted by half a dozen camera crews. Such fame, and so soon. Alas for Johnny, 33, his visit had coincided with the news of the arrest of several jockeys. Last weekend at Cheltenham, however, the cameras were there for Johnny when he sent out the tail-swishing, reformed 'character' King of Sparta to win his fourth consecutive chase.

My first question to anyone just embarking on a career training horses is simple: Why? 'I don't know why,' Johnny says, shaking his head. 'If your nearest and dearest tell you not to run under a bus, you don't do it. But if they tell you not to train, you promptly go and do it.' So last spring, he and his future wife Sophie set out on the rocky road to financial ruin, physical breakdown and mental torment by leasing Hamilton Stables in Compton, Berkshire.

Physical breakdown was very nearly achieved during a midsummer staff crisis. 'I had no intention of letting Sophie anywhere near the yard when we started,' he says. 'However, she was keen to prove she was capable. The next thing, she's riding out my best horse. There were, of course, one or two teething problems which led me to comment at our wedding that Sophie never knew when to stop loving, when to stop giving, when to stop caring or when to stop at the end of the gallop.' Six weeks into the staff crisis, Johnny dislocated his shoulder while unloading a yearling. Apart from putting the wife to work, he was rescued to some degree by jockey Andy David, who took it upon himself to drive down from Cardiff to ride out three times a week. Johnny reflects, 'I kept reassuring myself that things could be worse.'

Things immediately got better, though. His first winner came in a two-year-old fillies' seller on the all-weather at Wolverhampton. 'I'd hate people to think I missed it because we set off too late,' he recalls, 'but we met every traffic jam going and there was a pile-up outside the track. Not wanting to lose her in the auction, I got out of the car and ran. A policewoman sent me the wrong way and I couldn't find anyone in Wolverhampton who could speak English to ask the way. I eventually got there as she was being led in and it transpired that Sophie, who had stayed in the car, had got there in time to see the race.'

When Johnny bought King of Sparta for £13,000 he did so despite being advised against it. He then turned 'Sparky' out for a break, and when he got the firm-ground specialist in we immediately had the wettest autumn in twentieth-century history. I thought Johnny was doomed. Of course, there is nothing like a horse to make an idiot of you, but three of his wins have come on ground the soft side of good. Tactically, he has gone from only hitting the front in the last few yards to making almost all at Cheltenham, and I anticipate Johnny being sent every 'dog' in the country to sweeten up.

'Sophie and I are quits now,' says Johnny. 'She's watched the wedding video 170 times, and I've watched the Cheltenham video the same number.' ▣

PETER WEBBON, the Jockey Club's chief veterinary adviser, came across very well at Cheltenham's Centenary Conference last Monday. In a world increasingly dominated by bunny-huggers, he realises more than anyone else in the sport that National Hunt racing's survival for another 100 years depends largely on public perception of the racehorse's welfare. Pro-active and far-sighted, he is just the man to ensure that racehorse welfare in Britain is the very best in the world. The role of chief veterinary adviser is, it seems, going to be increasingly important in the next few years.

Webbon, 50, was appointed to the job in July 1996. His greatest achievement so far is the introduction of microchips. As from 1999 all thoroughbred foals will have to be microchipped for identification purposes. At the moment there is scope for mix-ups at the sales, and in years to come, when it has filtered through the system, it will have huge welfare benefits too, particularly for retired racehorses.

So much for the job; what of the man himself? Webbon, from a family of farmers and butchers, was a student at the Royal Veterinary College in London and returned there as senior lecturer in equine medicine and director of the college's hospital. His first contact with the racing industry came when he was awarded a Levy Board research scholarship, for which he studied horse tendon injuries. In practice, however, he cut his teeth as a vet for a circus. One of his first jobs was to castrate a black panther between performances because it was becoming aggressive towards its trainer. Did it make a difference, I naively asked? 'It does to most people,' he replied. His best patient was a performing horse which he had to treat for set-fast (muscular cramp). One of its tricks was to lie down and get up on command. When he suggested to the horse's trainer that it needed a rest, she told the horse to lie down and didn't give it the command to get up again for 24 hours.

His most worrying case was a safari-park lion with toothache. 'While I was dealing with it, one of the keepers was meant to keep an eye on the rest of the pride,' recalls the vet. 'When, after a while, I looked up, the keeper was engrossed in what I was doing and behind him was a semi-circle of lions all licking their lips.' The racing industry should be a doddle after that. ▨

MANY TRAINERS' DOGS would sooner take a chunk out of a journalist's backside than greet him with a grin, so it was quite comforting to be met with a lick by Lily, James Fanshawe's white husky – until the trainer pointed out that her last port of call was probably buffet breakfast from the muck heap. His other husky, Puffa, is a singular dog (she has one eye and one hip). Bored waiting all her life for the winter snows to arrive in Newmarket, she took up hunting. She became quite proficient at it and once killed all of John Gosden's guinea-pigs. Following the headline 'Killer Dog on Loose' in the *Newmarket Journal*, which put the wind up all law-abiding guinea-pig owners, Fanshawe put up a deer fence around his Pegasus Stables to keep the dogs in.

Fanshawe, 37, is having, numerically, his best season, with 50 winners, if you include two in France. It's the first time he has hit a half-century and he has five runners today, including Almond Rock in the Cambridgeshire and Arctic Owl in the Jockey Club Cup. Given his present form, it will be no surprise if one or more wins. Fanshawe is the world's thinnest trainer. Facing south and viewed from the east he is invisible. His skeletal figure could be a prop from *The Addams Family*. At Stowe School he was in the same economics class as Michael Bell (clearly, neither learnt anything because they both ended up as trainers), and during the holidays he rode out for David Nicholson (the Duke's wife Dinah is his aunt). He was at Josh Gifford's for the year in which Aldaniti won the National and was with Michael Stoute for seven years.

It was there one morning that Michael Dickinson, taking copious notes before taking over at Manton, was late in for breakfast.

'What held you up?' said Stoute.

'Ah,' said Dickinson in that considered way of his, 'I've been watching the world's greatest trainer [meaning Stoute] in action.'

'What, so you've just come back from Warren Place [Henry Cecil's yard] have you?' interjected Fanshawe, while John Ferguson, now Godolphin's bloodstock agent but then the other Stoute assistant, choked on his cornflakes. Stoute has only just forgiven Fanshawe.

It was also while he was at Stoute's that Fanshawe broke his neck in a point-to-point fall. He spent a fortnight in hospital and the following eight weeks wearing a halo (that is two months more than any other trainer has ever been seen under a halo). He recuperated at home in the Cotswolds walking the dogs. One day, when a mile from home, he got caught in a thunderstorm. 'I had visions,' he recalls, 'of being a mobile lightning conductor and my parents finding a pile of bones on a patch of scorched earth.'

He started training in 1990, having bought Pegasus Stables, the yard built by Fred Archer. 'I was one of the last assistants to inherit good owners,' says Fanshawe, as unassuming as he is thin. 'Michael encouraged them to send me horses. You can't blame trainers now, but everyone wants to hang on to all the horses they can.' Success was instant. He won the Solario Stakes, both divisions of the Westley Maiden at Newmarket (one of them with Environment Friend), and the Horris Hill Stakes. The next year, he won the Dante, Eclipse and Gordon Stakes while Royal Gait won that winter's Champion Hurdle. Expectations became too high; then the horses didn't run with much consistency, and he lost 20 horses when Sheikh Mohammed cut back. 'I became a miserable git and people started avoiding me,' says the trainer. 'My winter job was to make sure I wasn't miserable. I don't know whether the turning point was having a child or whether it was moving the portrait of Fred Archer from the loo to the sitting room (I'm quite superstitious like that). Fred must be a lot happier where he is now. Since we moved it, the horses have been in great form and I'm really enjoying it again.'

So there you have it, the key to training: if you're having a bad run, check out the site of the portraits. But at Pegasus it is a little spookier than that. Because they say (cue hairs rising on the back of your neck) that Fred's still around. 'The lads say they see him from time to time,' says the trainer. 'The older we get the more whisky we drink and the more ghosts we see. The lads tend to see him on a Friday night.' When the lads called him up on the ouija board, Fred told them to back Unblest the following day (he won at 6–4), where his grave was and where he committed suicide. Sounds like we could all do with a benevolent ghost. ■

SPONSORS DON'T REALLY GET A RUN FOR THEIR MONEY IN THIS DIARY, but then again not many of them are former trainers like Lee Amaitis, chief executive of Cantor Fitzgerald International. Today they have coughed up not just once but twice at Ascot for the Long Walk Hurdle and the 'nervous' chase. With Lee at the helm – his most recent share acquisition is in a two-year-old with Michael Bell at Newmarket – they should be called 'Canter Fitzgerald'.

The son of a coalminer, he is living the American dream having risen up through the Wall Street ranks. The only financial blip in his curriculum vitae is the ten years he spent in racing between 1967 and 1977 as a trainer and then racing official at Penn National racecourse. There's hope, then, for Jamie Osborne to become rich eventually, but it requires his giving up training, er, before his first runner, and going into the City. Most British trainers are famous for their lack of commercial sense, so much so that a week spent learning accounting is now mandatory for a licence. Until recently most of them believed 'budget' was somewhere they hired cars when they arrived at Dublin airport on horse-shopping trips.

The way things have panned out it was a great decision to quit training, I suggested to Lee. 'Well, not necessarily,' he replied. 'I almost regret it every day. I enjoyed the animals but not the commercial aspect. I was a claiming trainer, training for people in the finance business – a bit like myself now. I couldn't quite crack the blue-blood circuit and one thing led to another.'

His greatest claim to fame as a trainer was as the man who nearly discovered Steve Cauthen – in much the same way as people who sat in orchards and had apples hit them on the head before Isaac Newton nearly discovered gravity. Lenny Goodman, a friend of Lee's, was agent to the great Braulio Baeza, the man who shot to fame here by riding a masterful race on Roberto to inflict the only defeat Brigadier Gerard ever suffered, in the 1972 Benson and Hedges Gold Cup at York. Baeza was about to make a comeback after a spell out with weight problems and Lee had just the horse for him to make it a winning comeback. But at the last minute the jockey cried off.

'Tell you what,' said Goodman to Lee, 'I've got a young bug-boy [apprentice] from Kentucky who is meant to be very good.'

'Listen, Lenny,' replied Lee, 'I've got people gambling on this horse. I can't put up a bug-boy.'

When the bug-boy did ride Franglais, in a six-horse race at 9–1 on, he was such a certainty that all he had to do was stay on board for the horse to win. With hindsight, anyone could have ridden it. As luck would have it Franglais stumbled out of the stalls and the bug-boy was unseated. The bug-boy, for whom it would have been a first winner in New York, turned out to be Steve Cauthen. ◙

ONE OF THE MORE PLEASING ASPECTS OF THE LAST COUPLE OF SEASONS has been the emergence of the likeable Tom George as a National Hunt trainer. It is quite possible that the improving Tremallt, named after an Irish village and something of a misfit with other trainers, will give him his biggest winner so far in today's Rehearsal Chase at Chepstow.

I always wonder in the column whether to call the subjects by their first name or their surname, and usually, quite incorrectly, end up doing both, randomly. However, I suppose in this instance – Tom or George – I can't really go wrong. Both sound pretty matey. Home patch for him is Slad in Gloucestershire, the valley made famous by Laurie Lee in the book *Cider with Rosie.*

Venetia Williams may disagree, but establishing oneself as a trainer can be a long, drawn-out process. Tom, 32, started in 1993 with three horses; now, six years on, he has 35 in full training including horses for high-profile owners Stan Clarke and Brian Kilpatrick. Before that he had an eight-year apprenticeship with Arthur Moore, Michael Jarvis, Gavin Pritchard-Gordon, François Doumen and Martin Pipe. It was while working for the latter that Tom informed his friends of how well he was getting on with the maestro. Soon after that, one of those friends plucked up the courage to ask Pipe how Tom George, whom he had been led to believe was a vital cog in the Wellington wheel, was getting on. 'Tom who?' replied a mystified Pipe. 'Yes,' admits Tom, 'I learnt how to sweep leaves there.'

He also had a brief career as an amateur rider. He never rode a winner, and the height of his achievement came in the Aintree Foxhunters'. His mount took an instant dislike to the place and after cat-jumping the fifth and ploughing through the sixth he refused at the seventh, catapulting himself into the ditch and his rider on to the fence, uninjured. Finding himself on what was effectively a giant mounting block, Tom hopped back on his horse and walked towards the gate at the side of the ditch to get out. He was, however, engrossed in watching the continuing race, which was by this stage somewhere between Becher's and the Canal Turn. The gate was duly opened by a fence attendant, but so distracted was Tom that he failed to see a crossbar above the gate, and as he and horse exited it gloriously swept him off the back of his mount. To come off your horse once in a race is to be expected, but twice? That's really sporting.

Doumen had a rule that no one greased the feet of a horse for two days after it had been shod. I'd never heard of this one before and Tom certainly hadn't either, but according to Doumen oil lubricates the nails and the shoes come off a lot easier. There is, I concede, a certain logic to it, but I still think it's a bit extreme. Anyway, as a new boy unaware of the rule, Tom greased a horse's feet. Doumen became mildly hysterical, as only Frenchmen can, and scolded his new and apparently useless pupil with a lecture that Tom swears went on for an hour.

That afternoon, Tom took the same horse out for a pick of grass in the paddock. It had a bit of a frolic and when it had stopped mucking around Tom noticed that not just one shoe had fallen off but two of them had. 'It was just too much of a coincidence,' he recalls. 'I'm sure he undid the clinches on those shoes just to prove a point. The trouble is he still remembers it to this day, and if we meet at the races he mentions little else.' ◘

IT IS A WELL-TRODDEN PATH – well-swum if you're going to be pedantic – from the Emerald Isle to Lambourn or nearby Faringdon, where there appears to be an enclave of Irish jockeys. The latest to undertake that journey is David Casey, who has replaced Jamie Osborne as stable jockey to Oliver Sherwood and who rides Him of Praise in the Tote Becher Chase at Aintree tomorrow.

Waterford-born Casey, 23, is a product of the Irish Apprentice School. After that he spent two seasons with Tony Redmond. When Redmond retired, Casey moved on to Michael Hourigan – which he describes as 'an experience' – for a year. For the last five years he has been with Willie Mullins, and by last year he had graduated to the position where he shared the rides there with Ruby Walsh. He first caught the eye here when riding She's Our Mare to win the Swinton Hurdle at the end of last season, but it was Charlie Swan who put Sherwood on to him. 'I've been patient for the first time in my life,' says Sherwood of the pair's quiet start to the season, 'and most of my horses have needed a run, which hasn't really helped David.'

The big decision for anyone moving to a new country is where to live. For Irish jockeys coming to Lambourn it is a question of who to lodge with until you're established enough to afford your own house. There is a good network of fellow countrymen willing to take in the new boys for a while. Able to ride at 9st 7lb with ease, an obvious factor in Casey's choice of digs was the standard of catering. 'I started off with Norman Williamson but his cooking wasn't quite up to scratch so I had to look elsewhere,' says the jockey, who rode a winner at Warwick on Thursday. 'So then I moved in with Tony McCoy – where I am now – and that is worse, a total disaster. There is no cooking because he is always wasting.' Williamson is a great admirer of Casey's artistry in the saddle, but not his palate. 'He wouldn't know what good food was,' says Norm. 'I do all the cooking round here and I swear by it. Casey would only be used to Burger Kings and KFCs.' Like Williamson's cooking, I think we'll leave that little argument to simmer for a while.

Casey has also filled the right-back spot for the Commitments (jockeys) FC with just that, commitment. Judging by the way he keeps coming out of 50–50 tackles with the ball, I wouldn't want to sneak up his inner too often on a racecourse.

IT IS BECOMING SOMETHING OF A TRADITION at this time of year for an Australian to slip quietly – if, indeed, that is possible for an Australian – into the country with one of the biggest expense accounts you've ever seen and start wining and dining our trainers in the hope that they will enter a few horses for the Melbourne Cup. Entries for the 'race that stops a nation' (after the 1993 Grand National, were we the 'nation that stops a race'?) close on 28 July.

The man selected for this onerous task used to be little – a word I use in a relative sense – Les Benton. Last year, you'll remember, he found himself canoeing up one of the more polluted tributaries of the Snowy River without a paddle when he encouraged two British horses, Taufan's Melody and Yorkshire, to come for races for which they weren't strictly qualified. Some of his countrymen reacted as if they'd been scratched by a koala – with surprise and annoyance – when Taufan's Melody landed the Caulfield Cup. Benton is now running the Emirates Racing Association for Sheikh Mohammed, and one thing I can guarantee is that the Dubai World Cup will never again be contested, as it was this year, by as few as eight runners.

His replacement ambassador from Racing Victoria is the ex-Aussie Rules footballer Greg Nichols. If Nichols wanted you to enter a horse in the Melbourne Cup I wouldn't have thought a paid-for lunch as an inducement was necessary. At 6ft 4in and a fine exponent of the game that seems to have inspired some of the more violent scenes in *Mad Max*, his handshake alone should be enough.

Aussie Rules – a cultures amalgam of rugby, Gaelic football and wrestling – was designed in the last century to keep cricketers amused during the winter. Nichols, now 41, played as a semi-pro for Geelong before he was 'cut' in the late 1970s for being too semi and not enough pro. Now, that is quite an achievement for a player from Geelong, a team which over the past three decades has been the metaphorical winners of the FA Cup for, in Nichols' words, 'social antics and bedside manner'. He even played alongside the great but aloof John Newman, the George Best of Aussie Rules. 'There was a great team spirit,' recalls Nichols dryly, 'and we were a very cohesive unit. We were playing Melbourne and there was another player having his first game. Two minutes before kick-off Newman, who had no tolerance of ordinary folk, went up to the new player. "Well, sonny," he said, "what's your name?" That's how cohesive we were.' Nichols admits his playing career is best summed up by a pre-season friendly against Darwin when he, the equivalent of a centre-forward, chalked up only one goal while a defender scored twice.

He has since become a successful businessman, and worked as a racing administrator in South Australia before replacing little Les. 'There won't be the same guarantees about horses getting in races this year,' Greg points out. 'But I can guarantee a fantastic time for the connections. We welcome Pommie invaders.' ■

IF THE GOD OF RACING WERE A GOOD BLOKE he would ensure that Wednesday's Coronation Stakes at Royal Ascot goes to a farmer's son from Devon. Victory for Golden Silca would be just reward for her jockey Steven Drowne, and for Mick Channon for putting him up when the temptation must have been to hire a jockey who rides in Classics at least on an annual basis.

Drowne, 27, is at Bath today, and believe me, the *Telegraph*'s sub-editors were tempted to headline this story 'Jockey Drowne's in Bath'. He may have ridden 68 fewer winners than Pat Eddery at the royal meeting but he is no stranger to that hallowed winners' enclosure. He's already won the big one there – actually, make that the long one – by steering Sea Freedom to success for Toby Balding in the 1997 Ascot Stakes. This season he has had a flying start with 18 winners. Thanks to Richard Quinn's first opting to ride a runaway French filly at Newmarket, then opting to go to Italy instead of the Curragh and, for Wednesday, getting banned, 'The Wonderful Steven' has already partnered Golden Silca in the English and Irish Guineas. In the latter, he was a neck away from having his greatest moment when she just failed to nail Hula Angel.

Flat jockeys come and go, but few have ever earned a 'wonderful' prefix from Toby Balding's wife Caro. Toby says, 'You can safely say he's the only one. Steven is a straightforward, hard-working, beautifully mannered product of the Racing School. He's a good schooling jockey too. I think he'd ride over hurdles – and it might happen – but while he's trying to do 8st 11lb on a daily basis we don't let thoughts like that enter his head. He reminds me of Bill Elliot who used to ride for me when I first started.' Toby then had to remind me who Bill Elliot was.

A journeyman jockey like Steven also encounters more dodgy horses in a week than a Dettori in a season. Steven was at the start at Nottingham one day. His mount had just turned over and laid on him for the second time. The rider was lying there, uninjured but contemplating what injury he could fake, when a partially sighted 90-year-old man who had been walking his dog came over to him. 'I wouldn't get back on that one if I was you,' he advised. 'I thought,' recalls Steven, 'if a blind old man can spot a nasty one, then so can I. I limped off the track and refused to ride it.'

This is a busy time for The Wonderful Steven. Yesterday he started his day in Newmarket with riding work, drove to York for two rides, and then down, through all that traffic, to Chepstow for a couple more before going back to his Hungerford home and wife Clare. She works for OJOCS, the national jockeys' booking agency. 'It comes to something when your wife knows where you're going before you do,' he says.

Such a demanding schedule needs a few lighter moments. At Yarmouth, for instance, Steven and his mates rubbed tiger balm into Gary Bardwell's Y-fronts while he was out riding a race. It was the sort of practical joke that spawned the phrase 'hot pants'. Despite his colleagues humming the Jerry Lee Lewis hit 'Great Balls of Fire' on the way home, Bardwell didn't so much as shift awkwardly in his seat. 'We were going to do it to Seb Sanders,' said Steven, 'but no one dared touch his pants.' ▩

NEXT WEEK COULD BE MOMENTOUS in the life of one London medical student. As it stands, Mark Bradburne, a fourth-year physiotherapy undergraduate at King's College, will ride former Grand National winner Rough Quest in Thursday's Martell Foxhunters' and, hopefully, a future National winner, Blue Charm, in Aintree's big one.

Not only will the pair be Scotland's finest, they will be Scotland's only. Blue Charm is trained at Cupar, Fife, by Mark's mum Sue, and as such will carry the weight of Scottish housewives' pound notes from Gretna Green to John O'Groats. The nine-year-old, twice a winner over Aintree's tiddlers – so he clearly loves Liverpool – would be only the second Scottish winner (Rubstic was the other in 1979, though Freddie and Wyndburgh were both heroically second twice apiece) were he to triumph on Saturday. He has the credentials: the speed to win over two and a half miles, and the stamina to win over three-plus.

Mark, 22, has ridden 40 winners so far in an amateur career interrupted by four years of lectures and practicals in central London. When other amateurs have been cutting each other up around Plumpton, Mark has been doing it for real, dissecting ex-humans on a hospital slab. As a former student at the Royal Agricultural College at Cirencester who tried to combine further education with riding, I can sympathise. You always hear of medical and veterinary students having fun with body parts, like the vets who were reputed to have walked into a Chinese restaurant one evening, slapped down two dead cats on the counter and, before scarpering, announced that the restaurant would receive no more until the last batch had been paid for. Any such pranks at King's College? 'Some students in Scotland put a hand in a postbox with the fingers sticking out,' says Mark. 'After a murder inquiry had been instigated there was a big fuss, so I think we have to be fairly careful about that sort of thing now.' A hand with the fingers pointing out strategically placed in the kitbag of Joe Tizzard on National morning could sort out one quietly fancied rival, I'd have thought.

Mark went into physiotherapy with the intention of ending up looking after injured horses, which is where the money is. 'I actually quite like the human side now,' he says, not surprisingly, after pointing out that there are seven females to every male on the course and many of their practicals involve stripping down to their smalls and groping each other. Would working on injured jockeys as a 'flying physio' appeal? 'I think the jockeys would prefer a female hand, if you know what I mean,' he says. Not sure I do.

Student life isn't always conducive to fitness, unless of course you're in the Boat Race. Is Mark fit enough to give it his all next week? 'My principal mode of transport in London is the bicycle,' he points out, 'although my last four have been stolen. So I've been running around Kensington Gardens. Aintree should be a doddle compared to avoiding rollerbladers.'

AS A GENERAL RULE OF THUMB great jockeys don't make great trainers. Fred Winter was perhaps the exception. Without being disrespectful to his prowess in the saddle, if you take Martin Pipe as an example, you could argue that the worse the jockey the better the trainer.

In the north, two former jockeys, Dandy Nicholls and Richard Fahey, are turning out to be much better trainers. Joining them as a force to be reckoned with is Kevin Ryan, who two years after taking out a licence has made a stunning start. Not only has the Tipperary-born Kevin, who employs the wily former jockey Mark Birch as his assistant, sent out 27 winners from Hambleton Lodge near Thirsk this season, he can also pronounce Amamackemmush, his Musselburgh second earlier this week. It means, he says, 'I'm a Sunderland supporter', though he is not clear if it is in Gaelic, Geordie or Azerbaijani. On Thursday, neither of his runners in the Group One Nunthorpe Stakes, Easter Purple and Manobier, was disgraced. He's getting the numbers, and as sure as Monday follows Sunday the quality won't be long in coming.

His riding career was not distinguished. Kevin, 33, rode a grand total of 47 winners. Although he rode the useful Humberside Lady in her dotage, the names of his other mounts don't spring readily to mind. His main claim to riding fame occurred during a handicap hurdle at Newcastle when he suffered two falls in as many minutes. He was at the back of a 24-runner field when Richard Fahey, nearer the thick of the action, fell. Every horse proceeded to gallop over him with the exception of Kevin's, which galloped broadside into Fahey's mount as it got to its feet. As sod's law often decrees, Fahey walked away without a scratch while Kevin, who had the softer fall, was left clutching a broken arm. To get from the hurdle to the ambulance the stretcher bearers had to negotiate a steep bank, and that is where Kevin unceremoniously slid to the turf for the second time in as many minutes. ▣

THERE IS, BELIEVE IT OR NOT, a tiny village in Tipperary called Horse and Jockey. Naturally it consists of a pub of the same name and a few houses, a bit like our own Elephant and Castle, albeit without the tube station. However, unlike Elephant and Castle, if you are born in

Horse and Jockey there is a strong chance that, depending on the number of legs you arrive with, you'll be either one or the other.

Jimmy FitzGerald, a jockey before he became a trainer, was born there, and racing's latest prodigy Jamie Spencer hails from said village. In fact, he owns a good deal of it. By my reckoning – and I could possibly be wrong on this – the last farmer to make a significant name for himself in the saddle of anything but a tractor was Dick Saunders, who won the Grand National on Grittar. Jamie has already clocked up 77 winners this season and now fills Frankie Dettori's boots as stable jockey to Luca Cumani. He has caught Aidan O'Brien's eye sufficiently to have ridden Freud in the Dewhurst, and in a fortnight he will have his first Breeders' Cup spin on Arkadian Hero. Jamie's career really took off, though, when Barney Curley took a shine to him.

On a horse, Jamie is anything but agricultural. Colleagues say he's so bright that he's good for at least £250,000 in *Who Wants to Be a Millionaire?* Like any number of Irish horsemen he has an impeccable pedigree for racing. His father, George, who died seven years ago, trained the one-eyed Winning Fair to win the 1963 Champion Hurdle under Alan Lillingston, who returned the favour by getting Jamie the job as an apprentice with Liam Browne. Jamie now lets the yard to Edward O'Grady and 200 acres to a local farmer, but one day might slip into the green wellies himself.

Apart from horsemanship – he's had twenty rides over hurdles – what puts him above other twenty-year-olds is a cool head for the big occasion. Pulling up, having beaten Kinane a short head, he'd be just as likely to turn round to him and say, 'Mick, you losing your touch?'

Jamie's two passions in life are sleeping and hunting. He recently declined a day cubbing with Paul Carberry. Why? 'Well, he'd be sure to try and get me buried and I don't think it would have gone down too well with the boss if I'd missed the Breeders' Cup through injury.' See, told you he was bright. ◈

RACING HAS A NEW, albeit slightly chaotic messiah in its training ranks. Having delivered us a treble at Uttoxeter last week, a Newbury winner the day after and one at Southwell yesterday, Tom George is a man whose horses are in such form that I paid a visit earlier this week on the off chance that something would rub off on me. Even his friends, who used to ring him up when they'd had a bad day because they knew Tom would have had a worse one for one reason or another, are wary about picking up the phone for a comfort call now.

Slad, home of the late Laurie Lee, is like an Alpine village in that no two houses are on the same level, and steep banks, as we know, are ideal for training jumpers.

'I don't know if you ever read *Cider with Rose*,' said Tom, pointing to a field, 'but that's where Laurie Lee had it away with Rosie.'

Tom is enjoying a fine season. Tremallt won the Charisma Gold Cup, and High Mood, who has been winning in the north because he wasn't thought capable of winning south of Sedgefield, was so relieved that he didn't have to undergo a six-hour road journey that he ran away with a handicap chase at Newbury, despite the less-than-optimistic aside from Tom beforehand: 'I wouldn't want to ride mine in this.' He explained, 'When I started six years ago, High Mood was the first horse I bought. I sold him to my best friend as a juvenile hurdler. He wasn't the most precocious, because he's just coming to himself now, aged ten.'

Tom knows that in this game, just to stand still you have to go forward – if you know what I mean. So while the horse markets of Ireland, France and New Zealand have been plundered by every other Tom, Dick and Minty, he and a vet with contacts took off to Warsaw for a weekend recently. The highlight of the trip was a bout of female mud-wrestling – it's about all Chepstow will be good for today – but Tom returned with Cobbet and Corletto, top lots at the sale. They sound like an ice-cream manufacturer but are, in fact, a Czech-bred four-year-old and Polish-bred three-year-old, both off the Flat.

Each one set him back roughly £6,000, but as horses go they look cheap. They are not bad sorts either, and seem to have taken the move from Nissen hut at the desperately flat Warsaw racecourse to a Cotswold barn overlooking a steep, wooded valley without the slightest sign of vertigo. When Tom finds owners for them, Warsaw's mud-wrestling emporium will get a better idea whether it should expect more visits from Slad. Of course, Tom already has some prominent owners, including Brian Kilpatrick. The first time Kilpatrick visited the yard, he went with the trainer to the top of the gallop.

'What's the main difference between you and Martin Pipe?' asked Kilpatrick.

'Well,' said Tom, launching into the usual marketing overdrive, 'excellent facilities, miles of riding, wonderful views, et cetera, et cetera.'

'No,' said Kilpatrick. 'The main difference is that you charge more than he does.'

I, for one, think it's worth it. ◼

IT IS ONE THING when the horse (Katarino) that you (Nicky Henderson) think has a half chance of upsetting Istabraq in the Champion Hurdle gets beaten in its Festival trial (the National Spirit Hurdle at Fontwell last Tuesday), but it is quite another when it is beaten by a horse (Male-Ana-Mou) trained by someone (Jamie Poulton) who in two years' employment with you never really progressed beyond mucking out. I should think Henderson put something rather stronger (VSOP) than milk on his cornflakes the following morning.

Lewes-based Jamie, 34, has, after four years with a dual-purpose licence, finally struck gold – much to his regret. If only it had happened during his stint as a gold miner in Sierra Leone, how different things might have been. Nevertheless, Male-Ana-Mou, one of the jumpers in his predominantly Flat yard, now heads for Cheltenham as third-favourite behind Monsignor for the Royal & SunAlliance Hurdle.

It always seemed likely that Jamie (not to be confused with his brother Julian, who is in the same business) would end up training, which he now does on his wife's family farm – the same spot from where Shannon Lass was trained to win the 1902 Grand National. But not before exhausting a few other, shall we say 'alternative' avenues first.

After leaving school he worked on a marine salvage boat as a diving tender without once, he says, (in descending order of importance) getting seasick, losing a diver or sending one out with an empty bottle of oxygen. Then came Africa, where he and a geologist did find deposits of the shiny stuff, though they were too deep down for the Poulton bucket, spade and gold pan. In fact, they were so deep down that they would have required the combined digging equipment of six mining conglomerates to get it out. Nice try all the same. A long-haired phase followed during which his mother, quite rightly, refused to be seen with him in the paddock at point-to-points. He spent his time selling pop records, buying returns from record companies and selling them on to market traders (Eastenders rather than City).

His smooth sales patter soon earned him the nickname 'Geeza' at Henderson's. There, though, his biggest claim to fame was that he and Eddie Hales – now training in Ireland – had to look after See You Then on his regular lad Glynn Foster's weekends off. See You Then took Jaws as his role model. Make no mistake, it was a life-threatening task: if you dozed off, you could end up with a severe maiming. 'It was a two-man job,' he recalls. 'One of us would make faces and distract the horse while the other crept in, did his water and fed him.'

Poulton's career as a rider began with him getting unseated at the first fence in a point-to-point and never really progressed significantly from that point on, though he was placed a few times. Four years ago, his uncompetitive riding career came to an end when he broke three vertebrae and his coccyx on a horse of his own which he was schooling.

His training is gradually gaining momentum, and that is reflected not so much in horses like Male-Ana-Mou but in the state of his horseboxes. When he started it took his twenty-year-old Bedford TK roughly six hours to crank its way to Wolverhampton from Lewes. His new lorry does a steady 70mph and makes the journey in half the time. 'I'm not sure whether to look back on the old lorry with great affection or try to forget it,' he says. The latter option is suggested. ■

WHILE THE CAREERS OF SOME NEW TRAINERS are announced with a fanfare of trumpets, psalms sung by choirs of angels and impossible expectations, Ralph Beckett has slipped quietly and successfully into the role. As he is following Peter Walwyn at Windsor

House in Lambourn, there is only one man with any expectations of him – his bank manager.

Yorkshire-born Beckett, 28, has the pedigree. His uncle bred 1,000 Guineas winner Mrs McArdy, his grandfather owned Cheltenham Gold Cup winner Fortina, and his cousin Teddy manages Khalid Abdulla's horses. I'm not sure why he hasn't already had a box-load of bluebloods from Juddmonte Farms, though I guess it is just a matter of time. But with three winners so far from fifteen runners, all those games periods spent in the bookmaker's while at Marlborough College are increasingly looking like time well spent. Waterloo may have been won on the playing fields of Eton, but Bath's 3.30 last Monday was largely masterminded in a smoke-filled dive in Marlborough.

Ralph (pronounced 'Rafe' – the 'l' is like a Nigel Twiston-Davies television interview: silent) methodically went through a *Who's Who* of trainers to gain experience: Colin Hayes in Australia, Jimmy FitzGerald, Arthur Moore in Ireland, Tommy Skiffington in America, Martin Pipe, David Loder, and last but not least, three and a half years with Big Pete. It was Jimmy Fitz who did more than most to knock him into some sort of shape, and he was the first to congratulate Beckett after Malleus won at York last week. Following Beckett's fourth point-to-point ride, in which he had been pile-driven into the ground again, FitzGerald took him to one side. 'Listen, Ralph,' he said wisely, 'there's more chance of you becoming a dustman than a jockey.' Beckett retired after his fifth ride.

Beckett was there when FitzGerald asked a lad why he hadn't been in the previous day.

'My wife was having a baby,' explained the lad.

'Why were you there?' demanded FitzGerald. 'Did you have to effing deliver it?'

When Beckett was working for Big Pete, the patriotic trainer was driven to distraction by a new electric gate fitted by a Kiwi electrician.

'Now listen here,' said Pete. 'I'm fed up with all you effing Australians. You try and get rid of our Queen and all you give us in return is Rolf effing Harris.' ■

CHAPTER THREE

UNSUNG HEROES – NEVER PUMPED UP

Dropping his hands too soon

IN MANY SPORTS you are considered over the top at the age of 31, but for jump jockeys it's a pretty good age. You can draw on a few years' experience yet you are still brave, riding the sort of horses the Jockey Club sought to outlaw earlier this week, the type whose form figures look like a bad hand at Scrabble.

With long-term injuries to Mark Dwyer and Lorcan Wyer, there is a new pecking order in the weighing rooms of the frozen north, and to the top has risen a 31-year-old who is more Yorkshire than Geoffrey Boycott. Step forward, and not before time, Russell Garritty.

Garritty, first jockey to Mickey Hammond since August, was a late starter – he didn't ride his first winner until he was twenty – and has spent most of his career being second jockey. At Peter Easterby's, where he spent twelve years, he was even known for a while as 'second-hand Russ' after he rode six consecutive seconds. He has ticked along since, riding about twenty winners a year, until midway through last season when he started riding most of Hammond's horses and finished with 35. He has already passed that total this year, and his last six visits to the racecourse have resulted in ten winners, including a four-timer at Hexham on Wednesday. Until then, the highlight of his career had been a treble at Sedgefield. Nothing wrong with a treble, but, I think you would agree, we would have regarded his career as slightly sad if he'd got to the end having enjoyed his finest hour around the ridges and furrows of Tony Blair's constituency racecourse.

Russ, who was attracted to racing after his dad took him to Pontefract, is now riding out of his skin. His confidence is up, he's getting on good horses, and the killer instinct he may have lacked when riding six seconds for Easterby is now very evident in his determination – and in his haircut. It is very short. 'The wife cuts it,' he explained yesterday at Doncaster where he was at his strongest, winning on Cumbrian Challenge. 'I'm going a bit light on top and I was buggered if I was going to pay the hairdresser £3 for trimming what there isn't much of anyway.' It is a trait for which he is legendary, one he shares with his fellow Yorkshiremen. Colleague Jason Callaghan remembers, 'We once stayed in a bed and breakfast at Perth. It was £2 cheaper to stay in the room without an ensuite bathroom, so Russ took it.' And cutting her husband's hair is not all the long-suffering Andrea has to do either. The other day when his car got stuck in the car park at Wetherby, Russ was last seen at the wheel while Andrea pushed.

Like most things, he likes nothing more than ribbing colleagues. After his four-timer, he rang up his mate Adie Smith, out for six days with concussion, to see if he had seen the results from Hexham. Smith, who'd been expecting the call and was keen that Garritty should not put one over him, replied that he hadn't. 'I've got concussion, Russ,' he said. 'I didn't even know there was racing today.'

JUMP RACING IS A CHARACTER SHORT THIS WEEK following the news that David Walsh, last season's champion conditional jockey, is to take a 'sabbatical' from the sport – as a brickie. He follows in the footsteps of his brother Michael, who was a good show jumper before quitting equally suddenly, and, of course, Walter Swinburn, who is still taking time out.

'Walshy', who by his own admission didn't care much for school in his youth, had the potential to become a good, brave jockey, and he was manna from Heaven for a column like this. You may remember when we reported, shortly before the Gold Cup in which he rode Barton Bank into second place, that he was told he had been backed to be champion jockey by the millennium. 'When's that then?' he replied. Looks like that bet is off – for the time being at least. The day after Cheltenham he set off for Fakenham but cried off his ride when he arrived at Falkenham, about 100 miles away, an hour before the first at Fakenham. And on another occasion an owner arrived at Nigel Twiston-Davies' yard on Sunday with a sack of apples and carrots for his horses. He also brought with him his dog called Boots.

'What sort of dog is Boots?' asked David.

'An Old English Sheepdog,' replied the owner.

'How old would that be?' enquired David.

Although everyone will point to his riding of Barton Bank in the Gold Cup and Martell Chase, which he won, as good examples of Walsh's riding, his effort on Ballydougan at Towcester in May was more typical. Ballydougan has a mind of his own and had run ten times that season without success. Even *Raceform* alluded to his dog-like characteristics, and Timmy Murphy had already been banned for excessive use of the whip on the horse – just trying to keep him in a race. True to form, Ballydougan whipped round and lost fifteen lengths at the start of the three-mile novice chase. While others might have accepted the situation, Walsh did not, pushing and shoving for three miles until he hit the front over the last. As he landed, Ballydougan put the brakes on and dived for the rails, crossing the mounts of Richard Dunwoody and Jim Culloty in the process.

Somehow, Walsh got him going again to win by a neck. He then managed to blind the stewards with science and kept the race. When asked why he hadn't done what 99 per cent of jockeys would have done and given up, he replied, 'By Jaysus, you can't let a horse get away with that.'

His generosity became legend at Liverpool this year when the Grand National was delayed two days by the IRA bomb scare. He still had a room booked for Saturday night at the Adelphi in town and when he saw fellow jockey Carl Llewellyn, by that time dressed in the clothes of an inhabitant of Melling Road, Walsh took pity on him. 'Carl, you've looked after me in the past, now it's my turn to look after you. I've a spare bed in my room and it's all yours,' he said. At the end of that long evening in the Adelphi's nightclub, Llewellyn eventually sought out Walsh's room, the ultimate target being the spare bed. However, it transpired that Walsh had made the same offer to about half a dozen other jockeys; what's more, he'd told them to bring their friends. Consequently Llewellyn was one of about twenty (I think twelve of them had rides in the Grand National) to bed down on the floor of room 301 that night.

Walsh is now living back at his parents' pub, the Swan and Rushes in Leicester.

We all hope he makes a comeback before it is too late. ▣

RACING PRIDES ITSELF on attracting racegoers and participants from all social backgrounds. It is also fair to say that the sport attracts people from all levels of intellect, from the pea-brained to boffins.

Proximity to either end of the scale is dangerous, and I remember one particularly bright, delightful but slightly absent-minded university don who used to own horses. He wrote Greek poetry on the loo, sometimes forgot to shave one side of his face, and has turned up to the races wearing odd shoes. That's as dangerous as the chap who can't spell his own name or write a cheque.

At, or possibly over, the top end of the scale is the currently in-form Newmarket trainer John Berry, 31. From a stable of nine, his last six runners have yielded two winners, two seconds and a third. His yard has just been swelled by the arrival of two horses from Jersey. People ask if he is related to Jack Berry, and he is, of course, very close to him in alphabetical listings of trainers, but that's all. John's father Claude was, until recently, a director of the Tryon Gallery in London, and his mother owned one of the country's foremost Shetland pony studs, exporting ponies to America and Japan.

John has just had his 50th letter to the racing press published, and I'm hoping there are enough factual errors in this piece to prompt an upgrading to the *Daily Telegraph*. 'I enjoy writing and imposing my views on people,' says Berry, who also pens a weekly article for the *Winning Post*, an Australian racing magazine. 'With only nine horses I also have a lot of spare time on my hands.' He doesn't have any particular crusades, but whatever the political hot potato of the moment he'll pen a 'Dear Sir' on the subject. Presumably he gets sent a few 'Dear Johns' by return of post. Look out for something on the subject of going descriptions in the next day or two.

At Wellington College he was an 'exhibitioner' (a spelling mistake short of a scholarship), but it all started going pear-shaped when he turned down the opportunity to study theology at Oxford in favour, of all things, of becoming Luca Cumani's pupil assistant. While there he used to take his toothbrush to work so that he could clean his teeth after breakfast. He also used to take his dog along Newmarket High Street on a 40ft leash, which meant a number of shoppers had a 'B' added to their form figures. John can be seen wearing wellingtons on even the hottest day in summer, and he is not afraid to buck other trends either. He is, for example, along with Saeed bin Suroor and Captain John

Wilson, one of the few 'beards' to hold a trainer's licence.

His old boss probably has him best summed up. Recently, Berry was checking out of the supermarket ahead of Sara Cumani, who spotted him buying some mussels and a pizza.

'How was your meal the other night?' asked Luca on the Heath a few mornings later.

'I was sick for two days,' replied Berry, who had been struck down with food poisoning.

'You should realise,' said Luca, 'that Italian food and English eccentrics don't mix.'

I have always regarded anyone who trains racehorses for a living as eccentric. It's just that some are more so than others. ▣

AT THE END OF A RELATIVELY QUIET NEWS WEEK IN RACING, the King George VI and Queen Elizabeth Diamond Stakes has enjoyed an unprecedented build-up. Even the astronauts in the Mir space station must have a fair idea that it is an eight-horse contest and likely to be the best race since the United States beat Russia to the moon.

It may, therefore, be pertinent to take a look at how the various jockeys have prepared themselves for 'The Race of the Century'. Frankie Dettori has just got married, so we all know what he's been doing, but on Thursday he, John Reid, Ray Cochrane and Pat Eddery were at Sandown, Mick Kinane was riding at Naas, and Gary Stevens was in action in California. Brian Asmussen – who changed his name to Cash by deed poll in the late 1970s – was at home in Chantilly counting his money and preparing an invoice for Helissio's owner for slightly more than the jockey's set riding fee of £61.50 (i.e. moving the decimal point two or three digits to the right). Shantou's jockey, Gary Hind, a compulsive tidier, was relaxing at his Newmarket home like only he knows how – with a hoover in one hand and a duster in the other. A ride at Sandown had been hard to come by.

It was lucky for the spick-and-span nineteen-year-old, and indeed the number board at Ascot today, that his parents christened him Gary and not Barry. Had it ever crossed their minds? 'I don't think so,' says Hind, one of the weighing room's only part-time comedians and a man so immaculate he combs his hair between races. 'I've an uncle called Bob, and he's a bit of an arse.' Hind's mother worked, until two years ago, in a Ladbrokes betting shop – not the ideal place for a sensitive, protective mum when your son gets beaten on a favourite. 'She's heard me called a few names over the years,' he adds.

The son of a power-station engineer, born in Glasgow, brought up in Middlesbrough and apprenticed in Malton, it is little short of a miracle that the least known of today's octet is a jockey at all. Like most grandstand jockeys, a fifteen-year-old Hind thought, having never sat on a horse, that he could just get on one and ride. That was pretty much what happened. Now he spends his winters earning a tidy living in Dubai working for Sheikh Mohammed – he rode Flemensfirth for him in the Dubai World Cup and won the Racing Post Trophy last year on Medaaly for Godolphin – and summers with John Gosden. For every one of Hind's thirteen winners this season, Frankie has ridden seven more, but even the ever-optimistic Hind does not expect to waltz back to Britain every May and find himself with six mounts at each meeting.

It all started when he joined Pat Rohan, along with apprentice colleague Jimmy Quinn, in Malton. Within two years they had, between them, finished Rohan off and he retired from British racing. On one occasion, Quinn was giving a helmetless Hind a lift home on his moped when they passed a police car. Quinn, in a scene not remotely reminiscent of Steve McQueen in *The Great Escape*, dumped his pillion and made a swift exit through a cemetery on his scooter. Instead of legging it, Hind, arms aloft, surrendered and volunteered to the police Quinn's name and number. There were three consequences to this action: it earned Quinn three points and a fine; it earned Hind the temporary nickname 'Grass'; and thirdly, he decided to invest his life savings in his own scooter. Twelve hours later he wrote it off on Rohan's drive.

One of Hind's greater claims to fame involved being left at Maisons-Lafitte by Lester Piggott. They had flown there in the same light plane from Newmarket. As Piggott was riding in the later race than our already-changed hero, Hind volunteered to save time by organising a taxi while the great man changed. If you think Piggott was famous for riding horses, he was even more famous for taxi-fare avoidance. After half an hour of waiting, Hind began to smell a rat and went back to find Piggott. 'He went quarter of an hour ago,' said one of the jockeys. Piggott had got a lift (free) to the plane and instructed the pilot to fly home. Hind, who had not brought much in the way of cash, was left stranded in France.

Earlier this season, Hind won the biggest prize of his career – a new, top-of-the-range Saab – in a draw at a charity dance. There are two ways of looking at that: either our man's luck is in or he used it all up in one evening. We and Shantou will find out today.

JOHNNY KAVANAGH, erstwhile second jockey to Nicky Henderson – a part of the furniture there, Mr Dependable and, at the same time, Mrs Mop – has retired from race-riding. At least I think that's what he said. Despite having ridden out with him on countless mornings, I, in common with many an owner, trainer and colleague, have never quite got to grips with his County Laois accent. For all I know he may have said he had six rides at Stratford today. Shortly, he will leave Faringdon, Oxon, to join his great mate Adrian Maguire in Cork, where they will have fourteen point-to-pointers in training and will no doubt form a double act to rival Abbot and Costello.

Johnny, 35, rode his first winner for Henderson at Cheltenham in 1991. He subsequently notched another 101 for the trainer, riding horses such as Geos and Landing Light when Mick Fitzgerald wasn't available. His winning total stands at more than 300 altogether, including ten for the Queen Mother. Before his first ride for the Queen Mum, Henderson instructed his assistant to give Johnny an etiquette lesson: on no account let him (a) kiss the Queen Mother, or (b), although it was probably an accurate description, describe her horse afterwards as 'an awful f***ing t'ing'.

Johnny took over the position of Henderson's number two rider from John White. It is not always the easiest of jobs, especially when you are overlooked for promotion, and it requires a good, loyal team player to fill it. The first thing he was required to do after losing out on the number one spot to Fitzgerald was act as best man at Mick's wedding, a union that never really recovered from the day when Mick said winning the National was better than sex. Johnny's speech was, however, excellent.

On the whole, you don't have to be a forensic scientist to recognise a jockey's house. There is usually a trail of straw, shavings or hay, and most jockeys don't know the meaning of housework. Johnny, the exception that proves the rule, is the owner of an immaculately kept house, free from any sort of horse bedding. Nothing is out of place. So much so, in fact, that when Timmy Murphy once gouged out a blob of butter with a knife rather than scrape it neatly in thin layers from the top, Johnny refused to speak to him for a week. 'Johnny's a great bloke,' said a weighing-room colleague, 'even though he used to prefer staying in at night doing some hoovering rather than come out with us.'

It took Henderson, working in close proximity with Johnny, a couple of years to work out his accent. You can't blame Johnny – anyone brought up in a place spelt Laois but pronounced 'Leash' is going to be difficult to understand. Many of his owners just looked on bemused during his post-race descriptions. For all they knew they might have been listening to a weather forecast in Latvian. While Johnny was already coming to the end of his summary, his owners were still two sentences behind, trying to work out what had happened at the start. Carl Llewellyn once won on a horse at Plumpton, and when he hopped off the owners told him that the last man who rode it had given it a cracking ride, it was just that they hadn't been able to understand a word he said afterwards. Carl did not even need to look up who the previous jockey was.

Johnny will not be leaving a vacuum at Henderson's Seven Barrows. He will be taking it with him.

THE SMALL TRAINER IS ALIVE AND WELL AND SKINT. Godolphin may be on the brink of hardship, having collected only £40,000 in prize money this season before shutting up shop, but unlike Charles Booth (big man, small trainer), Sheikh Mohammed does not have to duck every time he passes Barclays Bank in Malton.

Booth, 51, is an Italian count and trainer of a dozen horses for twenty years, but a man whose wallet winces every time vets invent a new disease. The produce of a Yorkshire soldier and an Italian noblewoman, he has inherited the title of Italian count. 'Some people would vary the spelling of that,' admits the Marchese di Castel Betere. 'It entitles me to just about nothing. What property there was got flattened in an earthquake.'

Inspired by a great uncle who bred the mighty Gainsborough for Lady Jane Douglas, he married Gill, bought a farm and trained under permit. Friends insisted he become a professional trainer, but when he did, those who had promised him horses were not then seen for dust. Two decades on, he is still here.

Booth's first winner, Ruddy Drake, beat Fred Winter's Easter Eel in the Kestrel Hurdle at Ascot. He has had plenty of winners since, many of them at Cagnes-sur-Mer, and landed quite a few gambles. Unfortunately, his best horse, Mademoiselle Chloe, was a contemporary of a hot crop of sprinters, headed by Dayjur.

Booth has now had a couple of lean years. You know you are not going that well when one of your mates, Mark Tompkins, sees you at the races and says, 'I didn't know you were still alive.' And you know your fate is sealed for another season when you take the two-year-olds to Filey Beach and your two pet Dalmatians beat the horses over three furlongs. 'We knew we were in trouble,' he recalls. 'The season hadn't even started.'

Despite this, the mood at Foston, near Malton, is positive. Of his dozen horses, he reckons half of them should greet the judge at some stage. If Blenheim Terrace gets his act together, he should improve on his five seconds from his last seven starts. 'I was watching on Sky and they had Nick Cook on,' says Booth. 'He said the horse needed blinkers. Bloody marvellous – cricketers telling me how to do the job now.'

His allergy to jockeys is legendary. When Lindsay Charnock had just been beaten on one of his horses at Wolverhampton one day, Booth said, 'Charnock, if I was your weight I'd be champion jockey.' To which the jockey replied, 'If you were my weight I'd punch your lights out.'

This has been a busy week for Booth. He has been working for Raceday Radio at York, tipping like a demon for them, and entertaining owners. 'Win or lose, we have the booze' is his motto. On Tuesday, he took a bunch of them to one of his favourite restaurants. 'Big mistake,' he reflected. 'They went from racecourse to restaurant without a break. The restaurant, a straightforward place, was not prepared for singing or for people who began dropping off at nine p.m. onwards only to wake up with a start and shout, "What have I backed in this one?"'

THAT THE MAJORITY OF LAMBOURN TRAINERS have been able to keep their horses on the go at all during the past fortnight is due, almost entirely, to head gallopman Eddie Fisher, 61, and his team of four assistants. Fisher himself, a doer rather than a delegator, has been up at three o'clock some mornings to ensure that the village's Fibresand gallop is fit for use at seven o'clock.

On 19 February, Fisher will have been a gallopman in Lambourn for 42 years and head of the operation for four decades. When he started, Charlie Pratt, Fulke Walwyn, Majors Nelson and Champneys, and Peter Payne-Galwey were the principal Lambourn trainers; there were about 200 horses using the turf gallops; 'all-weather' was a term that hadn't been introduced to the English language; he earned £4 a week; and the crash helmet had yet to be invented. In those days everyone who rode out wore a flat cap – some turned backwards, some sidewards – and after a breezy work morning he'd collect half a dozen from the Downs. 'If the lads or jockeys lost a cap they'd usually come and ask for it back at lunchtime,' he recalls. 'If they didn't ask for them they didn't get them. I remember one cap wasn't collected for a few days and Richard Pitman came up to me and said, "Eddie, have you seen my cap? It's a bit like the one you're wearing on your head." I laughed and said it was the one I was wearing on my head. He said if that was the case I should keep it – so I did.'

Now, besides the 450 acres of gallops owned by Lady Eliza Mays-Smith, there are more than 1,000 horses, six all-weather gallops, a huge schooling ground and a fleet of tractors to maintain. Fisher, who does not believe in rolling the turf unless absolutely necessary – experts in grass management will tell you that constant rolling has ruined many racecourses – walks at least ten miles a day forking back divots. He gets more fresh air than Tony Bullimore when his yacht is the right way up, has never had a cold, and is so fit that the only person in Lambourn who doesn't know him is the doctor.

He is famed, though, for moments of high blood pressure when someone tries to 'sneak one past him', or 'steal a piece of fresh ground' by going the wrong side of the carefully marked-out gallops. Let's just say hell hath no fury like Eddie Fisher (who even has the three-pronged fork to go with it) when he finds a divot and the culprit the wrong side of a marker. It is not unknown for him to throw the F-word at lads, trainers or ladies. A colleague of his on Henry Candy's neighbouring estate (technically in the next county) always knows when Eddie is upset: the skylarks are quiet and distant ranting can be heard. 'I used to fling my fork everywhere,' admits Fisher, with a great smile. 'They used to know and it used to be a bit of a game for some of them, seeing if they could get one past me. One lad who used to work for Fred Winter called Bandy Bob always used to say, "Fisher, I'll get you one day." One foggy morning Mr Winter's string were flying round Mandown bottom and Bandy Bob came past outside the markers on the fresh ground. He was flicking Vs and shouted, "I got you, Fisher!" I was so angry I threw my fork down and broke the blasted thing.'

Every winner trained in Lambourn is his own, and he has witnessed some of the greatest exponents of the art of training. 'I think Fulke Walwyn and Fred Winter were the best,' he says, reflecting. 'Duncan Sasse was a bit of a devil, and Rod Simpson one of the great characters,' adds the man who has caught as many couples (who thought it was just them and the larks) in compromising positions in the long grass on the Downs as he has moles. 'I remember all Rod's lads flying past up the six-furlong gallop on Neardown with their pants down one morning. We had to stop working we were laughing so much.'

One of the most famous (I mean oldest) Lambourn Downs stories involves trainer Doug Marks, who found himself with a bit of time on his hands at the top of the cantering grounds while he waited for his string. The Downs are fairly bare by definition, and putting himself in the boots of an escaped criminal, he wondered where someone in such a predicament would go for cover. An old oak tree caught his attention. 'I couldn't climb that if I were half my age,' he reasoned. However, that inspired the daring side of his nature and he set about climbing the tree. He was successfully hidden when his lads arrived. 'Where the hell is the old bastard this time?' said one lad – and that, it seems, was one of the kinder things said about the trainer while he perched precariously above his encircling string. Eventually, after hearing enough said about himself, he revealed himself. 'Up here, you f***ers!' he shouted, much to the embarrassment of his lads. ■

BACK AT THE START OF 1990, *Racing Post* journalists, which at the time included me, were asked to name someone they thought would make a big impact during the twentieth century's last decade. My choice was the then leading conditional jockey (he won the title twice) Derek Byrne. Seven years later, *On Saturday* takes a look at that prediction and discovers it bears a remarkable similarity to many of my tips. Now, I'm not saying you let me down, Derek. I'm a patient man, but you've only got three years left.

Navan-born Byrne's British career is now back to where it started, in Lambourn, where he is first jockey to the upwardly mobile stable of Merrita Jones. Byrne, 30, first arrived in the village at Jenny Pitman's yard a decade ago, after weight problems had brought his promising career on the Flat to a halt. The intervening period, after nine months at Weathercock House, has been spent working for Jimmy FitzGerald in Malton, and even took him to Germany. For a while it looked like the ginger jockey would go all the way to the top, and in fact his present job gives him another welcome opportunity. At one stage he was jocking off Mark Dwyer for the cream of the FitzGerald horses, Sybillin, Boutsdaroff and Meikleour. Dwyer, enduring a terrible run at the time, admits that he expected a P45 to plop through the letterbox.

Byrne's biggest success came in the 1990 Scottish National on Four Trix, for Gordon Richards. It was a last-minute spare ride. Byrne had been due to partner a horse for John Edwards, but the day before the race Edwards rang Byrne's agent and told him that the owners thought Byrne was 'too short in the leg'. Two hours later he was on Four Trix.

The big day started badly when he fell from his first ride for Richards. When he came into the paddock to ride Four Trix, the worried owner asked Richards what instructions he was going to give Byrne. Richards thought for a moment. 'What can I tell him?' he said. 'He's just fallen off the first one. I think I'll tell him to try to stay on.' And those were the instructions he carried out to perfection. Afterwards he was offered the job as second jockey to Richards, but he turned it down, thinking he might get the FitzGerald job. If, in the words of the song, you could turn back time . . .

In some ways, though, Byrne did make a major impact – on Mrs Pitman's television. He and a few of the lads were returning to their digs after an evening in the local when they saw Mrs Pitman's son Paul watching the TV with the curtains open. Byrne immediately spotted the opportunity for a practical joke and rushed home to get his remote control. Crowded at the window, they changed the channel. Paul changed it back. They changed it to another; he changed it back again. This channel 'tennis' went on for five minutes until, in mad frustration, Paul kept his finger on his remote button for two minutes. When he had taken it off and begun to relax, they switched channels again. This time Paul gave up the unequal struggle, switched the television off with his remote control and went upstairs to bed. Byrne let him get to bed before switching it back on, turning it up to full volume and legging it.

And there, you might think, the story ends, but it doesn't. The following morning while the horses were circling the house for second lot, a television repair man arrived. To this day Byrne wonders what he found wrong with it. ■

THERE IS A RACE TO BUILD A NEW ALL-WEATHER TRACK NEAR LONDON. You can bet that wherever it gets the go-ahead it will be saddled with some appallingly dreary or, worse, commercial name. Not for racing, please, Boring Sands, East London or Reebok Park.

Australia has, thanks to its Aboriginal origins, the most colourful racecourse names in the world. Wouldn't it be interesting to go picnic racing at Onkaparinga, Warrnambook, Wagga Wagga, Wangaratta or

Wycheproof? Or how about a trip to Bedgerbong or Gooloogong, a six-race card at Come-By-Chance or a meeting in Queensland run under the auspices of the Banana Jockey Club? (Don't they have first cousins in Portman Square?) Then, of course, you could drink a 'spider' (ginger beer and brandy) at the Belyando and Mistake Creek Races. Bong Bong – Aboriginal for a 'rough relief of human buttocks', so one assumes it was hilly – was, alas, closed in 1988. Last but not least is Goondiwindi. Takes three days to get there and you'll only find two blokes and a dingo when you do. Only two good things ever came out of Goondiwindi: Gunsynd, the legendary grey Cox Plate winner who was immortalised in song as the 'Goondiwindi Grey', and Terry Lucas.

Lucas, 48, is something of a legend himself, but that fact has yet to reach British folk singers. It might were he to win today's Ayr Gold Cup on Westcourt Magic. He is the only professional jockey riding who doesn't employ an agent, and is to self-PR what Apollo One was to the space race (didn't get beyond the launch pad). *But* he is the only former champion operating out of the north. He may look a little washed-up, but he is wily, and with 1,600 successes he has ridden more winners than Frankie Dettori. And there are few better judges of a horse. Put him on one trotting-up lame and he'll tell you, or more precisely Mick Easterby, what trip it wants and how it should be ridden.

Lucas is a man of many winners but few words – or, as they say in Yorkshire, he 'never says owt', which probably suits Mick well. Throughout his career, Lucas has been attached by bungee to Singapore, where he has twice been champion in six separate stints. To be asked back to Singapore so many times is an advert in itself because too many cock-ups and you're likely to be asked to clean out the equine pool in concrete riding boots.

Though his parents ran Goondiwindi's Railway Hotel, Lucas wanted to be a jockey when he was knee-high to a platypus. The first of those 1,600 victories came at his local track on a horse owned by Mum and trained by Dad. Since then he has led something of a nomadic life. On a previous stay in England he won the Magnet Cup on Amyndas for Bruce Hobbs. He's done several stints in Australia and several here, but every time he has gone back for another sling at Singapore.

Does Sheriff Hutton compare favourably with Goondiwindi? 'Different world,' he said, before adding dryly, 'Different climate.' Is he settled now? 'We'd never like to say for good,' replied his wife Christine. The 'Welcome Back Terry' banners in Singapore may have use in them yet.

As for London's new track, Goondiwindi's out. Mistake Creek is a possibility, but in their current mood the British Horseracing Board might insist on calling it Buggajump Racing. Though of course the only fence will be around the perimeter.

MICHAEL BLANSHARD, 44, is enjoying one of his best seasons, and in the giant Locombe Hill he has potentially his best horse in eighteen years. So before the colt steps out in York's Acomb Stakes later this month, I thought we'd better fill you in on the trainer.

The son of a Dorset vet, Michael learnt his trade via Henry Cecil, Barry Hills and Henry Candy. For a while he rented a yard in Lambourn and eventually bought Lethornes from Doug Marks, who remains his neighbour. He lists archaeology as his hobby, which is just as well living next door to that old character. 'I remember going to Lingfield with Doug before the M25 was built,' recalls Blanshard, who has disappointingly just christened his third son Patrick after having had sons called Tom and Harry. 'We stopped at a garage to fill up with petrol and I asked if Doug wanted anything. He said a glass of sherry. I thought it was strange but I went to the pub next door, bought him one, he drank it and we drove on.'

As is so often the case with trainers who never put a mature foot out of place once they get a licence, most of the 'action' with Blanshard occurred during his formative years. For example, he is one of the few people to have crashed on all five roads leading into Lambourn. When he got the full set he was restricted to a moped. He was once kicked in the face, which necessitated his jaw being wired up. Mates being mates, Colin Brown and others used to bring delicious food into hospital for him to drool over. They then had little option but to eat it before it went off.

Brown recalls Blanshard's infrequent dinner parties before marrying

Philippa. 'He used to set a table up in his garden which was a wilderness, serve ham which tasted like rubber, and put out three lettuce leaves and cider which he had left until the plastic barrel had blown up. There was method in that madness though. It was so appalling that everyone thought they should feed him and never expected a return match.'

HERE'S A QUESTION: who has been racing every day of the Flat season for 30 years but has never seen the finish of a race? Answer: Peter Hickling, 62, leader of the southern starting stalls team.

Today, a second before the off at the Vodafone Stewards' Cup at Goodwood, there will be about fourteen tons of pumped-up horseflesh impatient to burst out of the gates. Not all of it, however, will have been quite so keen to enter the stalls in the first place. It will have been cajoled, pushed, pulled, shoved, blindfolded or persuaded by a combination of the above-mentioned methods. Before the runners have covered the six furlongs of today's big sprint, the stalls will have been dismantled and sent on their way to the mile and three-quarter start for the following race.

It has not been an easy month for this close-knit bunch of backroom boys who eat, sleep and drink in each other's pockets for the length of the summer. On the same day in July two of their number died from heart attacks, 'Wiggy' Wigmore at home and Colin Richardson while towing the starter's rostrum at Windsor. But few horses ever beat Hickling and his merry men, even though rules now permit only five men to a horse, one at the front and four at the rear. 'Only time and having to get a race off on schedule beats us,' he says, though he recalls once being unable to get Jimmy Lindley's mount in the stalls in a two-horse race, which then became a walk-over.

Lester Piggott won the first experimental race started from stalls at Newmarket in 1965, and Hickling has been working on them for almost as long. Originally he was a handler, then he progressed to technician before becoming team leader. A combination of their skill – all the handlers have worked in yards except Keith Barber, who was a goalkeeper for Luton – and a little divine intervention has helped avert the worst disasters. Heavy ground is always likely to cause an upset, because at one and three-quarter tons a set of stalls doesn't act on the going.

One day at Folkestone's six-furlong start, with the stalls across the course, Micky Dillon, chivalrously thinking of madam starter, opened one stall for her to pass through to save her from having to walk all the way round. No sooner had he opened the gates than a bolting horse appeared over the horizon. Five yards before the stalls, Richard Quinn bailed out and the horse galloped flat out through the open stall without touching the sides, jumped a fence and ended up in a farmer's field. Now, when the stalls stretch across the course, a gap is always left until all horses have arrived safely at the start.

My own best memory of the stalls as a jockey was also at Goodwood in an amateur race when Richard Hannon Jr (how did he do the weight?) was in the stall next to me. He forgot to take the blindfold off his horse before the gates opened and the poor horse (there's such nice scenery at Goodwood) didn't know whether it was night or day for the first half-furlong. I was incapable of riding any sort of a race – not for the normal reasons but because I was laughing so much.

GEORGE MARGARSON RUNS ABOUT 15 PER CENT OF HIS STRING in the first two Classics of the season, Speedfit Too in today's 2,000 Guineas and Jay Gee in the fillies' equivalent tomorrow. Should they both win and you've optimistically had them in a £10 double, then at current odds you'd stand to win £203,000. That is, however, not a suggestion that you do it.

Margarson, for fifteen years a travelling head lad to Mick Ryan, is now in his third season as a Newmarket trainer. He has already won two £20,000 nurseries with the pair – at last year's July meeting – and Speedfit Too finished a creditable eight lengths third behind Xaar in the Prix Salamandre last season. That, some people will tell you, is close. If it was experience that won Classics then Speedfit Too would be home and hosed, having run seven times last season. 'He was a bit of a lad,' recalls the trainer, 'and I had to run him to get the fire out of him.' Margarson is encouraged that this season Jay Gee has started getting her head in front on the gallops, something she didn't do last year.

In this day and age, when former footballers seem to have no problems getting a trainer's licence, Margarson is almost over-qualified for the job. He started off as an apprentice and rode winners over jumps before spells as an assistant and travelling head lad. 'Dedicated and hard-working' is how Mick Ryan describes him. And it was for precisely those reasons that he got into trouble when travelling a horse to the Cappanelle one Sunday.

With time on his hands he decided to take the train into Rome to do some sightseeing before returning to the course in plenty of time for the 4.30. At eleven a.m., having admired St Peter's and the Colosseum, he decided it was time to return to the course – a journey not dissimilar in distance from Newmarket to Cambridge. He hopped on a train and was slightly disconcerted when it hurtled past the stop for the races. Disconcerted became distressed when in his best pidgin Italian he discovered he had boarded the Milan express. After lengthy conversations with the train driver he was eventually deposited at a station an hour up the line. Two trains and a taxi later he arrived at the racecourse an hour before the race and just in time to declare the horse. 'I don't think Mick would have been too chuffed if we'd gone all that way and missed it,' reflected Margarson, understating the case somewhat. That day he saddled the horse in his T-shirt and shorts. Today he will be more suitably attired. ■

THE CAREER OF TOM JENKS, which looked dead in the water when he managed to ride only four winners last season, has taken a turn for the better. His eleven winners so far this season – seven in the last three weeks – have included the Welsh National on Earth Summit a week ago and a double at Leicester on New Year's Day.

That the only jockey who wears Gucci shoes is flying again has to be great news for racing. When Steve Smith-Eccles retired, they mourned the passing of the last cavalier. With 'Jenksy' around, I'm not so sure 'last' is a totally accurate description of Smith-Eccles, although against that our hero did spend New Year's Eve at home alone being dedicated. But how many other jockeys ride a Honda CBS 600 motorbike, spend their hard-earned percentages on a speedboat called *Twinkle* that is powerful enough to pull chicks as well as water-skiers, have a shark tattooed below the pantline (rear), and, when you ask them how many winners they have ridden, reply with the question, 'Do you mean nocturnal winners or ones on the racecourse?'

Jenks, 25, is the grandson of Bryan Jenks, who used to own horses such as Rouge Autumn and Coral Diver with Fred Rimell, and son of Bridgnorth trainer Willie. His aunt Jane is married to trainer Hughie Morrison, and Jenks is godfather to their young daughter Amber. Such is Jenks's interest in his goddaughter – birthdays forgotten; no present this Christmas or last – that Jane is threatening to put Amber in an identity parade to see if the jockey recognises her. Safe to say, though, he'll take a more avuncular interest when she's in her late teens.

Jenks left public school (Shrewsbury) at sixteen, joined David 'The Duke' Nicholson and rode his first winner on Monsieur Le Curé in a bumper. In his second season he won the Kim Muir at Cheltenham for the Duke on Strong Beau. It was, however, trips to the races with the Duke, Warren Marston and Robert Bellamy that he enjoyed most at Jackdaw's Castle. About twenty minutes into the journey, the young jockeys would ring up the trainer, who was driving, from the back seat of his car and hang up as soon as he answered. The Duke, not a gadget man, would start by grumbling, 'This f***ing phone's useless.' By the fourth time one of them had made a call and hung up on him, he'd be apoplectic with rage. He would then dial his secretary and demand that she order a new phone. As soon as it arrived, they would repeat the practical joke.

Before Jenks was found out, he joined Nigel Twiston-Davies as conditional jockey and has remained there as third/second and occasionally, when Carl Llewellyn is injured, first jockey. He is also pretty much number one to Ginger McCain, so had he been around 25 years earlier he might have ridden three Grand National winners by now. As it is, he has had three unplaced rides in the race. That, however, may all change with Earth Summit.

During the summer it is to Abersoch in Wales that Jenks drags his weighing-room colleagues to impress them with his prowess on a set of water-skis. Tricks, mono, jumping, barefoot – he can do just about everything on water except walk. Last summer, however, with a bevy of beauties cooing at Jenks's talents from within *Twinkle,* Mick Fitzgerald, who was steering the boat, slowed down to admire some dolphins that had swum alongside. As soon as he eased down on the throttle, Jenks sank, slowly, into the Irish Sea. All Jenks could see from his vantage point were a lot of dorsal fins. Believing they were sharks and that his career really was about to be dead in the water, he lost all credibility by bursting into tears and screaming to be removed from the sea. 'It's all sadly true, I'm afraid,' he confirmed yesterday.

IN THE STRESSFUL, NERVE-JANGLING WORLD – earthquakes on land and storms at sea – in which trainers imagine they live, one man has been a constant, a barometer stuck on 'set fair'. Not for him kicking the dog, bawling at the secretary or blaming the clerk of the course when things go awry. When Martin Fetherston-Godley sends out his last runners on Tuesday the title 'Most Laid-Back Trainer' will be up for grabs.

Kieren Fallon may have ridden a double-century of winners three seasons on the trot but the monumentally relaxed East Ilsley trainer has held his particular title since he took over Kennet House Stables in 1986. He may only have been a 'small' trainer, but the 42-year-old, who will shortly move to Pewsey, Wiltshire, has had his fair share of success. His vintage year was 1995 when Royale Figurine won the Ayr Gold Cup – backed from 33–1 to 8–1 – and Native Welcome the Magnet Cup.

On the morning of the Ayr Gold Cup he received an anonymous fax asking him three questions. Was he happy with the draw? Was he happy with Darryll Holland? Was he happy with the ground? Out of nothing more than curiosity, he replied that he was happy with all three. The following Monday a van owned by some market traders from Essex arrived and started delivering food to the back door. It started with whole salmon and sides of meat and ended with trays of asparagus and peaches. Presiding over an office that looked like Harrods' food hall the trainer had to give most of it to his lads. 'A lot of it just wouldn't keep,' he recalls. 'But it was a worthwhile exercise replying to the fax.'

Until he arrived as a tubby pupil-assistant to Gavin Hunter, he was training as an accountant but decided against taking the final exams. 'The first morning I arrived Gavin put me on the quietest horse in the yard,' he remembers. 'It proceeded to go the whole way to Compton and back on its hind legs, and I thought to myself, if this is the quietest then I'm not going to be able to ride too many of these.' Much of his training has been conducted from a car since.

One of his principal owners was the late Craig Pearman, who owned Royale Figurine and another good horse called Takenhall. He was never shy about celebrating a big winner in style. On one occasion after a Takenhall win, trainer, owner and entourage were 'flying' in a local hostelry. When Craig tucked into his steak he found it extraordinarily tough. In order to make a small point to the landlord he placed the steak in a shoe and sent it back to the kitchen with the note, 'Guess which one's the leather?'

Although he has two runners on Tuesday, Martin is confident that his last winner will be Shanghai Lil, who won at her beloved Wolverhampton a week ago today. 'I got given the tape of her winning by the racecourse,' recalls the trainer, 'and watched it a couple of times. As it was possibly my last winner I decided on Monday I'd watch it one more time, for posterity. It turned out that the children must have pushed the record button on the video. It's now got the *Teletubbies* on it.' A bit of bad luck there, but looking on the bright side, I suppose every time he sees La-La in action he will at least be reminded of his last winner. ◘

RICHARD PHILLIPS, THE LAMBOURN TRAINER currently recovering from a particularly spotty dose of chicken pox, is, we are told, one of the favourites to take over from David Nicholson at Jackdaw's Castle next summer when the Duke retires. When rumours first started circulating that Phillips might be in line for the job, his friends started calling him 'Son of Duke'. Now this has been refined. He is known as 'The Marquis' – one down in rank from a duke, and a title often bestowed upon their sons.

Having shared a house with him, I know a thing or two about Richard Phillips. For instance, he can't swim. So those who have said it will be sink or swim time come next June don't realise how hurtful they are being. We even went further than sharing a house: we had a joint mortgage because neither of us could afford the full whack at the time. When we went to see the bank manager about it, at a time when HIV Aids had just been discovered, he asked us a lot of questions. His final question was, 'And what is the address of your new cottage?' The answer – and its significance hadn't dawned on us until that moment – was 2 Queens Cottages. For the rest of our time there, although we tried to prove categorically that we weren't, we were known locally as 'the two queens'. I think he'll do very well at Jackdaw's Castle. ◘

AFTER 28 YEARS OF TRYING, the night classes in 'how to stay cool in a big race' have finally paid off for Lindsay Charnock. On Thursday, he rode his first Group-race winner when Tim Easterby's Jemima won the Lowther Stakes at York. Despite having ridden 700 domestic winners, and another 120 in India, the lack of Group-race success was beginning to annoy the north's favourite lightweight, especially after being touched off in a few.

Charnock's career, as it tends to do for the 7st 10lb boys, was ticking along steadily with the occasional Ayr Gold Cup and Cesarewitch when, about three years ago, it suddenly took off. He turned 40, and before you could say 'Cock of the North' he became the new kid on the block, as it were. Now 44, he is one of the old school.

Born in Wigan, he was one of the last generation of children whose career prospects were working in a coal mine or, er, working in a coal mine. His father was down the pits for 30 years – prepare for appalling joke – after which he needed a damn good bath. He refused to let his son follow in his footsteps and the young lad was packed off to Cheshire trainer Ronnie Barnes, with whom he signed up for an eight-year apprenticeship.

The modern apprenticeship consists of about three weeks at the British Racing School. In those days, though, an apprenticeship was at worst medieval, at best Victorian. You worked twelve hours a day and were locked up in a dark cupboard (to prevent you from growing) for the other twelve. The only way the contract between trainer and 'boy' could be broken was if the trainer retired or died – Barnes opted for the latter – or the boy left for the French Foreign Legion, where lads seven stone wet through were not in huge demand. When Barnes died, Charnock crossed the Pennines and joined Denys Smith.

Kevin Darley is not about to lose his 'Cock of the North' title to Charnock, but it is nevertheless refreshing to see Charnock, the master of the one-liner, rewarded by riding horses such as Pipalong, Flanders and now Jemima. In India, where he also met his wife – her five brothers all rode there – racing was disrupted one day by 2,000 rioting punters. Charnock, riding a first-time-out two-year-old, had to beat off the punters to get to the start and prevent himself from being lynched.

Once there, he turned to a fellow jockey, the appropriately named Kipper Lynch. 'It took a lot of getting to the start,' Charnock said. 'How the f**k are we going to get back?' He also once won a race at Newmarket despite having broken his ankle in a fall on the way to the start. 'Everyone said it was very brave,' recalls Charnock. 'I knew the connections had backed it, and I can tell you it would have been a lot braver to get off the horse than it was to ride it in the race.' ◙

MARK RICHARDS HANGS UP HIS BOOTS AT WORCESTER TODAY AFTER 22 YEARS in the saddle to concentrate on a career in the media. His final mount will be Sleigh Ride, who may have different ideas about the precise speed at which he whisks our man out of the weighing room and into the studio: he pulled up on his only previous outing in a bumper.

Richards, 39, is already an established member of the Racing Channel team. During a career which spanned 328 winners (I think we can safely assume that will be the final total despite a ride for Martin Pipe early in the afternoon), he has rightly earned a reputation for being the jockey best able to read – I was tempted to end the sentence at this point – a form book. Given a choice of two in a race, colleagues would often turn to him for advice. Jockeys are notoriously bad tipsters, but Mark was an exception to the rule.

In jockeydom, though, he is the 'missing link'. His first ride was in 1977, and other 7lb claimers at the time included Paul Nicholls, Charlie Mann, Shaun Keightley, the late Paul Croucher and Graham Bradley. At the time he was attached to another blast from the past, Ian Dudgeon, which doesn't make me feel too young either because I can remember when he assisted my father. 'Richard Dunwoody says I should ride on until 2000,' he says, 'so I can say I've ridden in four separate decades. I don't think it's really worth hanging on for. You've got to draw stumps at some stage.'

His total of winners is nothing short of amazing when you realise he has never been first jockey to a major yard, though he was first off the bench for the Sherwoods whenever Jamie Osborne wasn't available. Though he rode horses just short of the top such as Muse and Kilcash, his biggest claim to fame is riding a double at the 1992 Cheltenham Festival. Duke of Monmouth, who took no little persuading, won the Triumph, and Repeat the Dose won the Cathcart. At some Festivals, that would have been worth a share in some crystal as London Clubs leading rider. Last year, however, Osborne selfishly chose to ride five winners, and for the first and only time a double at Cheltenham was made to look paltry.

His greatest achievement, however, was to get Pukka Major to start in the 1990 Grand National – although he lived to regret it. The grey had refused to start in several of his races in the build-up to the big race, but Mark and trainer Tim Thomson Jones knew that he would go anywhere providing he was being led by someone on another horse. The night before, Mark was chatting to an owner in a bar who bet him £50 he would be left at the start. 'Why don't we make it £100 if you're so sure?' said Mark. The next morning he found Jimmy Duggan, who was riding Young Driver, and offered him £25 to lead him in when the tapes went up. Duggan duly obliged, but there was a minor hiccup when the tape was broken and everyone jostled for a new position. Duggan could be seen trying to find Pukka Major like a headless chicken. The long and the short of it was that Pukka Major did start and Duggan did earn his £25 – an incredibly small amount for holding the reins of two horses at the start of the National when you think about it.

However, there was a sting in the tale. Pukka Major decided at the fourth-last he'd had enough and stuck all fours in the ditch. Mark was propelled through the air like a gymnast who had miscued a vault, and his wrist did what Rice Krispies do when you pour milk on them – it went snap, crackle and pop. ■

THE GREAT AND THE GOOD GATHERED IN SCOTLAND THIS WEEK – not for the historic opening of the Scottish Parliament but to say goodbye to one of racing's legendary characters, Ken Oliver, who died last month at the age of 85. When the Good Lord made Ken, He threw away the mould, for although racing may still boast a larger range of characters than many sports, few of the characters will ever match the incomparable 'Benign Bishop'.

When my great grandmother was in her nineties, she said she didn't want to be buried in the local churchyard, which was in the woods, because she thought she would get frightened in the dark. Well, 'Uncle Ken', as he was also affectionately known in racing, has been buried in a beautiful spot on a hill in Minto, near Hawick, and he will have the best view of his beloved Borders that any graveyard offers. He had requested that 'The Carnival Is Over' be played at his thanksgiving service, and so it was, as his mourners left the church. He had also insisted that no single-shot drinks be served at the party afterwards – they must all be family size – and that no one must go short. They didn't.

For those who missed the *Telegraph*'s obituary of Uncle Ken, I will just recall the quote he once made about his triple heart-bypass operation. 'One for blood,' he said, 'two for Tio Pepe.'

Briefly, for the younger readers, Uncle Ken was a highly successful trainer who saddled Wyndburgh to second place in two Grand Nationals for his wife Rhona, who had herself trained the horse to finish second in one. Ken also won five Scottish Nationals, and rode one of the winners himself. Wyndburgh was one of the unluckiest losers in the National when jockey Tim Brookshaw's stirrup-iron broke at Becher's. Despite kicking his other foot out, Brookshaw had a terrific duel with Oxo and was beaten only by a length. Brookshaw's only comment afterwards was that he would probably be a bit stiff milking the cows the following morning.

Frequently, Ken saddled more winners than he had horses in the yard – a rarely achieved feat these days. He once saddled five winners from five runners in a day at Wolverhampton and eight Cheltenham Festival winners.

Ken was a farmer, a single-handicap golfer, a tennis player and a director of the Royal Highland Show. As an auctioneer, he founded Doncaster Bloodstock Sales. He was a master of many trades. Harry Beeby, managing director of the sales company now, recalls that Ken had two gears – flat out or fast asleep. He would often fall asleep in the middle of a sentence at a dinner party and wake up to complete it three-quarters of an hour later. As two of the addresses at his thanksgiving were given by auctioneers, Beeby and Mouse White, the congregation, which included many trainers, stayed motionless for fear of having something knocked down to them.

In 1980, Cockle Strand was going through the ring as an Irish bumper winner. 'Here's one to win the Scottish National in 1982,' said Ken, who was on the rostrum at the time. A few minutes later, when he had taken the last bid for the gelding from one of his own owners, he added, 'He's got a big chance because he's coming back to Hassendean Bank with me.' Cockle Strand duly won the 1982 Scottish National, beating his stable companion Three to One. On another occasion, the bidding was beginning to slow down and he tried desperately to get one last bid out of the under-bidder. 'The bid is against you, madam,' he said, whereupon 'madam' promptly got up and left in disgust. 'Oh dear,' he exclaimed, 'it must have been a man.' It had been.

But perhaps his greatest *faux pas* was when Beeby was getting successful bidders to sign the chit. He had been unable to see clearly to whom one horse had been knocked down.

'Sorry, Uncle Ken,' he said. 'I couldn't see who got that one.'

'Over there,' said Ken, who had forgotten to take his microphone off. 'The fellow in the front row who looks like a baboon.' ◘

HERE'S A QUESTION. If you have spent sixteen years as a Master of Foxhounds and a land agent, and the following six years spreading the gospel as an Anglican priest, what are you uniquely qualified to do? Manage a racecourse is the answer I was looking for.

That is the curriculum vitae of Stratford's racecourse manager, Stephen Lambert, who is in charge of his second Horse and Hound Cup meeting today. Stephen, 50, has been manager and company secretary at the Bard's racecourse for fifteen months. When he arrived the Easter before last he was literally thrown in at the deep end: the course was under five feet of water and the repair and refurbishment bill came to £600,000. 'We were able to kayak over the top of the fences,' he recalls. 'It was all very well until I discovered our groundsman couldn't swim so we rapidly rowed ashore.'

Stephen's hunting career started off with the Taunton Vale. He moved on to the Warwickshire and finally ended up as joint master and huntsman of the Heythrop. One day, although it probably was not quite as dramatic as this, while looking for a fox he found, instead, the Lord. To members of the Heythrop, this gave a new slant to the Sermon on the Mount – the mount being a seventeen-hands hunter. Stephen then trained to become a non-stipendiary Church of England vicar, was ordained as a deacon in 1990, as a vicar the following year, and was a member of a team looking after half a dozen parishes in the Stow-on-the-Wold area. He restricted his Sunday sermons to the same time that it takes to run a three-mile novice chase on good ground – about seven minutes. If he went on longer, a friend in the front pew would start tapping his watch. Extensive research failed to find out which were more exciting, his sermons or three-mile novice chases.

He married trainer Henry Daly to Clarissa, with whom he now has a couple of horses, and was known as the Galloping Vicar when he rode out for Nigel Twiston-Davies. When Stephen was an Anglican, he was reported to the local Catholic bishop for going into a hotel room with a woman. It was his wife, Jane. On another occasion he was travelling by train from Newcastle to London for a religious gathering. As it approached London he went to the loo to change into his clerical kit. When he returned to take up his seat the old lady opposite him, to whom he had been talking most of the way, stopped him. 'I'm terribly sorry, vicar,' she said, 'but there is a terribly nice chap already sitting in that seat.'

In 1996, Stephen became a Catholic and his present situation is that he is a Catholic layman. 'The Catholic Church does not allow an ex-Anglican who is married to be a priest,' he says, 'but it is considering its position with me because they haven't come across a racecourse manager before.'

As a Master of Foxhounds myself I'd rather given up hope of salvation, but this news has brightened my day. ◼

THERE LOOK LIKE BEING ABOUT FIFTEEN RUNNERS in tomorrow's Marlborough Cup at Barbury Castle. The race has attracted entries from here, France, Ireland and the United States. The only female rider among all the boys is Lt Lucy Horner, but that is the last thing that will bother her on outsider Master Crusader.

On Thursday, when I tried to contact her on her mobile – is that what signals have come to in the British Army? – she was about to take her platoon of 28 male soldiers jogging for a couple of hours. When she failed to return the call later that night, I thought she might have been posted to Kosovo. Luckily not.

A veteran of two Grand Military Gold Cups – she finished fourth both times – and a winner of three races under Rules, Lt Horner, 22, has considerably more bows to her string than any other jockey in tomorrow's big race. She is a qualified pilot, but when she dropped out of university she had no TA or cadet experience. 'I was a military idiot,' she says. 'I didn't know whether to join the army or the air force.' The RAF's loss is the Royal Irish Regiment's gain, however, and Lt Horner is shortly to become one of the first female platoon commanders in the infantry, until now about as much a woman's arena as the MCC. 'The army is pretty much gender-free now,' says our Lucy. 'In the old days we might have been there for the flower arranging, but today we do assault courses with the best of them.'

The army's current advertising slogan is 'Be the Best'. As Master Crusader is thirteen and likes very firm ground, it is unlikely the pair will quite aspire to that tomorrow, but you never know.

IF THIS COLUMN IS A LOAD OF OLD RUBBISH – and it usually is – then there is one trainer who will be salivating at the thought of it.

Demolition is also a favourite topic of ours. You know, the jockey who flattens a fence on a horse or in his car; the horse that knocks down a block of stables by leaning against a wall or gets loose, gallops off down the lane and ends up trashing its owner's gleaming Porsche. Well, this week we've found the ultimate: a man who gets paid for demolishing things and whose company moves 1.5 million tons of London's rubbish annually. Cue the theme tune from *EastEnders* and step forward increasingly successful Epsom trainer, businessman and workaholic Terry Mills.

He will have the proudest moment of his six-year training career a week today when he sends out 50–1 shot All the Way for the Derby. The one thing All the Way won't get is travel sickness. Other things in the colt's favour are that we know he gets the trip and he has already demolished one Godolphin hotshot, Rhagaas.

Mills, 60, oversees two lots at Loretta Lodge before having a swim and popping off to the office in Mitcham, where he runs A. & J. Bull, one of the capital's waste management companies. It is one of the great rags-to-tons-of-rags stories of our time. Mills started off with one lorry in 1962, bought a three-truck concern in 1969, and his fleet now consists of over 200 vehicles including dust carts, low loaders, road cleaners and skip lorries.

He had his first horse as an owner with John Sutcliffe 25 years ago and called it As Dug, the raw state in which much of the sand ballast he was digging out of the middle of Kempton racecourse at the time was sold. Later on he bought Loretta Lodge, installing David Wilson and Wally Carter before taking out his own licence in 1993. This season he has had thirteen winners at a 25 per cent strike rate, but what proves he is deadly serious are the prices he is paying for yearlings. Norton, a Woodman two-year-old colt, cost 350,000 guineas, and Bid for Fame cost 130,000 guineas. You wouldn't underestimate Terry Mills in a bulldozer, and I don't think we should underestimate him on a racecourse. ■

THERE'S BEEN PLENTY GOING ON so we haven't, until now, had time to record the fact that Enda Bolger, who has ridden more point-to-point winners in Ireland than anyone else, has hung up his boots. He said that Risk of Thunder would be his last ride in public, and the horse gave an exhibition of bank jumping before romping up in the La Touche Cup at Punchestown ten days ago.

I was once asked, by what I presume was a slightly dyslexic racegoer at the Cheltenham Festival, what the hell a bird called Edna was doing riding in the National Hunt Chase. The follow-up question, before I'd had time to reply, was whether she was attractive or not.

On his return to the Punchestown winner's enclosure, Enda, a favourite with the locals and equally popular among the professional jockeys, was given a hero's welcome. Among those applauding was Istabraq's jockey Charlie Swan. When, much like the winner of Wimbledon does with his tennis racket, Bolger threw his whip into the crowd, everyone roared their approval, nobody more enthusiastically than Charlie – until he remembered that he had lent his whip to Bolger. Charlie then had to dive into the crowd and retrieve it for his following day's engagement with Istabraq, all but reducing the whip's ten-year-old new owner to tears. Such was the stick that Charlie received about his stick that when he returned victorious on Istabraq he had no option but to fling the whip back into the crowd.

This brings to mind a story about Lester Piggott. On Piggott's retirement, a foreign gentleman who was present at Nottingham in 1985 thought it would be a good idea to get his 'last' whip so he could auction it for charity. He realised it would make a lot of money, so in order to secure it he offered Piggott a few hundred quid for it. The legendary jockey, so the story goes, gladly accepted. A few months later Piggott was at the Newmarket sales, spotted the gentleman, tapped him on the shoulder and, bearing in mind he had already sold him his 'last' whip, mumbled in that inimitable, almost inaudible way of his, 'You remember that stick? I've got a few more if you're interested.' ▣

ONE OF THE FEW INVOLVED in today's Martell Foxhunters' who knows what it is like to win round Aintree, other than Rough Quest, is first-season point-to-point trainer Gary Brown. As an amateur jockey he won the 1994 Foxhunters' on Killeshin for John 'Mad' Manners.

It was no mean feat for Brown, 32, for two reasons. Firstly, he did not sit on a horse until he was 23. Secondly, his instructions were not the most inspiring. He and Manners set off to walk the course, taking in The Chair first. Manners turned green and made his way back, leaving Brown to walk on alone. The jockey didn't see the trainer again until he legged him up. 'Pull up before The Chair,' Manners instructed. 'I could drive my Land Rover through that ditch. It can't be jumped.' Brown disregarded the orders and romped home.

He turned professional the following season but within eight months ruptured his pancreas and spleen in a fall at Uttoxeter and retired. He now trains near Lambourn. ▩

ONE OF THE YOUNGEST JOCKEYS taking part at this year's Cheltenham Festival will be Sam Stronge, who reached the tender age of seventeen in January. He sprang to some kind of prominence ten months ago when he won a hunter chase at Ascot on his second ride under Rules, and a bright future seemed assured. That has, to some extent, been confirmed by seven winners this season.

Comparisons were made with his stepfather and proud mentor Robert Stronge. Luckily for Sam, when it comes to style the similarities are mercifully few. Robert, 37, rode 120 winners in sixteen seasons and rode deeper than Andy Thornton before Thornton had made the Aubrey Brabazon look of the late 1940s fashionable again.

To his credit, Robert usually gave his mounts an enthusiastic ride, and if the 500–1 outsider you picked in the Grand National office sweepstake had R. Stronge on board it invariably gave you a run for your money by making the early running – remember Big Brown Bear and Rupertino? – and they usually got round too.

He retired once to start training, but when he couldn't find suitable jockeys to partner his horses he took out his riding licence again. One horse on which he made his comeback ran the wrong way around Windsor, during a race, taking him perilously close to the banks of the Thames and proving that you can indeed take a horse to water. Robert, whose training is now on a small but successful scale, didn't think it through too carefully and ran the horse next time out at Worcester, where he broke the landspeed record for a towpath, this time alongside the Severn.

One of his greatest claims to fame was not so much a day as a trip to the races. At the time the IRA were particularly active in mainland Britain. He, Tony Carroll and Martin Lynch were off to Market Rasen and arranged to meet fellow jockey and member of Mensa Gerry Newman in Towcester, to give him a lift. Unbeknown to Newman he had parked his pink number-plated car on the forecourt of Towcester police station. When the jockeys returned they found that downtown Towcester had been cordoned off for most of the day while bomb disposal experts carried out a controlled explosion on what was by then Newman's ex-car. All four were then subjected to the longest interview of their career. Unfortunately the interviewer was an anti-terrorist police officer, not a eulogistic racing journalist like myself.

I wasn't sure how to put my last question to Stronge Sr in case it caused offence. Do you, er, think Sam might turn out to be a better jockey than, er, yourself, for example? 'I hope to hell he does,' said Robert modestly. 'It wouldn't be too hard.' ■

AS THINGS STAND, at a time when it is popular to pigeonhole trainers and jockeys with a superlative, if Martin Pipe is the winning-most trainer of all time then Jamie Osborne, until he trains a winner, is, jointly with a few others no doubt, the winning-least trainer of all time.

Somewhere in between, but somewhat nearer Osborne (isn't every trainer?) than Pipe, is Malvern farmer-cum-trainer George Yardley. He's trained a small number of horses, either with a permit or licence, for nigh on 33 years now. Once in a blue moon he comes up with a very good, fun horse, and blow me if there wasn't a blue moon the other night.

In point-to-pointing's heyday he rode one, Gelderland, who won seventeen races. In the early 1970s he trained one, Deblin's Green, who won the National Hunt Chase at Cheltenham, the John Corbet Cup at Stratford and the 1973 Welsh National, ridden by Rupert Wakley's father Nigel. He was second in another Welsh National but not so lucky in the real thing. One year his jockey, David Cartwright, was kicked in the leg in mid-air over The Chair and had to pull up – the only time in 160 years of National history that this excuse has been used. Another year, when Deblin's Green went left at the Canal Turn, Nigel Wakley, for some reason best known to himself, went right. (They do like to be slightly different, those Wakleys.) Royal Russe was second in the 1982 Welsh National, and last week River Wye absolutely romped home at Kempton. The Mildmay of Flete now beckons, provided Cheltenham is not a bog. If it is, then George will wait for Aintree.

George was born at Upper Woodsfield Farm, still his home, in 1934. 'Right here by the telephone,' he says. 'I've got a good memory. I don't actually remember being born but I can remember the dog barking when the doctor left.' Valentine's Day 1967 stands out in his impressive memory. His horse Woodmanton won at Leicester at 25–1, his first daughter was born, and part of his house burnt down. All on the same day. The local paper headlined the story 'Farmer George's Red Hot Treble'.

Another occasion stands out. An old man who lived in a Keeper's Cottage miles from anywhere in the Malverns died one Christmas Eve. He was discovered on Boxing Day night during a snowstorm, and as the local farmer it was George who was called upon to precariously ferry the police, a doctor and undertakers up to the cottage on a platform on the back of his tractor. The tractor was overloaded as it was going up so of course the body just tipped the balance on the way back. Every time the tractor came to a bump or uphill stretch the front wheels reared up off the ground and the body rolled off the back. If life hadn't quite been extinguished before the body set off on its last, unceremonious journey, it most certainly was afterwards.

MONSIGNOR STANDS BETWEEN MARK PEILL and a glorious first Festival winner with Barney Knows in the Royal & SunAlliance Novice hurdle on Wednesday. Now I realise that's a bit like saying to a casual swimmer that only the English Channel stands between him and France, so we'll go with Mark's more realistic opinion that his horse is a good each-way prospect.

Mark, 30, was born within a few furlongs of the Knavesmire in York, left school at sixteen and joined Bill Haigh in Malton, where he learnt step one: how to ride. Mark qualified for a long-service medal when surviving two seasons with Jenny Pitman. During that time she won the Gold Cup with Garrison Savannah, so he is no stranger to Cheltenham winners. Mark then looked after Master Oats as a novice chaser at Kim Bailey's, and, edging his way up north again, was travelling head lad to Lynda Ramsden. He took the plunge to go it alone about five years ago.

Gradually, Mark has built up a string of 25 horses and he has recently moved them to the famous Whitewall Stables in Malton. It may not be strong on Festival winners but the place boasts 40 Classic winners, having been the home of John Scott, the outstanding trainer of the Victorian era. Between 1827 and 1863 he won five Derbys and sixteen St Legers. It is said that Scott's ghost still haunts Whitewall. 'Well,' says Mark, 'I've only been in the house a fortnight and I've already heard him walking across the breakfast room with his walking stick.' Let's hope Scott imparts some of his wisdom rather than – and this is slightly more likely, I suspect – his walking stick on the new incumbent.

It is not the only thing that haunts Mark. When at the age of sixteen he worked for Haigh, he shared digs with Willie Dwan, a jockey who used to work for Jimmy FitzGerald. One night they bought a bottle of Scotch, took a glass each before bedtime and placed the bottle in the fridge. The following night, when they went for a nightcap, they noticed that some of the whisky had gone. The following night a bit more had gone, and so on until after seven days half the bottle's contents had disappeared. Feeling slightly cheated, Mark decided they should get their own back on the thief by peeing into the bottle. This he did, filling it up to the top, so that the mix was roughly one half Scotch and one half Yorkshire, as it were.

As deterrents go it was useless: a week later another two-thirds of the bottle had gone. At the end of the month the pair were moving out of their lodgings and the landlady was devastated to hear that they were leaving. 'I have a small confession to make,' she said as they stood at the door with their bags packed. Ah, they thought, she's going to own up about the Scotch. 'I knew you boys liked it,' she said, 'so I've been putting a wee drop of whisky in your trifle every night.' ▩

AT AN AGE when most professional jockeys are counting on the fingers of one hand the seasons they have until retirement, Alex Charles-Jones, a self-taught equine artist, was contemplating his first ride in a point-to-point. On a spare ride at Andoversford it soon became apparent, after the animal had hit two Land Rovers between leaving the paddock and getting on to the course, why it was spare. Nine years on, not far from Andoversford actually, he joined a select band of accomplished amateurs to have ridden the winners of the Aintree and Cheltenham Foxhunters when he brought Cavalero with a late run to pass eight other horses after the last fence and pip the brave Real Value on the line. In contrast to most horses who win at Cheltenham and then go on to Aintree, Cavalero has already won the Aintree Foxhunters, two years ago in a bog.

Now aged 40, Alex is hoping he will get the call-up to ride the John 'Mad' Manners-trained Cavalero in the Grand National in three weeks' time. He has, after all, painted a few National winners; now it's time to ride one. Manners seems pretty agreeable to the idea, 'Providing I haven't sold 'im by then,' he says – joking, I think. 'Farming's not going very well as you know, Mr Marmytage.' Last year Alex was barred from riding in the National because he had not had the required number of winners. Sean Curran rode instead. The saddle slipped approaching The Chair – there is never a convenient moment for a saddle to slip but, relatively speaking, a more convenient moment could have been found – and he pulled the horse up.

Alex was anything but a late developer as an artist, gaining his first commission, of a local stallion, at the age of eleven. Since then he has painted most top horses. His 'Desert Orchid' represents January in this year's Injured Jockeys' Fund calendar, and for fourteen years the owner of the Racehorse Owners' Association's Horse of the Year was presented with a Charles-Jones portrait of the said animal.

At one stage sister Lucy, an interior decorator, used to bring on young horses. She was lunging a particularly wild one when brother Alex arrived. 'Stop faffing around with that horse,' he said dismissively. 'I'll get on it.' His next instruction to his sister after an act which displayed aspects of both bravery and stupidity was, 'Fetch me an ambulance.' The horse had set off like a bucking bronco and fired him off. He was about to hit the ground when it kicked him with both barrels fifteen feet back up in the air, breaking his nose and ribs.

Last Thursday, like the day when as a five-year-old he discovered matches, is an occasion the Charles-Jones family won't forget in a hurry, although for different reasons. He and year-younger brother Gareth, the former jockey, had been shown 'these wonderful lighting sticks' by an older sibling and thought that the new barn, where straw for the horses and his father's sparkling Bristol motor car were kept, would be the ideal place to try them out. For stunning effect they were right in their belief that it would be the ideal place. The barn and the car never did recover. ▪

MONICA DICKINSON IS THE ONLY WOMAN to have trained a Whitbread Gold Cup winner, and that was fifteen years ago. Today it wouldn't be a great surprise if she was joined on that roll of honour by Lydia Richards. In what is possibly a first for racing, she will be both running and wearing Eau de Cologne.

I know he'll be rather disappointed by this statement, but, with apologies to Josh Gifford who I dare say is pretty fragrant himself, Lydia is unquestionably the best-looking trainer on the south coast. What is more, since moving to Funtington, near Chichester, three years ago – it was built by Derek Kent who trained Grand Canyon there – she has become a major force to be reckoned with at places other than Fontwell.

She has a good riding pedigree. Her father, Mike Cooper, was a permit-holder in Hampshire, while her grandfather owned a racecourse at Paulsgrove near Portsmouth. Like many ex-racecourses – unfortunately that doesn't include Wolverhampton – it is now a housing estate. For most of her time, first with pointers, then with a permit and even for a decade with a full licence, total capacity for her yard was eight. As you know, racing is more of a numbers game than *Countdown*. Gradually she is increasing her string and branching out on to the Flat.

Last year, with just three Flat horses, she won six races with Brilliant Red and Secret Spring. Brilliant Red won at Ascot and Sandown Park, and last November famously touched off Running Stag at Lingfield Park where Pat Eddery had got off him in order to ride the runner-up.

Both will be back this season, Brilliant Red possibly on Monday and Secret Spring when the ground firms up – which, come to think of it, might not be this season.

Flying the flag for Lydia's jumpers is the novice Eau de Cologne. He and trainer both went to Ayr for the Scottish National a fortnight ago but, despite having travelled the length of the country, she took him out because of the fast ground. That decision could reap its reward today.

Though she was married to one for a time, her own career as a jockey was very short-lived. She had one ride, fell at the seventh on a horse that had never got round, and both lay there for dead. In the subsequent medical examination the doctor discovered there was only one thing wrong with her: she was four months pregnant. Her son Daniel, now 20, studies business and beer drinking at Bristol University. So, despite the fall, he is clearly normal. ■

IF THE WORLD ENDED TODAY or something even more cataclysmic happened and racing was banned for ever, then Francis Norton would be champion jockey in this last, truncated Flat season. We are almost halfway through May, and with 34 winners so far (his best season is 47 winners) he is setting a cracking pace. Granted, plenty of those winners have come on the all-weather while other jockeys have been sideways on a sun lounger, but Franny's winners have not altogether dried up since the turf season opened nearly two months ago in March.

At Chester this week he was almost on home territory, having been brought up in Liverpool's Belle Vale – 'The word "Belle" is the only glamorous thing about it,' he joked. He is as popular in those parts as Robbie Fowler. Unfortunately, he missed out on winning the Chester Cup by a short head.

His current position, at the age of 29, is down pretty much to hard work and sweat. His father worked for Dunlop (tyres, not John) and horses did not play any part in the Norton household. Remarkably, instead of his mates suggesting that he was the right size to get in through small windows, they were constructive enough to tell him he was the ideal size to become a jockey . . . more than once. This carefree careers advice was heeded by Franny, and when he was told he didn't have enough experience he sought it in a job with Peter Arthur, in Didcot, for twelve months. Franny then went to Charlie Nelson as an apprentice, but he retired, so Franny joined Alan Bailey, in Newmarket. When Bailey moved to Cheshire, Franny had come to like Newmarket so much he decided to finish his time with Geoff Wragg.

Last season his victory on She's Our Mare in the Cambridgeshire was voted ride of the season. He has continued in that sort of form this year, though there was a stage when racing might have lost Francis Norton to another sport, and I don't mean as the projectile in the popular Aussie sport of 'small people throwing'. You see, and this is one of the reasons I'd never be anything other than polite about him despite his ability to do 7st 11lb, he was six-times stable lads boxing champion (never once knocked down) and was selected to represent England in the Kuala Lumpur Commonwealth Games. He declined the latter to concentrate on riding, which is looking like a good decision. ▣

NOT LONG AGO, if you blessed a trainer with the words 'May the Lord remain with you', he would probably have thought you were referring to the hope that one of his larger and trickier owners, probably a Jockey Club member with a few acres in London and considerably more in the country, would keep patronising his yard with his lordship's homebreds for some time to come.

Since January, however, and hallelujah, horse racing has had its own chaplain in the shape of the Rev. Graham Locking. He is now more of a regular on Newmarket Heath during first lot than the most fervent work-watcher, and can often be spotted at the races in his dog collar.

It has been quite a big week for Graham: York on Thursday and a guest appearance on the BBC's *Songs of Praise* tomorrow evening. It will be the *Vicar of Dibley* next.

His previous form suggests his new parish of stud and stable will be a doddle, though of course it never is. A minister for 22 years, and extremely approachable, he started in the East End of London, running a centre for homeless alcoholics and their pet lice. Between 1980 and 1985, during the miners' strike and the running down of the steel industry, he worked in Sheffield. For the last fifteen years he has done stints in Paisley and Birkenhead. If he could do us fifteen minutes in the press room some time, that would be helpful.

Apart from the Good Lord, Graham is answerable to SCORE (Sports Chaplaincy Offering Resources and Encouragement), a charity set up nine years ago by the chaplain at Manchester United (no wonder they're top of the League).

In the past – and there's a slight irony here – he has had to deal with the damage wrought by one man and his pitchfork. Now he's having to cope with lots of people with lots of pitchforks. 'At the moment I'm getting known and building up relationships,' he says, 'so that people can approach me when things go wrong. Young people in stables do have a feeling of being at the bottom of the pile, often having come into the sport with aspirations of becoming a jockey. The first joke I was told when I came here was about the lad who had moved yards so often that the only stable he hadn't worked in was the one at Bethlehem.' ◼

COLIN WEEDON, second-hand car dealer and trainer, is giving up the training. Though he sent out Miracle Man to win at the Cheltenham Festival, he has concluded that training a dozen horses is bad for the wallet.

He caught the bug when he bought a one-twelfth share in a horse with Kim Bailey which eventually developed into a barter system, he supplying the trainer with cars, the trainer looking after his horses at a reduced cost. After Kim had crashed another, this one within a fortnight of getting it, head on into a cement mixer, the thought occurred that it might be cheaper for business if he trained his own.

If you're trying to sell a horse, advised Kim, you must convey to the prospective owners that racehorse ownership is fun. With this in mind he had some people new to the game down to see a horse.

'If it won a race,' asked one lady, 'would we be able to celebrate?'

'Of course,' said Colin. 'We had eleven winners last year, eleven celebrations, and I had eleven hang-overs.'

This marketing was not lost on the Irish lad who was leading up the horse. 'To be sure,' he said, 'it's a good job you're not Martin Pipe!' ◼

THAT NOT INSIGNIFICANT LITTLE BUSINESS which supplies racing with its raw material – breeding the nag – rarely gets much of a mention outside specialist magazines. For all the information I've given you about racehorse breeding in the Diary, you'd be forgiven for thinking that *Pacemaker* was something heart transplant patients subscribe to for an update on the advances being made in cardiac surgery. It is, in fact, a monthly racing magazine with a strong emphasis on pedigrees.

Did you know that when Looks Like Trouble runs at Down Royal today he will, in a way, be going home? He is by Zaffaran, who stands at Scarvagh House Stud in Northern Ireland. I've always thought – though I'm assured it's a misconception – that the breeding of jumpers must be as frustrating for the breeder as it is for the teaser pony, who has to warm the mares up because an equine stud like Zaffaran hasn't got the time for foreplay.

Breeding jumpers is no short-term affair. When a stallion has proved himself with a Gold Cup winner, he is often old, has a grey beard, gets around with the use of a Zimmer frame and has the sex drive of a neutered cat. If you're lucky he's up for it once a year with a favourite old girlfriend. In Britain it's doubly frustrating because Ireland has such favourable tax advantages. At Doncaster Sales on Thursday, nine of the ten top-priced jumping mares were on the next boat to Dublin. The incentive to use British-based stallions is a pot of £1.68 million in breeders' prizes for certain races, but that's still nothing quite like putting one over the Inland Revenue by upping sticks to Ireland.

None of this has put off Simon Sweeting, 34, who has just taken a lease on the Overbury Stud near Tewkesbury. If he does really well, he won't become a millionaire; he'll become slightly better off than skint. Sheikh Mohammed has sent him Ascot Gold Cup winner Kayf Tara, who will be given a good chance of becoming a Flat stallion but, at a bargain £3,000 a mating, should attract some decent jumping mares. Kayf Tara's full brother, Opera House, is a leading sire in Japan, and full brothers have a good record at stud – for example, Fairy King and Sadler's Wells, Kris and Diesis.

Having been to America and Ireland and spent time with Henry Cecil and Luca Cumani, Simon has spent considerably longer learning the ropes than brain surgeons do before their first frontal lobotomy. He also rode in point-to-points, though he was overshadowed by his brother Rupert, who single-handedly transformed hunt racing as a spectator sport because of his penchant for riding through wings. Simon's first ride was for his father at Larkhill. The race included David Loder, who after a French sabbatical is about to be unleashed on Newmarket again. After the race, Simon, who had been a close second, was debriefing his dad, Christopher, when Loder, a close friend, marched up. Ignoring Simon as if he wasn't there, he was nothing if not to the point: 'Christopher, do you want me to ride that horse next time?' said Loder. 'I think I'd have won on it.' Some things never change. ▣

WHAT DOES A CLERK OF THE COURSE DO apart from walk the dog around the course and then field calls from trainers enquiring about the going? That is the question I put to Mark Kershaw, who will be overseeing his second Hennessy today.

Having been in charge of four Derbys, he is an old hand, but no less relaxed because of it. There are, it seems, more banana skins around a racecourse than there are in a Fyffes container ship leaving Honduras. 'Hang on a second,' he said at 7.30 yesterday morning, having already walked the dog. 'I'm moving furniture into the new stand [cost £9.1 million and designed by Lord Norman Foster].

'My recurring nightmare is leaving all the hurdles out for the bumper. It stems back to the first bumper we ever ran at Sandown. The runners went so wide round the top bend that one of them ended up jumping the downhill fence. We immediately reduced the maximum field for bumpers.' Thus was the life expectancy of the bumper jockey proportionately increased.

Mark was a land agent minding an estate at Hopetoun House, near Edinburgh, when he answered an advert for an assistant at Sandown. After being promoted, he left Sandown in 1988 to join the Tote, and in 1992 he returned to his calling, racecourse management, running Ayr and Musselburgh before the opportunity arose to join

Newbury in 1999. That's a bit depressing – 47 years in two sentences.

Underpinning the whole shooting match is the trust of the trainers. 'For the trainer, the ground is the most important thing, prize money is secondary, so he can make a constructive decision to run or not,' points out our man. 'At Ayr, it was even more important because 80 per cent of runners had travelled over 100 miles to get there.' Telling a trainer the ground is good when it's good to firm is like telling a size 10 female she's obese – it doesn't go down well.

He also has to look after his sponsors. At Ayr, the winner of the Ladbrokes Gold Cup is traditionally draped in a rug bearing their logo. Theses rugs had a habit of going missing, so Mike Dillon of Ladbrokes rang up on a daily basis for a fortnight to check it was there. Every time he was told it was in a cupboard, safe from harm. The big day arrived, Mike and the Ladbrokes high brass were taken to the cupboard, and the box was opened with some ceremony. Inside, in all its glory, was a, um, frilly tablecloth. ◘

IF TED HEATH was the much-respected 'Father of the House', then Jimmy Frost is the equivalent of the National Hunt weighing room.

Not far behind him with a 40th birthday on the very near horizon is a man who knows Market Rasen better than I know my garden path. He supplements his income from riding with a demolition business – on some of the horses he rides the distinction between the two jobs is sometimes blurred – and he is already (and neither of us can work out why) enjoying his best season ever with thirteen winners.

More clues? If impending birthday celebrations are not enough, his son had his first ride in an amateur steeplechase recently. Ladies and gentlemen, I give you racing's Peter Pan, a fine wine getting better with age (though I believe his name is more synonymous with beer), the evergreen – and before I tarnish his good image with any more clichés – Billy Worthington. Everyone knows who he is, yet I suspect few know that if he's not demolishing open ditches he's demolishing buildings and reclaiming the bricks.

He had his first ride in 1977, the same year in which Red Rum won his last National, and does not intend to have his last until he has caused some confusion and ridden against his son – confusion because his son is also called William Worthington.

Billy is not your stereotypical jockey. In fact he breaks just about every mould. For a start he lives in Hinckley in Leicestershire where, unlike Lambourn, you're unlikely to get bowled over by a loose racehorse stepping out of the house first thing in the morning and there aren't 25 colleagues within a five-mile radius with whom to share lifts to the races.

He has another job when most jockeys won't even glance at 'situations vacant' for fear of being written off. And unlike most jockeys he has, to the best of my knowledge, never complained, even though during his 23-year career he has probably ridden more yaks than a Tibetan herdsman (if that's what they ride). He's brave, seems completely unfazed if the horse needs three handlers in the paddock, and gets on with it, mainly minding his own business.

The majority of his rides are for Michael Chapman, and the rest for Lincolnshire trainers. Hence he is the undisputed Victor Ludorum at Market Rasen. Chapman trains across the road from the course. When he runs his horses there they often hang badly left, tail themselves off down the back straight as they pass their stable and then sprint by the whole field up the finishing straight as they head back for home. The versatile Cromwell, whom Billy rides in the Arthur Stephenson Chase at Wetherby today, is a case in point. As you all know, Market Rasen is right-handed, but Cromwell hangs left and jumps left. Yet Chapman's five-year-old has won five times there, over every trip. ■

ON TUESDAY, Frankie Dettori took delivery of an old mate – Fujiyama Crest. The eight-year-old was the final leg of the jockey's Magnificent Seven at Ascot in 1996. Frankie has bought him as a hack for his wife Catherine, and it's no less than the old warrior deserves.

Fujiyama Crest has, in fact, had a few ups and downs himself since making all to beat Northern Fleet a neck to complete Frankie's 25,095–1 seven-timer. Initially he was sold for 69,000 guineas to go hurdling with Nicky Henderson, but on returning to Seven Barrows he slipped off the ramp of the horsebox and damaged himself almost beyond repair.

Since then he's won a hurdle, been point-to-pointing (unsuccessfully) and, most recently with Roger Curtis, has won on the Flat again, landing a lowly claimer at Nottingham in June.

He was once sold for 8,000 guineas at Malvern Sales and was about to return there when Frankie stepped in to buy his well-earned retirement.

CHAPTER FOUR

THE ART OF TRAINING A RACEHORSE

Excessive use of the whip

IF YOU POSSESS A BETTING-SHOP MENTALITY – e.g. a jockey can be both brilliant and crap within half an hour if he rides you a winner followed by a loser – it will have crossed your mind when you've backed a series of losers from the same stable, how the hell did that trainer get a licence? Do the Jockey Club dish out licences with the same generosity that Jenny Pitman gives out rollickings? With apologies to trainers Tate, Hern and Thomson Jones, can any old Tom, Dick or Harry get one?

The last fortnight in January is one of the most hectic in the year for Richard Smith, for eight years the efficient boss of the Licensing Department at Portman Square, for by 1 February all 500 public trainers in this country must have renewed their licences, at no little cost. A trainer with fewer than 25 horses is looking at posting a cheque for £703.91 this week, and the fee is on an upward sliding scale. In France you have to sit a written exam. Here there are six or seven criteria you must meet to join the 500, not the least of which is supreme optimism. You'll also need favourable references, proof of security of tenure, letters from owners confirming demand, and your yard must pass a rigorous inspection by the Security Department. Only two years ago the drawing up of a business plan became mandatory, as did the financial guarantee – without recourse to armed robbery or winning the lottery – that you could get your hands on £35,000 at a moment's notice.

The answer to the questions posed above is that one in five applicants fail. 'It's quite an emotive thing to be turned down,' says Smith. 'We've had people write to the Queen Mother and the Prime Minister, but more commonly it's to their MP or solicitor.' One man threatened to bring himself and his horse to Portman Square where he would chain himself to the railings; Smith, he said, would have to look after the horse. Another, who was given a licence, offered to chop off his little finger in front of the Licensing Committee if he was a failure. For another two applicants, all was in place except the financial guarantees. One, when asked what security he had, grinned, undid his cuff and revealed a gold Rolex watch. It wasn't considered good enough. Nor was the wallet produced when the other man was asked the same question. He pulled out a dozen different cards and began listing credit limits.

Experience is paramount. A jump trainer arrived before the committee one day requesting a dual licence so that he could train on the Flat. The committee was worried he hadn't the relevant experience.

'But I've spent time with Guy Harwood,' he said.

'How long did you spend with him?' the committee enquired.

'Well,' said the jumping man, 'I went to his open day.'

The final barrier is that interview. Once, the Licensing Committee and the Disciplinary Committee met on the same day. 'Victims' and applicants shared the same waiting room. The next 'applicant' was summoned and it was several minutes before both parties realised he should have been in front of the Disciplinary Committee.

'Our biggest file belongs to Rod Simpson,' reveals Smith. 'It's no secret he has moved yards quite often. He rang once and I told him he was causing me a headache. The next day I got a suspicious package in the post. It was a packet of aspirin with a note saying sorry.'

Ireland has a similar system. When their Licensing Committee sought to interview a dairy farmer from Wexford who wanted a full trainer's licence, they telephoned him to tell him the time of his interview. 'Jaysus,' said the farmer, 'I'm too busy then. Would it be all right if my brother attended instead?'

Being refused a licence, though, is a bit like a big losing bet: you don't tell too many people about it. Giles Bravery, the Newmarket trainer who does well with his small string, once applied for an amateur rider's licence and enclosed with it two written references, one from a trainer and another from his father's then stable jockey. The letter from the jockey contained the damning request to the committee, 'Don't give this man a licence to ride for all the tea in China.' And they didn't.

Finally, I remember one spiv, with more wallet than wisdom, who couldn't tell a fetlock from a forelock. After owning horses for ten minutes, he thought he would train them for himself. To train jumpers you are required to have, within hacking distance of your stable, at least one plain fence and an open ditch. When the Jockey Club security officer arrived at the stable to inspect the schooling ground he fell about laughing. There, as required, was a plain fence followed, about fifteen strides away, by a trench.

THE STIRK FAMILY have made more than the average family's contribution to racing. Anthony, who has patched up and put down some of northern racing's great horses, went with Michael Dickinson from Yorkshire to Manton as vet-in-residence. And contrary to public opinion, the first long-awaited winner out of the revamped training establishment back in the 1980s was not a Dickinson two-year-old; it was Maxine Stirk's Sealed in a selling hurdle.

When the Manton bubble burst and Dickinson sailed off in the *Mayflower*, Anthony and Maxine returned to Ripon, from where Maxine, as a permit-holder, sent out Simple Pleasure to win fifteen races under National Hunt Rules. As he was her only horse, she used to work him with her Border terrier Slipper. That was fine, but it used to infuriate trainers at Middleham: their yearlings would dive in all directions at the sight of a dog on the gallops. The other problem arose when the reliable and speedy Slipper got in the family way. Simple Pleasure had to have a couple of months off.

Maxine recently took a car-load of children to Ripon and – normal small-market-town problem – couldn't find anywhere to park. Particularly annoying was the fact that the normal car park, the market square, was roped off with ticker tape, so she got one of the children to lift the tape, enabling her to reverse in. When she returned from shopping, beside her car was an irate man from the council who started complaining.

'It's pure bureaucracy,' she retorted. 'You're just making life difficult for the shoppers in Ripon.'

'No, it's not madam,' the man replied. 'It's just that you're parked in ready-mix concrete.' ■

NO PRIZES, YOU'D HAVE THOUGHT, for guessing which horse is the apple of Luca Cumani's eye after last weekend, although it is a closer-run thing than you might imagine. Just in case you haven't got it already, it begins with F, is the winner of four races this season and, after a quiet few years, has helped return Cumani to the top. The self-esteem, the Italian confidence – it's all back thanks to this one horse.

Step forward, then, Falbrav – Milanese slang for 'be good' – winner of Saturday's Queen Elizabeth II Stakes and the 'best horse in the world', according to the trainer. Well, actually, no. Back in your box, Falbrav, you big brute. You're only the second most popular horse at Bedford House.

Step forward, daintily, Faraway Lady, who runs in a stayers' handicap at Nottingham today. Her latest win came in the prestigious Saffie Joseph & Sons Apprentice Handicap at Warwick on 8 September. If you need further information about the race it was a 0–70, class F, two miles, with no more runners than there are in the average greyhound race (i.e. six), and it was the object of the first, half-baked, owners' strike because of the lack of prize money.

Not quite the QEII then, but there were other advantages which make it very clear why the trainer, in Faraway Lady's case, wouldn't countenance a strike. Her owner, long-standing Greek patron Tony Antoniades, promised that every time the three-year-old filly won a race he would 'lend' Luca his Ferrari Testarossa for a week. Good to his word, the car, low and fast and red, is on its month's loan to the trainer, who occasionally struggles to get to Newmarket to see a horse run but is now likely to have an end-of-season spate of runners, which he will saddle himself, at Musselburgh and Carlisle. 'I've told people I bought it to get over a menopausal blip,' says the trainer, who is yet to be done for speeding in it. 'It's every Italian's dream to drive one of these. It was made in 1986 and only has 4,000 miles on the clock.' His wife Sara chipped in, 'It's great driving along the M25 only two feet above the tarmac.' One of the more debatable pleasures of driving such a low-slung beast in the wake of juggernauts.

Then, of course, there is the matter of the number plate. There's a hint of irony about it. It is 4 AGA. After Cumani's fairly public fall-out with the Aga Khan, we should like to make it clear that he doesn't any longer train 4 Aga.

HERE'S A TALE WITH A POSSIBLE MORAL OUTCOME – I'll leave you to work out that one – involving those qualities so cherished in our sport: athleticism, beauty, speed and, above all, Bravery.

With the nights lengthening and his girth expanding after another fine summer, Newmarket trainer Giles Bravery accompanied by his wife, Fiona, decided a few sessions in the gym would be to the benefit of both. Apart from cricket whites Giles's wardrobe is bereft of sports clothes, so he borrowed a pair of his wife's tracksuit bottoms, which she had last worn during pregnancy, and after a bit of selective surgery to the gusset region they almost fitted. So even before he'd mounted the treadmill in the sports centre he looked a bit of a sight among the lycra-clad fitness enthusiasts of Newmarket.

Initially all went well. Giles was jogging away, gradually going nowhere faster, while Fiona headed to the other side of the gym and an impressive selection of bikes, from where she could see Giles working up quite a speed. At an impressive 10km/h Giles began to glow and decided the time was right to discard his jumper. Now, any normal person would stop the machine, but not Giles. He'd got as far as getting the jumper half over his head when he 'became unbalanced'. In a split-second the treadmill, normally an innocuous belt of moving rubber, viciously spat him out backwards like a human cannonball into the brick wall of the gym where he slumped into an untidy, not to mention struggling, heap. He was effectively blinded because his jumper was still over his head. His arms, still in the sleeves, were pinned in awkward positions above and behind his head because the half-off jumper had created a straitjacket effect. The earlier surgery to the tracksuit bottoms added to the effect, making it look like he'd had a serious groin-ripping accident to boot.

'Oh, look,' said a lady biking next to Fiona, 'that poor man over there's had a heart attack.'

Fiona, quite rightly at this stage, denied all knowledge of the writhing man in question, looked the other way and kept pedalling. Meanwhile an alert young lady stopped toning herself and started administering a heart massage to the prostrate trainer, who was in no position to see, move in anything that resembled a controlled way, or, least of all, argue.

Heart scares being all the rage at the moment, this was, I'm glad to say, nothing of the sort. Giles is, however, carrying around a cracked elbow and has cancelled his membership of the gym. ▩

JOHN EDWARDS, WHO HAS ANNOUNCED THAT HE PLANS TO RETIRE, is not quite sure when he will saddle his last runner, but a tribute to his career over a Cheltenham meeting could not be more fitting. Few trainers, past or present, have bettered his twelve Festival winners. Horses don't win there by accident.

At 50, it may appear that Edwards has reached his sell-by date a shade early, but he started young, taking out his licence at the age of 21 in 1967, the year he rode Dunwiddy in Foinavon's Grand National. His mount trod on the reins, snapping them, at the third. Though he negotiated the Canal Turn without steering he pulled up before the others piled up.

Tricky owners are the bane of most trainers' lives, but Edwards had a good bunch, with a couple of exceptions. One was a big punter, which Edwards is not, and one day the owner assumed that his horse was 'not off' so didn't back it. It ran a blinder, finishing second under Richard Evans. From the stands to the winner's enclosure the owner berated Edwards. Worse followed: Evans objected and got the race. On another occasion Edwards went with jockey Philip Blacker to Perth with the same man's horse. Blacker asked where they would stay and Edwards replied that, 'courtesy' of the owner, they'd stay at Gleneagles. In the paddock for the race, the owner asked where trainer and jockey were staying. Blacker was about to blurt out 'Gleneagles' when Edwards trod on his toe and said, 'A pub down the road. What about yourself?'

'Oh,' replied the chap, 'I've hired a caravan, towed it up and parked it in the car park.'

His horse got stuffed, he had done his cash, and Blacker's abiding memory of the meeting is seeing the owner walking across a deserted car park, a picture of deflation, as they set off for Gleneagles.

Edwards had another owner who drank a bit. His horse, given the ride of Blacker's life, got up on the line to win at Cheltenham. The owner staggered into the winner's enclosure, walked up to Blacker and said, 'Well, Blacker, you nearly effed it up again.' Afterwards, Cheltenham officials asked the winning connections into a box for a drink. As they entered, the chairman held out his hand, and the owner, attempting to respond to the greeting, landed flat on the floor. 'Picking him up,' said Edwards, 'was the most embarrassing moment of my career.' ▩

THE JOCKEY CLUB OF KENYA sponsored the Molecomb Stakes at Goodwood last week. They are keen to promote British ownership (training fees £200 a month) and are continuing their leasing scheme after a filly leased to two British women won the Kenyan Guineas.

In Britain you occasionally find deer or hares on the gallops, but in

Kenya the wildlife is more exotic. It was Tony Ives who once got the shock of his life during a piece of 'swift work' near Lake Naivasha when a giraffe stepped into his path. His mount, used to such interruptions, swerved and carried on. In Newmarket, they talk about horses catching pigeons. Now, if a horse could catch a giraffe it would be fast. Giraffe have been known to clock 45mph, and of course we don't have to go into the advantages they have when it comes to photo-finishes.

A BIG BUT AWKWARD OWNER who never lasts much longer than a season at any one yard recently bumped into a leading trainer at the races.

'I must have a horse in training with you,' said the owner.

'Oh,' replied the nonplussed trainer. 'Must you?'

ONCE THE JAPANESE STARTED WINNING RACES IN EUROPE it had to happen sooner rather than later. With Japanese interpreters and fast-talking Europeans around, there was an embarrassing moment following Taiki Shuttle's convincing victory in the Prix Jacques Le Marois at Deauville on Sunday. It followed the equally emphatic success of Akiko Uenaka's Seeking the Pearl in the Prix Maurice de Gheest the previous weekend.

Taiki Shuttle is trained by Kazuo Fujisawa, who has more than a basic grasp of English, having spent four years as assistant trainer to Gavin Pritchard-Gordon in Newmarket. And having worked in a racing yard, he knows one or two words and phrases you will not find in too many Japanese–English dictionaries. Desmond Stoneham, the International Racing Bureau's man in France, asked Fujisawa if it was true that his horse liked French lettuce. To trainer and a blushing interpreter, neither of whom could believe what they had just heard, the last word of the sentence sounded extremely like 'letters'.

'I think,' said one of Stoneham's colleagues who had twigged exactly what the Japanese trainer was thinking, 'you ought to rephrase that question.'

Long may these lettuce-eating horses keep on winning France's best races. ▣

A LADY PERMIT-HOLDER HAD A MINOR GYNAECOLOGICAL PROBLEM so she rang her local lady doctor to book an appointment. 'She's on holiday,' replied the surgery, 'but a male locum is standing in for her. There's a spare slot in half an hour if you can get in on time.'

The lady permit-holder, who had spent most of the day with her horses, thought she'd better 'freshen up' first. She rushed into her daughter's bedroom, picked up the first spray that came to hand and squirted a little under her arms and all those other places ladies like occasionally to 'freshen up'.

As she was leaving her appointment, the doctor said, 'Thank you very much. None of my other patients takes so much trouble when they come to see me.'

This statement bothered her on the way home, so on her arrival she popped up to her daughter's bedroom to find out what perfume she had applied in such a rush. The bottle of spray read 'Glitter'.

THE SMART NEWMARKET TRAINER'S REBUFF FOR HACKS at the Craven meeting asking where their horse was going next was short and sweet. 'Home,' they would say, knowing the journalist had hoped for an answer more like York or Chester.

Other trainers have been more helpful – up to a point. When James Bethell's mare Hunters of Brora won the Lincoln Handicap, the trainer outlined his plans. 'She'll either go to Zilzal or Newbury,' said the Middleham man, thinking it was high time the mare went to see a stallion. Having seen this on TV, an owner of Chris Thornton's rang him. 'I've heard of Newbury,' he said, 'but where the hell is Zilzal?'

THE 1998 FESTIVAL LASTED THREE DAYS, but yesterday, racing's great and good gathered in College Chapel, Eton, to celebrate a lifetime, that of David Morley, who died from a heart attack during the winter.

Sir Mark Prescott, one of his great friends, recalled how, after Morley's second heart operation, he went to visit him in hospital one evening. Morley was in considerable discomfort having been opened up down the middle, and found it less painful to pace about the room than he did to lie still in bed. Having already been to two race meetings that day Prescott was, not surprisingly, tired, so he lay down on Morley's bed. Before long he had fallen asleep. It so happened that at about the same time the duty nurses changed and the night nurse was making her first tour of the evening. When she saw Prescott asleep she turned to the pacing Morley. 'Leave immediately,' she commanded. 'Can't you see how seriously ill this patient is?'

For the last ten years of his life, Morley, a great hunting, shooting and fishing man, trained for Sheikh Hamdan. The owner's first visit to High Haven, when he had just two horses in training, was one of the most memorable.

'What's this one like?' said the sheikh as they came to the first colt, an athletic-looking beast.

'Well,' said Morley with great enthusiasm, 'he's like an October grouse, and by that I mean he's fast, quick and agile.'

The sheikh and his entourage moved on to the second colt, a more burly type. 'What's this one like?' he asked.

'Well,' said Morley, by now warming to his theme, 'this one's like a well-fed autumn stag, and by that I mean if you cut him open he'd be full of fat.'

As the satisfied owner's party departed in their cars, one of the sheikh's men slowed down, wound down a window and winked at Morley. 'Normally,' he said, 'our trainers play themselves in for a couple of years before they start making suggestions about where they would like to go on holiday.' ◙

THERE IS A VERY GOOD CHANCE that 1998 will go down in Jockey Club history as the year it became paranoid about non-triers. It's almost as if it's a new concept introduced to the sport by the unscrupulous modern jockey. There is some evidence, however, that it's been going on for a little longer – since racing was invented, in fact. Without wishing to attract the attentions of WPC Dawn Raid of the Met, I'll risk the following story about the legendary Irish jockey of the 1930s and 1940s Phil Canty.

Canty was as famous for the winners he rode as he was for the non-triers he, to coin a currently popular euphemism, 'never placed to challenge'. One day, after he had finished third in a five-horse race, his trainer asked, 'What do you think, Canty?'

'Well, sir,' replied the champion, 'I'd have no trouble beating the two in front, but I'm not so sure about the two behind.' ◙

NOT MANY HORSES have won the Stewards' Cup from the number one draw, but Soba managed it in 1982 and Peter Calver will be hoping Perryston View can do the same at Goodwood today and provide him with a second triumph in the race (following Mandraco twelve years ago) before he retires from the training ranks in November.

Calver retiring? No, I didn't ask you to believe it. Calver, 65, is unique, for while some trainers such as Richard Lee are qualified blacksmiths and others such as Mark Johnston are qualified vets, Calver has been both since he held a permit in 1956.

Even in 'retirement' his veterinary skills will still be in demand at the yearling sales and he will continue to 'check eyes and heart beats, feel legs and count balls'.

Racehorse vets are incredible snobs when it comes to small animals. On the whole the best horse vets pretend not to know which end a cat pees from. So when Calver was fresh out of vets' school he, the new boy, ended up with the small-animal jobs. Imagine his concern a few months after doing a job-lot of cat hysterectomies when one of the felines from which he had extracted various tubes was returned to the surgery the proud mother of kittens. 'There was one occasion,' he recalled yesterday, 'which was probably worse. It was another neutering operation when we opened up a tom looking for its ovaries.'

It was Calver who trained the mighty Gospel Rock, who took off with Graham Bradley at Wetherby one day and failed to negotiate the bend. Instead, he took on an eight-foot chain-link fence, three strands of barbed wire, two concrete posts, a ditch and a hedge, and then galloped loose down the A1. He was retrieved with not a scratch on him. 'A lot of ability, but not a natural jumper,' says Calver of Gospel Rock. Just an observation, but I'd have thought there was something rather Pegasus-like about his jumping ability.

I rode out for Calver at his Ripon yard and, as a weak teenager, was run away with round his circular gallop. But I wasn't the first. Nicky Henderson, chequebook in pocket, decided he would try out Battlefield Band with a view to purchasing him. He didn't know at the time that Battlefield Band was the strongest horse ever to grace a racecourse. 'The gallop wasn't quite circular then,' says Calver, 'and after being carted, Nicky had to go across tracks and rough ground to get to the start of the gallop again. I was somewhat surprised when he didn't buy the horse.'

Another Calver claim to fame was to have sold Highland Wedding, the 1969 Grand National winner, to his great friend Toby Balding. Wasn't he the tiniest bit disappointed he wasn't training the horse when it galloped to Aintree glory? 'Put it this way,' he says. 'The only way I've ever made money out of horses is by selling them. So it's a bit like eating a wonderful cheese, going back to the grocer the next day to tell him how good it was and then asking him if he was disappointed that he sold the cheese and didn't eat it himself.' So there. Not the least bit disappointed. ▩

ONE OF THE GREAT LAMBOURN MOMENTS. That was how Oliver Sherwood described a practical joke by neighbour Kim Bailey, who departs from the valley for pastures new in three weeks.

Sherwood and his wife Tarnya were hosting about 100 people at their owner's open day at Rhonehurst. The last horse had just paraded when there rose above the stables a large sheet attached to 60 helium-filled balloons. On the sheet was a cartoon of a naked Oliver and Tarnya drawn by Peter Walwyn's artistic son and heir Ed, with the message 'Tanya and Ollie. Goodbye, I'll miss you'. Sherwood, who had been commentating on the parade, looked up in wonder and exclaimed, 'What's the bugger up to now?'

'He knows I can't stand being called Ollie and that Tarnya hates being called Tanya,' says Sherwood. 'I've got the sheet now but haven't got a wall big enough to hang it on. It will be kept sacrosanct. I just hope Ed Walwyn charged him a fortune for it.'

PENNY MORLOCK, amateur rider and New Zealand-born wife of Kingston Lisle trainer Charlie, got more than she bargained for last Sunday night.

For several days Charlie's string of jumpers had passed a large, white, lop-eared rabbit sitting beside the road. It was clearly an escapee, and Penny, a disciple of that well-known antipodean pet rescuer Rolf Harris, decided she would pick it up and take it home before it got squashed on the road, despite Raceyard Cottage also being home to several lurchers. The rabbit came quietly and was put in a dog basket for the night. The following morning Penny came downstairs to discover that the kitchen had become a maternity ward. During the night the rabbit had multiplied by a factor of eight. 'It's no wonder it didn't run away,' explained Mrs Morlock. 'It couldn't.' ▩

RACING LOST TWO LEGENDS IN A WEEK with the passing of Captain Tim Forster and Paul Kelleway.

I can't imagine how All Saints Church in Faringdon, Oxon, will fit everyone in for Tim Forster's memorial service, which is at 2.30 on 6 May 1999 – a day when there is no jump racing – even though the Captain wouldn't have liked anyone to go. The Captain was unique. I rode out for him for several years and was stable amateur for a while despite being fined £50 for excessive use of the whip on my first ever ride for him at Wincanton. I thought it would be my last because most of the stewards that day were his owners.

Some things you won't have read in his obituaries. He was an excellent croquet player but difficult to partner in doubles because it was always your fault if you lost. He was a hard man to work for, yet he invoked a tremendous loyalty among his lads. His loves were his lawn, which he often tended on hand and knee with a Tippex bottle of weed killer, and his gallops, so much so that he didn't really like his horses working up the turf. His hates were jockeys, women who wear jeans – with the exception of Venetia Williams – and people who use mobile phones on the racecourse. 'If it wasn't for jockeys,' he used to bemoan, 'I'd have been champion trainer many times.'

If something went wrong he would stand at the top of the gallops pulling his hair out and announce to the wind, 'I know there are some bloody idiots in this world, but why do they all have to work for me?' On one occasion, in a pea-souper, we had all got lost on the gallops and the lead horse, ridden by Luke Harvey, had been within inches of knocking the Captain over. When we pulled up and were circling at the end he drove over, got out and let rip. 'You're all as blind as me!' he yelled. 'You're all as deaf as Reg [a partially deaf lad in the yard] and you're all as thick as this fog! Now eff off home!'

On his first morning riding out there on secondment from the army, Dominic Alers-Hankey was bucked off at the bottom of the gallop and severely winded. In the distance he could see the Captain's Land Rover heading his way – to pick him up, he presumed. 'Dom' was still crumpled up on the floor when rescue arrived. The Captain wound down his window, leaned out and said, 'And to think I put you on the quietest bugger in the yard,' before driving off and leaving Dom still gasping for air.

Paul Kelleway was a tough jockey. He was pulled off Barona, whom my father trained, at Becher's Brook in the 1975 Grand National when Andy Turnell lost his balance on April Seventh and grabbed the nearest thing – which happened to be Paul's arm. There were no video replays or big screens in those days, so when Paul returned to the weighing room with this most original but implausible of excuses, Dad assumed he had had a bang on the head and reported him to the doctor, who promptly stood him down with concussion. It was not until the replay of the race on *Match of the Day* that Paul was proved right. He went on to win the next two Scottish Nationals on Barona and was fourth in the following year's Grand National. ■

THE FOLLOWING CONVERSATION took place over breakfast in Lambourn this week between an owner, who had just enjoyed seeing his horse cantering as the sun rose over the gallops, and his reasonably successful trainer.

'If I ever win the lottery I'm going to start training,' said the owner.

'If I ever win the lottery,' sighed the trainer, 'I'm going to stop training.' ■

MAXINE STIRK, the permit-holding wife of popular Yorkshire vet Anthony, will be familiar to regular readers. She it was who, in her haste to do the shopping in Ripon once, parked her car in a cordoned-off area without realising it had just been laid with quick-drying concrete.

The latest 999-style drama to unfold happened a few weeks ago when one of her store horses fell down a hole. One minute a laid-back four-year-old called Andrew was standing in a field eating grass, as you do if you're a horse; the next, somewhat surprised but still chewing, he was down an eight-foot-deep hole caused by a leaking water pipe with just his tweaking ears poking out above the parapet.

Ripon's answer to Pugh, Pugh, Barney McGrew, Cuthbert, Dibble and Grubb duly arrived with not one but two fire engines and proceeded to spend the next five hours, with the help of a local digger driver, trying to extricate him. When plan A, to dig a ramp for him to walk out of the hole, failed and the hole began to fill with water, Andrew's owner, by her own admission, began to get mildly hysterical. 'We're doing our best,' said the clearly niggled Captain Flak, trying to reassert his authority. 'If you don't mind, there can only be one chief around here. Please go and make the boys a cup of tea.'

Plan B, to dig around Andrew to enable one of the Pughs to put slings under him, was precarious, but ultimately proved successful. Eventually Andrew was dragged out, exhausted. Once he was freed, they quite expected him to lie down and die from stress, but not Andrew, who stood up, shook himself, had a long pee and tucked into a huge feed.

So how is Andrew now?

'Physically he has some muscle wastage from a trapped nerve, but people said he would be emotionally traumatised for life,' reports Maxine. 'The zenith of his emotional trauma was when he refused to go through a muddy gateway the next day. I think he's over that now.'

THERE ISN'T AN AWARD, AS SUCH, for the training performance of the season. However, had there been one last year then right up there among the top nominations would have been Charlie Egerton, seventeen, whose feat of sending out Mely Moss to finish second to Papillon in the Grand National following a 346-day break was a notable achievement indeed.

There is no doubt in my mind that, provided things continue to go the right way, 'Edgy' will be outright winner this year. So outright, in fact, there won't be any other nominations for this prestigious non-award. His task: to complete the London Marathon in aid of the Countryside Alliance.

You may have thought I underestimated his age by about twenty years, but I was, in fact, referring to his weight – in stones. But that's all about to change. Edgy had his last (alcoholic) drink on New Year's Eve, his last Irish coffee with double cream the same night, and his last banoffee pie (washed down with mineral water) on New Year's Day. He has already shed a stone and jogs a couple of miles every day. No sweat. Not bad for someone who went through the pain barrier at 150 yards on his first run back in December and reckons he hasn't been fully fit for fourteen years, when he last rode in a point-to-point, since when there has been a steady deterioration in his condition. 'We're talking about moving a mountain here,' says Edgy, the master of understatement, who is looking at a Cathy Freeman-style lycra bodysuit for the big day. 'When one trains one can lead a very narrow and restricted life without other goals. I'm beginning to enjoy it, and it is for a cause I strongly believe in.'

Edgy has hired a fleet of personal fitness trainers and a dietician. He has no target time for the 26 miles – just completion. 'It's a bit like climbing Everest,' he says, 'but in my case, starting in a submarine. I'm still some way off base camp. Projecting times is still a bit ambitious.'

The Countryside Alliance have been fielding runners in the London Marathon for years, often athletic, beagling types for whom 26 miles around our concrete capital has been a stroll in the park. This year they wanted a longer-priced target, a 100–1 shot, to run for them. Initially Edgy did the nearest thing he's done to athletics for a while and told them to go and take a running jump. They persisted, though, and after a lot of thought he accepted, with one proviso – that he'd have a month of secret trials, and if he felt at the end of it that he was fully committed, he would give it a crack.

His racing weight, he feels, is around the 13½-stone mark, and he is confident he will have lost three and a half stone by April. 'The marathon is a week before the Punchestown Festival,' he points out. 'All I can say is thank God it's a week before and not a week after.' ▣

THERE COMES A TIME – and my goodness we've delayed it as long as possible – in every racing journalist's career when he has to write about all-weather racing. Like an injection, I'll try to get it over with as quickly as possible.

However, with a string of mainly good-ground jumpers, the husband-and-wife team of Martin and Sarah Bosley have no complaints about it just now. Tonight at Wolverhampton, their Makarim, bought last July for 1,200 guineas and with a reputation longer than the run-in at Aintree, goes for his fifth straight win.

The Bosley family is well known to us. Martin's father John won the 'Adelphi Cresta' (fastest down the Liverpool stairs on a tray the night before the National) some time in the last century. Martin was the child, you might recall, who, aged eleven, was told to take National third Eyecatcher to stand in the stream for the benefit of her legs. So that he'd stay there long enough, John gave him a Havana cigar and told him not to come back until he'd smoked it.

'Bos', 36, rode for 12 years as a professional and his fourth ride was on his father's Flexibility in the Aintree Foxhunters'. Admittedly Mersey Black Cabs Ltd had to move their entire rank to Aintree that afternoon, but the pair finished a very good third to Grittar – and we all know what *he* did a year later. Early on in his career, Bos rode a 1–10 shot for Captain Tim Forster in a two-horse boys' race at Kempton. The prospect was having the same effect on his underwear as a leak in the waist of a deep-sea diver's suit. 'Don't worry, two-horse races can be funny things,' said the Captain reassuringly, before making it perfectly clear he didn't expect the horse to be beaten. 'But kick on in the straight so you've time to remount.'

On one occasion, his father had two runners in the same chase. He rode one, Stuart Shilston the other. 'The one thing I don't want,' said John, 'is for one to bring down the other. Martin, you take the inner. Stuart, take the outer.' Need I continue? Turning into the straight, bang, Martin's mount walked through a fence, and in a vain effort to prevent gravity doing her damndest drifted so far right that he fell at the feet of his stable companion. Hey presto, both ended up on the deck.

As a jockey he also struggled with his weight, for which he had an ingenious idea which also satisfied his sweet tooth. When everyone else sat down to a steak supper, he'd sit down to a Kinder Surprise chocolate egg, the beauty being that Kinder eggs consist of precious little chocolate, mainly fresh air and a toy. The toy amused him while everyone else finished their meal.

Makarim has been a revelation since arriving in Kingston Lisle, and he's by no means the first one they've sweetened up. How come? The trainer recalls, 'Though he didn't make a noise when we cantered him, in the vet's own words, he had a "soft palate like a floppy condom". We fired it, and though we tried to work on his head by taking him on long rides, we now know he likes routine.'

KEEPING UP APPEARANCES. Lynda Ramsden and a few other Yorkshire ladies who lunch occasionally were dining out last week when the trainer recounted to them how she had been driving, during the recent appalling weather, to see the vicar to make arrangements for her daughter Emma's February 2005 wedding to Ballydoyle jockey Jamie Spencer (at which, one hopes, he doesn't get to the front too soon, go too wide up the aisle, and various other Breeders' Cup mini-disasters). On the way from Breckenborough House her car was swept off the road by a tide of flood water.

'Were you in a ford?' enquired Angie Delahooke, wife of bloodstock agent James.

'No,' replied Lynda, perishing the thought, 'in an Audi.'

HERE'S SOMETHING WE WILL NO DOUBT NOT HEAR THE END OF. Graham Motion, the young English-born trainer who saddled Better Talk Now to win the Breeders' Cup Turf, and Film Maker to finish a highly respectable second to Ouija Board in the Filly & Mare Turf at the prestigious meeting last weekend, used to be Charlie Brooks's chauffeur. 'Yes, it's true,' said Graham, who now speaks with an American drawl. 'I spent four months driving him to the races. He taught me everything I know.' Needn't go that far, Graham.

'He was a top man,' confirms Brooks. 'He was already fairly Americanised when we had him. We called him the Tuxedo Kid. We were off to a black-tie dance one night and he said, "Do you mean we wear tuxedos?" None of us knew what a tuxedo was, so we said, "No, definitely not, it's strictly black tie."'

JOHNNY WARRENDER, an artist, is running in this year's London Marathon a week on Sunday in aid of Marie Curie Cancer Care in memory of his great friend, the trainer Alec Stewart. Johnny, 50, from south-west Scotland, is a landscape artist whose next exhibition, at St Andrews to celebrate the 150th anniversary of the Open before he takes it to Edinburgh for the festival, will be entitled 'The Great Links Courses of Scotland'.

As a youngster, he and Alec were playing a round of golf at North Berwick when the trainer shanked his ball up the opposite fairway and cursed loudly. As they went over the top of a rise to find the stray ball they met an irate golfer coming in the opposite direction who had nearly been decapitated. 'You have clearly never played this game before,' he said to the pair. 'You don't shout "duck", you shout "fore"!' On another occasion he was staying with the trainer and was out on Warren Hill in Newmarket with his easel. As a long string passed, one of the lads stood up in his stirrups, looked over the artist's shoulder and, to the hilarity of his fellow lads, shouted, 'Oi, Picasso, sharpen up your brush!' However, Johnny's response was not lacking either: 'Bugger off, Lester,' he said.

Johnny's own marathon training had been going well until he went to Glasgow to get some new running shoes. He was unsure about whether or not he liked the shoes, so the shop assistant suggested he take them for a 'test drive' down the street. So, with labels and price tags still attached, he set off from the shop front at a brisk pace only for a passer-by, thinking he was legging it with a new pair of shoes (as presumably happens a lot in Glasgow), to set off in hot pursuit, shouting, 'Stop, thief!' Some, it seems, suffer cardiac arrests during training for the marathon. Few, until now, have suffered a citizen's arrest. ▩

YOU MAY BE LED TO BELIEVE THAT at the age of 35, Tim Martin, trainer of 2004 Aussie July Cup hope Exceed and Excel, is something of a young boy in training terms. However, as you're probably well aware, in Australia they don't procreate around. He got his first trainer's licence at twenty, an age when most British trainers are not yet bored with their stint in the City, on a gap year in the unlikely event of being accepted by a university, or still in ever-desperate contact with a careers officer. 'Wish I'd never started so young,' reflects Tim, which will be good news to City boys, students and the generally undecided alike. 'It was a real battle for the first five years.'

Having started with nothing, Tim had to survive on his wits. Now at the all-singing-all-waltzing Rosehill in Sydney, he started off in the country. In 1990 he fancied he had a decent maiden to run at the Grafton Carnival, a place where 'you can get plenty on'. The one snag to this plan was that he didn't possess a witchetty grub, let alone 'plenty', so he hitched a ride for the horse with another trainer and sold his own lorry, putting all the proceeds on the horse. Had it not won, he says, Tim Martin would still be mucking out.

Thus began a reputation – one which he is now trying to shake off – for being a successful punting yard. However, as any trainer in a similar position knows, if your staff are half intelligent they take all the change. So in a brilliant ruse to confuse them he'd open up the track at Tamworth at one a.m., gallop a horse, and then when the lads turned up at 4.30 leave it in the box. He would then repeat the exercise a few days running. 'Ah, must be just giving it a run first time out,' the lads would think, wrongly, and it would start at wondrous odds with just the trainer on. 'There used to be quite a lot of that sort of fun in those days,' says Tim. 'I'd like to think we're a bit more professional these days.' Exceed and Excel confirms that. ■

TRAINERS ARE ALWAYS TRYING TO GET ONE UP ON THEIR PEERS, and Richard Phillips is no different. After saddling a winner last week he accredited the success to sports psychologist Michael 'Corky' Caulfield and former Champion jockey Richard Dunwoody, both of whom act on a consultancy basis at Adlestrop now. Having read this in the next day's *Racing Post*, winning jockey Warren Marston rang Corky to say how indebted he was to him for the winner and how, quite obviously, it was all down to psychology and nothing to do with the lads who'd ridden out, mucked out, fed and watered the beast for the last three months.

Knowing Richard reasonably well, I know his way with staff. He greets them in the morning, or certainly used to, not so much with a cheery 'Hello!' but a 'Why don't you eff off?' with an aside to the effect that it is a pity they weren't involved in some capacity with the latest disaster incorporating multiple fatalities. So Corky has been working on that, telling him to be nice to his staff. Richard Dunwoody has been working on improving the staff's riding. He comes in, gets the numbers of all the pretty girls, tells them how well they're riding, leaves an invoice for £500 and buggers off back to London. 'You may laugh,' says the trainer, who was busy writing staff appraisals at the time, 'but I'm trying to run a sporting academy here. It's all about raising standards. The staff have definitely started riding better, but I think they're also drinking more too.'

Warren is of the old school, where David Nicholson was headmaster, and can't quite see it. 'How can I take advice from two nutters who lie awake staring at the ceiling all night?' he asks – not unreasonably. Fellow trainer Martin Bosley had a different take on it after saddling a winner at Wolverhampton. 'We've killed two birds with one stone this week,' he said, 'by getting Simon McNeill [former jockey and all-round top bloke] in to do the two jobs.' ▣

HE WHO PAYS THE PIPER CALLS THE TUNE. An owner of a horse with a choice of Festival engagements was discussing the options with his trainer. The options were to run in the Arkle, a red-hot Championship race, or one of the handicaps in which the horse appeared to be very favourably weighted. 'Well,' he concluded to his trainer, 'you're the expert. You decide. But I want him to run in the Arkle.' ▣

AFTER A PARTY, trainer Jonny Portman tends to fall asleep in the passenger seat with his wife Sophie driving, wake up as they enter their yard in Compton, pat her affectionately and say 'Thank you, darling, well driven', despite having been unconscious for most of the journey.

On Saturday, they hired a lad to drive them to a particularly good party. True to form, Jonny awoke as they returned to the yard and, much to the driver's surprise, took his hand, patted it lovingly and thanked his 'darling' for such a safe drive. The driver left without waiting to be paid. ◙

HONG KONG HAS BEEN PARANOID about gamblers influencing results since the infamous Shanghai Syndicate was cracked in the 1980s. What the authorities discovered with the Shanghai Syndicate was that some of the jockeys on their payroll were using a 'semaphore' signalling system to alert the gang. For example, they would carry their whips in the right hand on the way to the start if they were off, and in the left if they were not off. Then, to avoid detection, they would change the sign and pull their goggles down going to the start if they were off, but leave them up if they were not off. Got it?

You may have, but the jockeys didn't. After the signal had been changed a few times the poor buggers didn't know whether they should have their goggles down and whips in the left hand, stay on or hop off at the start, scratch their noses or their balls, or whatever. The Shanghai Syndicate was subsequently shanghaied.

Soon after that a devout Catholic jockey was just about to load in the stalls for his first ride in the colony and, as he always did, he crossed himself. As soon as he returned to weigh-in he was summoned to the stewards to explain who he had been signalling to. They were rather impressed by the standard of modern race fixer when he replied, 'God. ◙'

AUDREY MANNERS ANSWERED THE PHONE. 'John's just having a pee – in his favourite place on the lawn.'

John 'Mad' Manners is a farmer, a permit-holder, a compulsive purchaser and a man who professes to love his horses, particularly the family pet Killeshin – who runs in the Tote Eider Chase at Newcastle – more than his wife. What he was doing when I called doesn't begin to do justice as an introduction to Manners, who turns 70 in April but still rides out daily. 'Come and have a slosh round the farm,' he said. Sloshing round Newcastle for Killeshin, who won the 1994 Aintree Foxhunters', will be like home from home.

If Old MacDonald ever did have a farm, it must have been something like the 400 acres Manners works at Highworth, near Swindon. His original three mares are responsible for a herd of about 40 'mainly useless' horses, whose winter quarters are a barn next to the cowshed.

In racing, Manners is more famous for his run-ins with authority than for his successes. In 1989 he named the 'worst horse in the yard' Sambruco after the three stewards of the disciplinary committee – Sam Vestey, Bruce Hobbs and Robert Waley-Cohen – who stood him down for three years for saddling a point-to-point winner without a weight-cloth. 'I got on so well with them I thought I'd only get six months,' he says. Another time he was fined for hopping over the rail and following his first Cheltenham winner up the course.

Killeshin, whom he bought at Ascot Sales for 1,200 guineas after a few drinks, thrives on the refreshingly agricultural atmosphere of Common Farm. Until Manners got hold of him he'd only been placed in selling chases. In a wet year you could see him being placed in the National – if he were qualified. With the Handicapper no longer able to apportion 'Aintree factor', Killeshin has missed out on this year's race despite a four-mile victory at Taunton and an Aintree success. 'People have been coming up to us as if there's been a death in the family. "We're terribly sorry …" they begin. I'm not. We'll do it next year.'

After we'd galloped round various fields and washed the horses off in the river, wading up to the high-tide mark on Manners' boots, we came in for a coffee. If blinkers help horses to concentrate, then it is possible they might do the same to Manners when he is talking. 'I nearly died during the summer, you know,' he began, taking off his water-filled boots. His soliloquy then took off at a tangent, and at tangents to the tangents. In an hour I never asked a single question. He touched on such diverse subjects as holidays in Florida (he took a couple of dozen of his own eggs and declared them at customs; 'Lay them all yourself?' asked the official), cruise ships, Edward VII, the Second World War, and how he'd given four jockeys their first winner in the last two years.

We never did quite manage to complete a story, and I never found out why he nearly died. I can only suggest that it was a good thing for racing that one of our most unpredictably eccentric permit-holders – 'I do some bloody mad things, you know' – survived. ▣

WARREN O'CONNOR HAS A SENSE OF HUMOUR. He needs it with some of the horses he's riding at the moment (my words, not his, lest they offend those people who have been good enough to give him a leg up). This was the man who witnessed a loose horse galloping up the Curragh after the lad riding it had dismounted and kicked it in the guts. When O'Connor met the lad concerned he asked him what, in the name of Jesus, had happened. 'Well,' answered the lad, 'the trainer told me to go to the five-furlong marker, jump off and give it a kick in the belly.' ▣

MIKEL MAGNUSSON, the Swedish businessman who bought Kim Bailey's Lambourn yard, is still getting to grips with some of the simpler journeys to the races here. For example, Lambourn to Sandown, by my reckoning, is roughly out of the village, left, right, left, right, left, left. Not, so it seems, if, as Mikel did recently, you plug the name Sandown into the state-of-the-art global positioning system in your new Range Rover.

The GPS, for those of you who still rely on the ancient art of cartography, talks to you as you travel, telling you which turn to take and when. Distracted for much of the way by telephone calls, Mikel did as he was told until the voice commanded, 'Stop in port and take ferry.' He was, in fact, in Portsmouth, and the ferry beckoning him was indeed bound for Sandown. Sandown on the Isle of Wight.

'It's very accurate,' says Mikel in defence of his equipment, 'but you do need to plug in the right address.'

And therein lies something of a problem with British racecourses. Sandown isn't Sandown at all, it's Esher. Likewise, Kempton is nothing of the sort, it's Sunbury. And if you went to Folkestone looking for the racecourse you'd be about ten miles out. Try Westenhanger. As most of these GPS things are an everyday application of weapons or astronautical systems, it must have been quite a worry for the inhabitants of the small village of Moscow in Scotland at the height of the Cold War when the might of America's nukes were aimed at the Russian capital. ◼

IF SIR MICHAEL STOUTE is sent the yearling own-brothers to his last half-dozen Classic winners this autumn, it's unlikely he will be as chuffed as he was when three sods arrived at Freemason Lodge. Likewise William Haggas. And I'm not talking about a brief respite from racing's well-publicised staff shortages with the arrival of three new lads. No, the sods in question are bits of turf, but no ordinary bits of turf. They are square feet of the outfield at Lord's, which is currently being relaid. You might have seen that Lord Archer bought three acres of it. To own a piece of Lord's, over which Don Bradman may once have strode purposefully to the crease, is to the cricketer what owning a slice of heaven is to the holy man.

'It's a man thing,' explains Haggas, who intends putting up a plaque in front of his three square feet, and tends it daily with nail scissors. 'There's no point even trying to explain something like this to the wife.'

As a result, Sir Michael had a men-only christening of his patch to which he invited William and a few cricketing friends like Jeremy Richardson, Newmarket's erstwhile wicketkeeper, and Julian Wilson, who still tweaks a mean leg break. The only man missing was Whispering Death himself, Michael Holding, the former West Indian pace bowler and now Newmarket work watcher who was in Miami trying to avoid the hurricanes in Jamaica. (Some opening batsmen might consider that poetic justice.)

'We cracked open a bottle of Bolly and I think the dog peed on it,' said Julian. 'Then we retired to the Chinese.' ■

CHAPTER FIVE

CORINTHIAN SPIRIT

Failing to weigh in

IT WAS NOT ONLY JUMP RACING that was seen for the last time at Windsor on Thursday. Hugo Bevan, Windsor's extremely popular clerk of the course, is now three-quarters of the man he was at the start of the week, with just Huntingdon, Worcester and Towcester in his portfolio. Windsor's loss is the other courses' gain.

There are few more likeable characters in racing than Hugo. Next year, 1999, it will be 25 years since he got the job at Huntingdon, and when he finally hands in his penetrometer a few years from now he will be going back to school, in Florence, to become an artist.

Bevan has led a fascinating life, and this week's Diary is a portrait of the artist as a young (62) man. His father, Geoffrey, was a good amateur rider before the war who jumped his first fence at the age of eight and his last at 80, and a famous raconteur who wrote a play that was performed on the London stage, but who basically 'hunted five days a week'. Hugo never emulated his father in the saddle. His 30 rides produced nothing more than a couple of seconds, and he was incapable of twiddling his stick from the carry to the hit position. To save embarrassment he would tie the stick to his wrist with an elastic band so that he could let it go without dropping it and re-grip it in the forehand position. An ingenious ploy, except that at Haydock one day the elastic band became very twisted, and when he let it go it spun round like an aeroplane propeller at a vicious ten revolutions a stride. It made Lester Piggott's two-hits-a-stride look tame, and the stewards had him in as the first ever case of 'excessive use'. Luckily for our jockey he was able to prove the whip hadn't once connected with his mount.

On one occasion at Worcester he rode his own horse, which was trained by Nan Kennedy, who had another runner in the race ridden by Andy Turnell. Her instructions in the paddock went something like this: 'Andy, you make the running and at the second-last take a pull and let Hugo past to win.' Hugo recalls, 'It went to plan, except that she hadn't taken into account the other eighteen runners. Turning for home, Andy and I were nineteenth and twentieth. Two out, his patience ran out and he turned to me and said, "I'm going on."' When Hugo looked to the River Severn on his right he saw a swan not only keeping up with him but overtaking. Discretion got the better of valour and he pulled up.

Before becoming a farmer, Hugo worked in the family brewing business for seven years. When it comes to cooking, Hugo, by his own admission, could spoil a saucepan full of boiling water. But for one year of the seven he was dispatched to be a trainee chef at the Cumberland Hotel, near Marble Arch. After three months he was finally allowed to prepare a full plate of food for a customer. He and all the other chefs crowded round a peep hole to see how the meal was going down. The customer, an elderly gentleman, took one bite and promptly – coincidentally, I might add – suffered a (non-fatal) heart attack. Few chefs can claim that their first meal made such an impact.

All manner of things have changed since Hugo started. Then, racecourse accounts were done on the back of a fag packet. Also, on his first day at one course, Jeff King was getting the better of a duel from the last when Hugo noticed three stewards in the side-on box screaming, 'Hit it, Jeff, give it another! Go on my son!' Of course they had all backed it, which is forbidden now, and probably was then. ▩

ONE OF THE GREAT THINGS ABOUT RACING as a sport is the diverse range of backgrounds of those involved. Last weekend, for example, County Durham trainer Paul Johnson, a dentist by profession, sent out his first runner, Hormuz, who won a handicap at Beverley. If Paul has any sense, he'll retire now, undefeated. By my calculations, if he and Dr Philip Pritchard both have a runner at the same meeting, you could go to the races feeling unwell and have Philip look up one end and Paul down the other. They'd have you sorted out in no time at all.

It's not so long ago that Paul's idea of a handicap was something to stick on the end of a broken tooth (a handy cap). 'It all started when I was in my mid-thirties,' says Paul, 43. 'Instead of getting a Harley Davidson, I deluded myself into thinking I'd ride in races.' He subsequently enrolled at the Northern Racing School as a mature student. When he began shaping up as a potential amateur – rather than, let's face it, an amateur of potential – his wife sent a letter, including a reference from the school, to local trainers asking if he could swing his leg over a horse for them.

Don Eddy agreed for Paul to ride out the following Saturday. When he arrived in his 4x4, Don's assistant met him. 'Where's your son?' she asked. 'I've been speaking to Paul's mum on the phone.' It was a crushing blow to his fledgling riding career from which he was never to recover. It just hadn't occurred to him that age might be a barrier. Instead, Don pointed him towards training, and a spell with Mark Polglase at Southwell means he should be as lethal with his all-weather team as he is with his drill.

The owner of two dental practices in Durham, Paul now runs a small string of horses and dentists (presumably that's a floss of dentists?). He's already resigned to the racing press's dreadful puns, of which I'm as guilty as sin. He has been described as 'getting his teeth into racing'. 'It's All Smiles for the Dentist' is one of the headlines that has appeared. However, if you had a horse with him I'd imagine it would be one trip to the dentist you'd enjoy. ◼

THE ICEMAN COMETH – A CROPPER. Polar explorer Richard Dunwoody, rider of 1,699 winners and survivor of a thousand falls, dislocated his shoulder last Sunday. Funny at first, he says, but by the time A&E in Crawley had kept him waiting for 90 minutes without so much as an aspirin, let alone morphine, it had become the most painful thing he's ever done.

Richard fell off while giving an after-lunch 'dressage demonstration'. His mount, The Assassin, 'didn't do a lot' and dropped him. He swears he hadn't been drinking, but if that's the case the communion wine in those parts must have some kick to it. In a vain attempt to hang on to the horse (Pony Club lesson one: though it may be heroic, especially if you're on a million-dollar yearling, don't), he remained on the floor while his arm, disconnected at the socket, went with the horse. Forget kids with saucepans stuck on their heads; it was the ex-champion who was crying in the waiting room. 'I was on my hands and knees begging for a painkiller,' he recalls.

It hasn't deterred him from taking part in the world's first ever polar race in April with two companions. This week they went for their psychometric tests to find out whether they're lunatic enough to do it. Though they found that Richard is still pounds and ounces, the psycho more than made up for it. They're hoping for a corporate sponsor for the venture, which will be the subject of a documentary. Obviously if the former champ steps on very thin ice or gets lost then there should be good ten o'clock news coverage too.

RICHARD DUNWOODY IS BACK and giving the impression that the Arctic is, to be perfectly blunt, lacking a bit in scenery. In a horse race, finishing second a day behind the winner would probably get a lengthy mention in *The Book of Heroic Failures*, but finishing a day behind the winners in the first polar race was no mean feat and anything but a failure for Dunwoody and his team-mate Tony Martin.

The Diary has kept a vague eye on Richard's progress, which was hampered during the early stages by a polar bear who lay down in their path and went to sleep. As it was in the middle of a 'rubble field', there was no way round it. 'We shot at it and it didn't blink,' says Richard, who now has a souvenir furry white hearth rug, which is very 'Fulham'.

If you weren't already full of admiration for him, you should be now. In eleven days, he and Tony trudged to the North Pole, 330 miles as the penguin waddles but about 350 as two disorientated humans go, pulling a sled. Richard lost 10lb on the trip, something he used to do in two hours in a sauna; Tony lost a stone and a half, so it's fairly evident who did all the pulling. The view, as you can imagine, doesn't change much – take a blank piece of paper and it could easily be a postcard from Richard – and you don't meet people as you might were you walking, say, the Ridgeway. During those eleven days he fell and dislocated his shoulder twice. 'Luckily, Tony was trained to put it back in,' he says, as if it were like extricating a small splinter. Trained Tony may be, but it took him four attempts to put the second dislocation back and Richard will now require an operation to tie it in properly. They might take a look at his brain when they do it.

We can just about wrap up the Polar Race 2003 now. Experienced race readers will put the Dunwoody–Martin defeat down to their lack of technique on skis. But the beard? That was a winner. 'In the style of Abraham Lincoln,' says Richard. 'The first thing I did when I got back was shave it off.' ▩

IT HAS BEEN A VINTAGE AUTUMN for the collectors or, for most of us who can't afford to touch, admirers of equine art. Peter Curling and Katie O'Sullivan have both held their first exhibitions for some time, and if you are in London this week you could do worse than visit the Arndean Gallery in Cork Street for Charles Church and George Bingham – Unbridled. The exhibition lasts until Saturday.

Both Church and Bingham are Dorset-based, but painter Charles, 32, once did time in Lambourn, where he lodged with the legendary Eddie Hales, now based in Kildare where he teaches the Irish how to sell horses. Returning home to Lambourn one night, Charles missed a bend on the ice and landed up in the middle of a field with significantly less exhaust pipe than he had when he left the road and, in the best *Dukes of Hazzard* style, his bonnet up and somewhat obscuring his vision. Before he had had a chance to ask how Eddie was, his lanky passenger had his head out of the window and was navigating, with some confidence, their way to the nearest gate. They went through another two fields before finding themselves on a completely different road at the back of a village.

'Eddie,' said Charlie with some surprise, 'how did you know where to go?'

'Oh,' Eddie nonchalantly replied, 'I came off at the same corner with Norman Williamson last Friday night.'

George, 45, a sculptor, is one of the few amateur jockeys to have been admonished by the stewards – for smoking in the paddock while waiting to mount. On another occasion he was very chuffed to survive the mother and father of all falls. When he got to his feet with a 'Wow, girls, I'm pretty tough' smug look about him, he was promptly mown down by a loose horse and knocked unconscious. George's sculpting career is, I'm glad to say, somewhat more successful than his riding career. ▩

SHARON MURGATROYD, authoress of *Jump Jockeys Don't Cry*, was entertained by Prime Minister John Major last week, but he had had a bad day at the office – isn't every day like that for him at the moment? – and it appears Sharon did the entertaining.

After the other guests, including Clive James and Rolf Harris, had gone, Sharon told the PM a story about his daughter Elizabeth, then a trainee vet, when she went to ride out for Dave Thom in Newmarket. Elizabeth had arranged to ride out through Alison Thom, and when Alison told her husband who was coming to ride out it went in one ear and out the other. Consequently, during breakfast, Thom turned to Elizabeth and asked what her father did.

'Um, my dad's John Major,' she said.

'No,' said Thom, 'I didn't ask what his name was, I asked what he did.' ◙

WHEN SOMEONE HANGS UP THEIR RIDING BOOTS it is a popular cliché to report that 'an era has ended', but one genuinely came to a grinding halt on Wednesday when Simon McNeill, at 42 the oldest jump jockey, retired at Chepstow.

When McNeill started in 1976, Jeff King, Philip Blacker, Richard Evans, Bob Davies, Tommy Stack, Ron Barry, Graham Thorner and Ian Watkinson were still riding, and Nigel Twiston-Davies and Genghis Khan were still 7lb-claiming amateurs, as was Graham McCourt. Jockeys (I think) still wore cork helmets, and the Sex Pistols had yet to be invented.

McNeill rode his first winner 22 years ago on Florida King at Wolverhampton, where, 360 winners later, he will begin his new career as a starter next Wednesday. One of the last jockeys not to have an agent, out with him will also go his trademark pair of white mittens, once worn by all but now about as popular with jockeys as wearing trenchcoats into the paddock.

The most respected and the least number (make that none) of enemies is how I would sum McNeill up. His career was back to front in that it was not until the latter stages that he really hit the big time, winning the Queen Mother Champion Chase on Katabatic in 1991. For much of his career he was confused with another jockey with a similar name, but as he was returning to weigh in after his epic victory on Katabatic, a friend turned to him and pointed out, 'Well, they'll never confuse you with Seamus O'Neill again.' As he walked through the weighing-room door, the old doorman congratulated him. 'Well done, Seamus,' he said. Anyone other than McNeill would have been deflated.

One of McNeill's greatest assets is his ability to laugh, often at himself, in desperate situations. At Aintree one day, John Tuck, for whom McNeill was riding later that afternoon, saw him circling at the start. 'I need a word with you later about my horse,' said Tuck. At the first hurdle, where Tuck was by now standing, McNeill took a shocking fall. 'Are you all right?' asked the trainer, adding, 'I know I wanted a word but I didn't mean that urgently.'

McNeill's feat of retiring from riding one week and starting another job the next should not be underestimated either. Off to Newmarket for his second interview with the Jockey Club for the post, McNeill was halfway up the M11 when he realised he had left the jacket of his suit in Lambourn. In a flash of inspiration he rang up his old Newmarket boss, David Ringer, and asked him to fit him up with one of his own suits. Ringer was only too happy to oblige. 'It was a bit in at the waist and slightly out at the bottom,' recalled McNeill, the master of understatement, earlier this week. In short he looked like the lead singer from Showaddywaddy. But he got the job.

PERHAPS IT DOESN'T AUGUR TOO WELL for Gatwick's chances in the 2004 Derby that the computers operated by Air Traffic Control went down on Thursday. However, should the colt win, he will be the first syndicate-owned winner of racing's Blue Riband.

His dozen owners, managed by Henry Ponsonby, also known as the 'SAS Major', are an eclectic bunch and include himself, Sir Alex Ferguson – one hopes the stallion rights have been formalised in the small print – Johnny Weatherby (who was also in Gold Cup runner Behrajan), Jenny Powell (who sold the horse to Henry), Felicity St Jean (one of his longest-suffering owners) and others scattered between Brussels and Londonderry.

So how did Henry, 55, become man-about-Lambourn and one of the country's leading syndicate managers? It's a long story. Brought up in Wensley, near Middleham in Yorkshire, he returned home from Shrewsbury School a dirty, spotty, unemployed teenager wanting to get into racing. The legendary Neville Crump fired off four letters for him to Tom Jones, Frank Cundell, Fred Winter and Fulke Walwyn. The first two had no vacancies, the third turned him down, and the last accepted him on £2.50 a week. After three long months Walwyn sent him packing saying he'd never make the grade. Forward the clock seventeen years and Henry returned to Walwyn's yard, this time as his second biggest owner after the Queen Mother.

In between it seems the army took a similar view to Walwyn, turning him down twice as officer material, so he joined the cavalry as a trooper. This involved escape and evasion exercises where Trooper Ponsonby was used as live targets for the SAS. He was, he says proudly, never caught during these grown-up games of hide and seek at Otterburn – hence his sobriquet.

Despite this marvellous addition to his CV he was rejected as an officer for a third time and quit the army after nine months to become a pensions and life insurance salesman in London. A chance meeting with Paul Cole in the Pheasant, a pub near Lambourn, in 1976 led him into racehorse syndication and the formation of Shefford Bloodstock. To survive in the business you have to do it well, and the fact that he rarely has fewer than a dozen horses on the go is proof of that.

The Gatwick story – all of Jenny Powell's horses begin with a G, so that's why he's not called Luton or Heathrow – is also a romantic tale. Henry's father's best man was a trainer called Colonel Wilfred Lyde who, when Henry was an impressionable young boy some 40 years ago, trained a horse called Brief Flight. Despite a deformity, the filly won the Jersey Stakes. She is the second dam of Gatwick and also bred Shotgun, which Lester Piggott rode into fourth behind Shergar in the 1981 Derby. When Sir Alex asked Henry to find him a horse to have in training with Mick Channon he picked Gatwick out of a field because of this connection.

YOU CAN SEE VINCE SLATTERY having sand kicked in his face at Wolverhampton tonight. You could have seen him at Huntingdon on Monday winning a chase on Super Sharp, and you could have seen him finish 23rd of 24 on Hever Gold Glory over a mile at York on Wednesday. Or, if you had been at Clonmel on Thursday evening, you could have seen him finishing 'completely tailed off' in the Powerstown Handicap Hurdle.

'Second-hand Slatts', as the valets call him, is the only jockey riding consistently (if that is the right word – the winner slightly spoilt that) both over the jumps and on the Flat in Britain as well as Ireland. And all the time he is riding, it means he is not being a handyman about home – which is just as well because when it comes to DIY he has the Frank Spencer touch: enthusiastic, undaunted, but a tad accident-prone. He may have ridden about a thousand fewer winners than Richard Dunwoody but the happy-go-lucky Slattery, 29, is one of the changing room's happier jockeys ('lucky' is open to question) and among the most popular. He has been attached to Owen O'Neill's Cheltenham yard for the past twelve years but is probably best known for his exploits around Ludlow on John Spearing's white charger Raba Riba, a runaway whom he reformed to win eight races. On one occasion, he hung around Raba Riba's neck for 100 yards after a horrendous mistake, climbed back in the saddle just before they reached the water, which he jumped ten lengths last, eventually got back into the contest and, against the odds, won.

Though his father, Tony, trains not far from Ballydoyle, it is thought he named his son after Saint Vincent, the patron saint of hospital workers and prisoners, on whose day Slatts was born. About fourteen years later Slatts left school and joined Jim Bolger for three months before he was packed off to agricultural college. There, he was told to plough a field. When he returned, justifiably proud of his straight lines and deep furrows, they told him that his lines were indeed straight and his furrows deep but that he had ploughed the wrong field. Spells with Frank Dunne and Arthur Moore then prepared him for race-riding, but not for artexing ceilings. He is among the select band of jockeys to have injured themselves schooling on Christmas Day (he broke a collar-bone). 'My father said it was wrong to bother the people at the hospital on Christmas Day,' he recalls, 'so he wouldn't take me in for 24 hours.' Once, after being quite badly concussed in a fall at Southwell, he hopped into the doctor's jeep, which was parked beside the fence, and drove it off. 'I had no idea what I was doing,' he says of the incident – a sentiment that could equally apply to his handiwork.

It is ironic really that the St Vincent he was named after was not the same St Vincent whose day is 5 April and who is patron saint of builders. Slatts is, by his own admission, the handyman from hell. He was once (only once) asked to paint his sister-in-law's window, which was three floors up. His ladder would not reach so he decided to take the window out, bring it in, paint it and put it back. Normally, painting does not require that degree of logic. However, he had just about unhinged the window when it plummeted through the tiled roof of the porch. As you can imagine, there wasn't much left to paint after that.

When Slatts was decorating his own house he made the error of putting in a new carpet first. When it came to moving his step-ladder he did so with an open tin of emulsion on the top of it. He tripped, the tin went flying, but he caught it. Unfortunately it was upside down and already emptying its contents. He stood back to admire the new colour scheme on the carpet, only to kick over his mug of coffee to add a brown stain to the mess.

A drill in his hands is to electric cables what a V-shaped stick in the hands of a water diviner is to underground streams. Most recently, he put a spade through a gas main while smoking. 'It didn't go up,' says Slattery. So he is lucky after all. ◼

THE WEIGHING ROOM IS SOMETHING OF A CULTURAL DESERT. This is not a criticism because the ability to recite poetry is bugger all use to you as you sail down to Becher's. But if you asked most jockeys for a line on Mozart it would be 'top sprinter, 2001'.

In this respect, however, David Dunsdon, who rides his 21st birthday present Joly Bey in Saturday's Hennessy Gold Cup, is something of a desert orchid. Returning from Auteuil on Sunday he was on the same plane as the well-known top-heavy model Jordan. 'She's not exactly Botticelli's Venus,' he commented on his close encounter.

What? I thought, reeling. Am I hearing him right? Quite apart from the moral question of whether it is apt for a gentleman amateur to pass such judgement on a 'lady', did he, a jockey, really say 'Botticelli's Venus'?

Yep, he did. David, 22, first cousin of Joly Bey's trainer Nick Gifford, is a student at the University of Surrey, Guildford – after riding out of course. But he's studying business management, not an arts foundation course. That stuff's self-taught. Yesterday he was attending lectures, something only Jenny Pitman's jockeys used to do as part of their big race build-up.

Though he still claims 3lb, David does not lack experience. He was Fegentri World Amateur Champion in 2002 and has ridden 25 winners abroad from Moscow to Madagascar. Riding trips abroad are rarely without incident. In Baden Baden he was walking the course with an Irish jockey and both were due to ride horses having their first runs over obstacles. 'At the start he was like Van Gogh's sunflowers – all orange and red and ruddy, a typical Irishman who spends his life outside,' said David of his Irish counterpart. 'But by the time we had come to the last he was like Monet's water lilies – a sickly, green mess.' He was, it appeared, terrified of the prospect of riding a bad 'un at Baden. Jimmy Quinn, the Flat jockey, decided to capitalise on this weakness and to play a prank by substituting the Irishman's long leathers for his own, which weren't much longer than shoelaces. Consequently, down at the start our Irishman found he was riding so short he made Paul Carberry look like a grand prix dressage rider. The end result was a hairy tightrope sort of ride for the Irishman and a stewards' inquiry at which, because no rules had technically been broken, the conspirators were merely given a smacked wrist.

In Madagascar, David's unfortunate Norwegian amateur colleague was kicked and developed a large haematoma which he decided to lance. That was an error, because the dirty local water could not be used to clean it. There was nothing either antiseptic or painkilling at the primitive course – except for the family-sized bottle of Jack Daniels which he had bought at Oslo's duty free on the way out.

The combination of loss of blood and the not inconsiderable flow of Jack Daniels absorbed into his system through the wound and down his throat soon began to have side-effects. Quite apart from ride, the Norwegian could hardly stand. At a reception in the evening, and by this time unable to taste, he compounded his problems by indulging himself in a local variety of tripe sausage, which was his second wrong judgement call. The following day, his guts no doubt twisting themselves in knots, he passed out in the plane loo on the flight home. His first ride on touching down in Paris was in an ambulance to hospital.

Riding abroad – you see it all.

So if David Dunsdon wins the Hennessy, what sort of picture would that paint? 'I should think,' he says modestly after considering the options, 'Malevich's "Black On Black" – for the punters. I can't imagine many of them backing an eccentric amateur to win it.'

NEXT THURSDAY BERNARD LLEWELLYN, owner of three of the last six small coal mines in Wales, secretary of the ever-dwindling Small Mines Association, magistrate, farmer and trainer, and his son John, who used to deliver the coal and consequently knows every address in a twenty-mile radius, will set out from the valleys of South Wales for Royal Ascot, where they run Suplizi in the 1998 Gold Cup. With only one set of top hat and tails between them – the same reason my father and I have never been seen at the same wedding – John, 27, will probably be leading up the seven-year-old full horse.

Suplizi, who is owned by Geraint Price, is stocky – a racing euphemism for small and tubby – horizontally laid-back and, despite being vertically challenged, as cool a dude as you will ever find on four legs. I don't suppose the favourite for the Gold Cup, Persian Punch, spent yesterday morning dodging sheep, rubbish left by locals, boulders and hurdling rushes (he's a great jumper, and it's primarily what he has been bought for) 1,600 feet up a mountain called Gelligaer Common. An ibex would consider this hilly; imagine what Suplizi thought on arriving from Newmarket. It is so open up there that when one of the lads is being run away with past the rest of the string, his colleagues put in an order for a McDonald's from Merthyr Tydfil, about five miles away. And winter or summer, it is an overcoat colder than any other part of Britain. John says, 'The first thing I ask when buying a horse is if they're any good with sheep. We had one brought down by a one-eyed ram not so long ago. We must have come at him from his blind side.' The other hazard Persian Punch probably did not encounter yesterday was a herd of wild Welsh Mountain ponies. 'Don't fall off him,' warned John, 'otherwise there'll be lots of little Suplizis running about these hills. It took three hours to catch the last colt to get loose with them.'

Last night at Chepstow, the Llewellyns ran their cheapest horse, Village Pub, who cost 500 guineas, and their most expensive, Prizefighter, who cost 6,600 guineas. 'I offered another trainer 2,000 guineas for a horse recently,' recalled John, 'and they said they didn't have one horse in the yard that they would sell for that. I replied that for £2,000 they could have three horses and the horsebox from our yard.' They also recently ran a talented but thinking horse at Hereford. After he had run disappointingly for the umpteenth time there, they asked the jockey on dismounting whether he thought the horse was getting wise to the track. 'Getting wise to Hereford?' said the jockey. 'He's so wise to Hereford he could drive the box home for you.'

In this part of the world, which has been hard hit by the loss of the coal industry, cheap is cheerful and remarkably successful – sixteen winners last jump season. One of the Llewellyns' two all-weathers is along the disused colliery railway; the other rises 350 feet over five furlongs. 'When we dug it,' says John, 'we let it settle for a year. It's so wet here that if we hadn't it would be in Bargoed [three miles down the valley] by now.'

Soon after Party Politics won the 1992 Grand National for Carl Llewellyn (no relation), John went to the local market to take orders for coal. He was told what a good ride he had given Party Politics. 'I saw the same bloke the other day,' says John. 'He still calls me Carl, thinks I rode Earth Summit, and still believes that Carl delivers coal part-time.' ■

ONE WONDERS WHETHER Amaryllis Goschen shouldn't be picking up a gold award at the Chelsea Flower Show this week rather than an engraved decanter from Gay Kindersley in the fading light at Stratford. Exotic it may sound, but with sisters Chrisula, Celeste and Mariora – an artist, a model and a masseuse-to-the-stars – testing the spelling skills of the clerk writing out birth certificates in that neck of the woods is the norm for Goschens.

Having ridden 60 winners in point-to-points, the majority for John Dufosee, 'Rilly' rode off the West Country point-to-point scene and into our living rooms earlier in the season by winning the Christies Foxhunters at Cheltenham on Earthmover. At the age of thirteen the horse, who has spent a lifetime parting birch like Moses did the Red Sea, seems to have finally kicked the habit. Proof, as it were, that you can teach an old dog new tricks? 'Not at all – my hands,' explained the rider, who is more direct than a cruise missile. She nearly completed a notable double at Stratford on Saturday when Earthmover loomed into contention at the last in the Intrum Justitia (formerly Horse & Hound) Cup. But he was brought down by the ill-fated Right to Reply. 'I made a tit's arse of it,' said Rilly (that, it seems, is a convent-school education for you).

Other than that it's all coming together for Rilly, whose mother runs a ceramic tile business. At the age of three she was given a pony. Both of them understood that kick meant go and pull meant stop. She would fell rhododendrons, make mini-Aintree fences and race round a course she had built, imagining commentaries on her winning the Grand National. To that aim she left the Dufosees and started riding out for Paul Nicholls. Stage one of the plan happened in April when she had her first ride round Aintree, coming to grief, like about two dozen others that week, at Becher's.

There is one problem, however – with most girls this is a no-go area – and that is her weight. John Dufosee says there's an eclipse of the sun every time she passes the stands at a point-to-point, and she, to give her her due, barely denies it. 'I can hardly hide it, can I?' she says. 'In those white breeches it's there for all to see. I'm a big bird, and the weight's concentrated in the backside.' Like most journalists, she's working on it. She's had a £100 bet with Paul Nicholls that if he puts her on a horse in the National she'd do ten stone on it. 'He saw me struggling to do eleven stone with a small saddle on Sunday,' she says, 'and doubled his bet.' ▣

LOOKING BACK ON THE 1996 FLAT TURF SEASON, you will agree that as far as we are concerned one horse stands out, a cigar among roll-your-owns. He is Montone, who has run 21 times and won five. In the process he has carried his owner, Dr Michael Mannish, self-confessed mug amateur, to victory in the Bollinger Series for gentlemen riders.

Dr Mannish, 45, can alter the way you smile, not only because he's a cosmetic dentist but because of the way he rides. He is publicity-shy, but you wouldn't think it if you read the *Racing Calendar* under the section 'Jockey Club Enquiries'. If he does not have a mention it is probably because he hasn't had a ride that week. His weighing-room sobriquet, Dr Death, has not been lightly earned, for in the early days, if he could go round the horse in front of him he invariably went over it. Indeed, my first encounter with the good doctor was in front of a panel of Lingfield stewards. If I remember rightly, I had a dual role as both victim and prosecution witness. He was regularly run away with going to the start, which prompted his trainer John Jenkins to insist he be led down, and he had to leave Chepstow quietly by the back door after his only outside ride. He broke the five-furlong course record there on a locally trained hot-pot. The only drawback was that the race was over a mile.

Montone, though, goes for no one else. After Pat Eddery had ridden him at Windsor one day, the rider came in and told Jenkins that the weight, 9st 2lb, had beaten him. A week later, carrying twelve stone and his owner in an amateur Flat race, he won. When Jenkins told Eddery this, the jockey enquired if it had been in a hurdle race.

Dr Mannish learnt to ride at the tender age of 38, when most jockeys are having internal struggles with their 'bottle', and his interest in racing only developed because the chap teaching him at a Sheffield riding school claimed to be a retired jockey. 'I'm Persian by birth,' says Dr Mannish, who is not without a great sense of humour. 'It sounds better than Iranian.' He dabbled in stockbroking and shipping and went to nearly every university in the country, except the British Racing School, before settling on the idea of dentistry. Now based in Highgate, London, he runs a successful practice. In his spare time he deals in antiques and scares the hell out of other amateurs.

He bought his equine partner at Newmarket in 1994, when he and a friend went to the sales with 3,000 guineas each to spend. His friend became bored with proceedings, fell asleep and woke up as the bidding was under way for Montone.

'Do you like that horse?' he asked Dr Mannish.

'Yes, I think he's magnificent,' replied Mannish, and up went the friend's hand, at which point the auctioneer said, 'Going, going, gone.' Mannish looked up at the scoreboard and saw that their single bid had secured Montone for 11,500 guineas.

'He ran away with me at home,' says Mannish. 'In fact, every horse I ever sit on at John Jenkins' does that. The first time I rode Montone, at Redcar, I asked Kieren Fallon how I should ride him and he told me to give him a long rein. The next thing I knew, on the way to the start, I was doing 45mph and heading for the stables' brick wall. That race was over a mile and three furlongs, and for nine furlongs nothing got near him, so we ran him over seven next time at Beverley and he won.'

And so began one of the horse world's great partnerships.

So if you have a horse who has lost his zest for racing, I have one piece of advice: stick him in an amateurs' race and don't book the pro-ams like Tim McCarthy, Lydia Pearce or even, dare I say it, me. Book Dr Mannish, and providing the horse does not break the course record going down to the start, it probably will coming back. ■

THE 1996 POINT-TO-POINT SEASON starts at Larkhill today without one of its greatest exponents, although he did toy with the idea of taking a ride in the maiden before going to Ascot. For Rupert Nuttall, 36, father of three, Somerset farmer, horse dealer, joint master of the Blackmore and Sparkford Vale Hunt, graduate of the Hard School of Knocks, and rider of 60 winners and one hell of a lot of dross, has hit on a partnership that sees the big time take precedence.

At an age when most jump jockeys are contemplating a life out of the saddle – Nuttall's done all that, having retired for four years in his early twenties – our hero's career is taking off again thanks to the quirky horse Harwell Lad, who lines up in Ascot's Peter Ross Novice Chase today – if he feels like it. 'The kinkiest but wisest horse I've ever had anything to do with,' says former international showjumper Nuttall, whose kid-glove treatment has seen them unbeaten in four races.

On their first meeting, Harwell Lad planted himself in a field so the rider gave him a kick in the ribs. The ensuing buck all but caused him to swallow his cigarette. Apart from teaching him not to smoke on horseback, the experience also gave Nuttall an important lesson: the less you do on Harwell Lad the sweeter he goes.

Powered by a fidgety, nervous energy, Nuttall is nicknamed Fred Scuttle because of his ability to eat, drink and smoke simultaneously. He is also one of only two people I know, other than some fading Lady Di sorts from the 1980s, who still turns his collar up because it's cool. He is acknowledged as one of the best schoolers of a young horse in this part of the world. Reputations like that are all very well, but more often than not it is the sacked jockey who has the last laugh. Nuttall once rode a point-to-pointer so slow that an outrider trying to catch a loose horse on an old hunter overtook him.

However, every once in a while it works to your advantage, and when Harwell Lad bucked Tim Mitchell off at the start of a race, trainer Robert Alner sought his assistance. 'You've just got to sit as quiet as possible,' says Nuttall, who, when he was 26, broke his neck in a fall at Southwell, drove home, had it manipulated the next morning, then spent the next eleven weeks in hospital.

At Wincanton last November, Harwell Lad's infamous character was brought to a wider audience when, in a three-horse race, he pulled up setting out for the last circuit because the other two runners had fallen. If one of the others hadn't remounted he would still be there now, but encouraged by the company of Ottawa, to whom he gave a twenty-length start, he soon had the race sewn up.

So if you see Harwell Lad in a tight finish today with the rider looking like an incompetent amateur unable to draw his stick, just remember that where this horse is concerned a little wisdom is better than a lot of strength. ▩

THE WHITBREAD GOLD CUP will be preceded today by a parade of winners which includes Docklands Express, who won on the controversial disqualification of Charlie Swan and Cahervillahow in 1991. If that was not Anthony Tory's greatest moment on the track, his performance in the stewards' room saw him short-listed for the part of Rumpole.

Tory, 29, retired ten days ago after 151 winners, a fight against increasing weight and, the final straw, a heavy fall at Cheltenham. Unable to get his breath for two hours afterwards his wife Belinda 'really thought I'd lost him'. Off stage, Tory's career was the stuff of legends from the moment he turned up for an interview with Tim Forster for the position of pupil-assistant. As you can imagine, the punk era had rather passed the master of the Old Manor by, and it still baffles people how a young David Bowie lookalike with peroxide hair driving a gold VW Beetle ever landed a job with a man whose fashion starts and ends with cavalry twill and brogues.

Accommodation for would-be amateurs during his two years there was a 'hut' in Letcombe Regis. His landlord, after Tory and a colleague had looked after his dogs for a couple of days, made the mistake of rewarding his tenant with a bottle of Scotch, which was drunk at one sitting. Feeling a bit whimsical, he and his pal took a fully clothed dip in a pond, which upset the ducks and the locals, who called the police. Alerted by the siren, they bolted for the hut leaving a watery trail. The local bobby let himself in and found Tory feigning sleep in bed in his wet clothes.

'What have you been up to?' he enquired.

'Nothing,' replied Tory, who obviously improved a stone in legal argument before crossing paths with the Whitbread stewards.

His *pièce de résistance* as an amateur was in the said Beetle, a car with the engine of a sewing machine. He bet the lads that he could get up to 75mph down the lane – unbeknown to Luke Harvey, who thought he was just getting a lift home. The lads lined the road, a still unknowing Harvey entered the 'missile', and to the strains of 'Nights in White Satin' they set off. So confident was Tory that he'd reach the speed that he reckoned he had time to swerve and put the wind up his audience. But in doing so he lost control and the car came to rest on its roof, Tory with his foot still hard down (up) on the accelerator, the Moody Blues still at full volume.

This column will always hold Tory, who is now married and really sensible, dear to its heart, not for the Whitbread but because he was one of the gentlemen who rode in that infamous Stratford hurdle when Jacqui Oliver split her breeches from backside to breakfast time. He, like all the others, had manners enough to let Miss Oliver cut out the running. All the best in retirement, Anthony. ■

WHEN JOCKEYS RETIRE, few take up a profession which increases the chance of a broken arm. It seems appropriate today to catch up with former Whitbread-winning rider Anthony Tory, who guided Docklands Express into second place in 1991 and subsequently managed to baffle the stewards into giving him the race. 'When he retires he should be a barrister,' wrote one journalist. That doesn't necessarily follow, for in 1975 John Oaksey, who was a barrister, managed to lose the race on Proud Tarquin for the most minor of infringements to Ron Barry and The Dikler. Although Ron could talk parrots out of the jungle, he would have been more familiar with the first syllable of 'barrister' than he was with legal argument.

No, Tory, who retired two years ago, a mere pup after having his stomach trodden on in a fall from the appropriately named Medina Swansong at Cheltenham, has taken up horse dentistry. For Tory it is now a case of have rasp, will travel. 'Some people will no doubt say that I extracted a few back teeth when I was riding,' says Tory who, having done ten stone for most of his riding career, now weighs in at a cruiserweight 12st 6lb. 'Like humans and their dentists, about one in 30 horses are not impressed with the service I provide,' he explains.

Tory, 31, learnt to distinguish his molars from his canines at the Academy of Equine Dentistry in Idaho, USA. He is now at the sharp end, trying to smooth it out and round the edges. 'The smoother a horse's teeth the more comfortably the bit sits in its mouth,' points out Tory.

What about today's Whitbread? 'Is it that time of year again?' asked a surprised Tory. Who says jockeys miss this sport when they retire? ◘

IT IS ABOUT TIME THIS COLUMN HAD A NEW HERO, and I think we've found him. He has been a candidate since 1982, when he partnered the front-running Spinning Saint around the Mildmay course at Aintree and all but succeeded in overshadowing Grittar's Grand National. Instead of turning sharp left to follow the Mildmay course like normal people, he set off towards the first of the National fences. His path, however, was blocked by two JCBs which were spreading grit across the Melling Road. To add to the tension of those viewing the impending accidental death, we knew that 'brakes' was not a word in Spinning Saint's vocabulary. Three strides away the JCBs parted, not like the Red Sea but by about the width of a narrow horse, and Spinning Saint and his intrepid amateur rider were spared from becoming the meaty filling in a digger sandwich. Instead they were faced with the first National fence.

Now Babbage is back – with a vengeance. Norman Babbage, budding trainer, took more finding than your average hero. If he doesn't live at the end of the world, he lives nearby. Nutterswood, which looks like a Stone Age settlement as you approach it over the cliffs of Cleeve Hill above Cheltenham, somehow seems appropriately named.

Whether it is because punters remember Spinning Saint or because Norman is not a name normally associated with success I don't know, but one of his six winners this season, Haya Ya Kefaah, started at 33–1. Another, Wannaplantatree, won at 25–1. Babbage, 33, is going through that early stage in the evolution of the trainer when most of his horses have been sent home as untrainable by their three previous trainers and sent to him as a last resort. If this is the sort of miracle he works with moderate horses with fantastic vices – won't load in the horsebox, won't eat, chews anything wooden or human – what is he going to do when he gets a decent tool?

'I didn't pick up the *Sporting Life* for five years,' recalls Babbage, who retired from riding at 24 and returned to the family building business. 'Then one night I went out with a few racing lads. We sat around talking about racing until four in the morning. I then realised how much I missed it.' Later that morning he sold his car, borrowed a few quid from a girl he had just started seeing – now Mrs Sarah Babbage – and went to Ascot Sales where he bought a couple of horses at 'knacker prices'. 'I started with has-beens that never were and wannabes that never would be.'

The first time he asked about a licence he was told no chance. A year later the Jockey Club Licensing Committee said, 'Mr Babbage, you're a borderline case.' He was given four months to produce three placed horses or one winner. Among the £700 horses was a decent one, Mathal, who won three. Our Norman's permit was upgraded to a trainer's licence and he hasn't looked back.

One of the keys to his success must be location. If you were trained on top of the world then surely you would feel on top of the world, and run accordingly. ◼

THERE WERE MIXED FEELINGS in the northern weighing room this week when Brian Storey, who makes his last trip to Cheltenham today, announced his retirement. Brian hangs up his boots later this month and joins the Jockey Club as a part-time starter – work that should fit in nicely with his other job as a farmer.

Now, it is the great McCoy who has perfected and legitimised – among jockeys at any rate – the art of lying-in in the mornings, and given a two-fingered salute to the tradition that his profession must ride out. What you may not fully appreciate when you see Brian, 40, riding today is that before McCoy even got round to scratching himself this morning he had done what many would consider a day's work and milked 70 Friesians. That's 4,500 pints of the white stuff in the tank – 'A lot of milk if you want to sup it,' confirms Brian. The money's in the bank before he's even sat on a horse. Takes the pressure off a bit, doesn't it? So while, by my counting, Brian has handled 280 teats before breakfast, McCoy can only dream of such pleasure. And when the champion gets the semi-skimmed out of the fridge for his cup of sweet tea, I wonder if he thinks, 'Thanks, Brian.' I'd like to think so.

Brian is a grafter and a horseman. Up north, no jockey is more respected, believe me. He's hard. Hard in the sense that he would have been riding out, after milking, in a T-shirt this week. On one famous occasion at Wetherby, following a fall in which he had dislocated his shoulder, he convinced the doctor it was nothing more than minor bruising, despite turning green when the doctor asked him to hold his arm level. Unfortunately it was heroically in vain and his mount in the next had to be withdrawn because he couldn't steer or hold it.

He has other claims to fame. His weight has always been good and, not one to miss a meal, he still stops for lunch on the way to the races. He's ridden 550 winners, 96 of them for Raymond Anderson-Green in an eighteen-year partnership that eclipses all other 'arrangements', apart from Sir Mark Prescott and George Duffield. He won the Scottish National on Mighty Mark and the Cathcart at the Cheltenham Festival on Sparky Gale. He also fell – the last to do so by my reckoning – at the water jump in the Grand National. He's rarely been in trouble with the stewards except for the ride he gave, or rather didn't give, to Flowing River one day – an epic of the genre. Richard Dunwoody thought he was so good he stuck him in for the ride on One Man when unavailable, and Tony Dobbin says he's the best man to follow in a race. The pair, Tony and Brian, have one of those 'deals' whereby they look after each other in a race, give each other a bit of light when needed, and so on. 'Brian retiring?' says Dobbin in horror. 'It'll be like taking half my winners away.' ■

WHEN THE UNBEATEN NOVICE CHEVAL DE GUERRE lines up for the Sun Alliance Chase at next month's Cheltenham Festival, one man will be taking more than a passing interest.

This is the serious side of racing's one-time wild child Gavin Wragg, who is now, with his wife Jonny, settled down and producing a very nice line in potential chasing stars for British trainers from his new base near Cashel, in Ireland. After Jonny – the last person to ride side-saddle in a British point-to-point – won the side-saddle championship at the Dublin Show on Cheval de Guerre, they sold the gelding to Lambourn trainer Kim Bailey.

Wragg, 44, veteran of eight Aintree Foxhunters', was back at Sandown on Thursday to partner Young Nimrod in a hunter chase. Sporting the same shoulder-length hair, the same distinctive riding style and still driving fast cars, only his new vocation and a recently acquired mid-St George's Channel accent were different. Welcome back, Gavin, if only briefly.

Sandown racegoers may not have realised it, but they were in the presence of a legend. After all, this is the man who once got unseated seven times on the way to the start of a point-to-point before winning the race by fifteen lengths. He also spent a night in the cells after riding in the Velka Pardubicka, and was once asked by the Folkestone stewards what the owner would think after he had dropped his hands in a hunter chase. 'He's furious,' he replied. 'I *am* the owner.'

Though – and this is vehemently denied – one rider on the southern point-to-point circuit claims to have had his nose broken when Gavin 'waved to auntie' over a fence and accidentally connected with his face, our man is not normally given to violence. However, after being brought down in an Irish point-to-point one day he slightly lost his Wragg and was on the point of hitting the man who'd brought him down.

'I wouldn't do that,' advised a friend.

'Why?' demanded an apoplectic Gavin.

'Because,' said the friend, 'he's just been let out of prison for shooting his wife's boyfriend.'

Wragg sensibly took the advice.

His car racing – current set of wheels is a Lamborghini – is now restricted to motor circuits. But it was in an Audi Quattro that he upset the Czech police. In a country where the Trabant was then the most sophisticated (and only) vehicle, an Audi Quattro travelling at speed was bound to attract attention. After leaving a restaurant and passing a stationary police car he looked in his mirror to see if it was following. Instead he saw the terrified face of Charlie Mann, with whom he had just dined, clinging on to his rear spoiler. By the time he had stopped and let a shaken Mann in, the police car had arrived and they were arrested at gunpoint. ■

NO MATTER HOW UNLUCKY YOU ARE, just remember it could have been worse. That's a mantra which has been sustaining jockeys for years. You know the sort of thing: an Irish jockey breaks two legs in a fall and thinks to himself, 'How lucky am I? A fall like that, it could easily have been three.'

Recently, a jockey was leading a field of 23 runners when he fell at the last hurdle down the back at Warwick. He took the mother and father of falls, was rolled on by his own mount, and several of his pursuers managed to get in a kick as they passed over, round and through him. But when he was checked over in the ambulance room the course doctor found nothing wrong more permanent than dented pride, because the jockey felt the fall had cost him a winner.

After tea and sympathy, the jockey was allowed back into the changing room, where he slumped into his seat, head in hands, digesting what had happened, a picture of abject misery and possibly mild concussion. One of his colleagues, who had been tracking him and had been unable to avoid hitting him, was pleasantly surprised to see him walk back in one piece and went over to commiserate.

'I was very lucky,' said the jockey who had fallen.

'Yep,' agreed his mate. 'You could easily have been badly injured or broken something.'

'No,' said the jockey. 'I missed landing in a dog turd by six inches.' ■

AT THE END OF THE MONTH John Blake officially takes over the reins at the Jockeys Association from Michael 'Corky' Caulfield, who after fifteen years in the job is off to set up a firm of sports psychologists. John is already putting in a couple of days a week familiarising himself with the role. However, unless something is sorted out between the jockeys, their mobile phones and the Jockey Club in a meeting today, then this little spat will not be so much a golden hello for John but, in rugby terms, a serious 'hospital pass' from Corky.

Nevertheless, despite this little unresolved blip, Corky's boots will take some filling. So, I hear you ask, is John, 37, up to the job? The answer appears to be yes, despite the fact that when it comes to riding he finds a rising trot a bumpy challenge. He is much happier with a football at his feet, which, if nothing else, should earn him an automatic place in the Commitments, the jockeys' football team for which Corky kept (picking the balls out of the) goal.

For the last two and a half years John has been racing editor of Teletext. Knowing a thing or two about racing is one thing, but John also brings that bit extra to his desk – a sound knowledge of turf and sods. I dare say no one else in racing can claim to have 'grave-digging' on their CV. As a schoolboy in Cardiff he took a summer holiday job, to gain work experience, in a graveyard. Digging? 'Well,' he says, 'more filling in than digging.' It wasn't the pick of holiday jobs – 95 per cent of the people he met were in floods of tears (presumably the other 5 per cent were over the moon) – and eventually, before he became emotionally scarred, he told the authorities he would be hanging up his spade for good. 'That's a pity,' said his boss, surveying acres of gravestones. 'One day you could be running this place.' The bereaved of Cardiff's loss is the jockeys' gain.

For stylish CVs, it doesn't end there though. His first proper job was for the Society for the Promotion of Christian Knowledge, a worldwide bookshop promoting religious reading. 'No, I'm not happy clappy, before you ask,' he says. And while posted to Chattanooga in the United States he got a part-time job in local radio. Cribbing World Service reports on racing, he broadcast interesting facts, such as Willie Carson riding a big winner, to the hillbillies of Tennessee, who remain baffled to this day. ■

FRANKIE DETTORI may have put a few thousand on Musselburgh's Easter Day gate with his first visit to the course for eleven years, but let's put some perspective on this. Would he cut the mustard in places like Angola, Chechnya or Eritrea? Would the Afghan warlord General Dostum let him loose on his finest mule? I doubt it.

There is, however – and it seems appropriate to single him out in this week's Scottish number of the Diary ahead of their National meeting at Ayr on Saturday – an ageing (relatively speaking), as yet winnerless under Rules amateur in Dumfriesshire who does cut that mustard. He is Guy Willoughby, 43, head of the mine-clearing charity the Halo Trust.

His role is more executive now, but he's cleared mines around the world without a scratch, although his heart may have skipped a few beats. He possesses two pretty potent weapons of his own, one of which – Lord Edwards Army – broke Guy's collar bone on his last visit to Ayr. The other, The Panjshir, named after an Afghan valley, broke Luke Morgan's collar bone in a point-to-point a week later. 'Mines,' as Guy pointed out rather dryly, 'don't tend to break your collar bone.'

Before Lord Edwards Army, subsequently a 50–1 second at Kelso, runs in the hunter chase on Friday, Guy must do his regulation six press-ups to pass the doctor. He's hoping if he wears a very smart suit, tie and hat, the 'doc' might not ask him to get down on the floor.

His fall there last time necessitated a trip to the local hospital, from where he was picked up by Umar, his Chechen bodyguard – another thing Dettori lacks. Now granted asylum in Britain after a run-in back home with the Russians, Umar is Halo's odd-job-man-cum-driver, but unlike your average bodyguard, who is no more qualified to protect someone from flying bullets than he is to dog-sit for his neighbour, Umar is, or rather was, the real thing. When Guy and other members of the Halo Trust came under attack from bandits in Chechnya, Umar, who had been assigned to them, killed two assailants and winged another brace.

It is on the cards that Lord Edwards Army will give Guy that elusive winner before too long. Guy plans to give it another couple of years trying anyway. 'At my age, most people either get a motorbike or change wives,' he reflects. 'This seemed the only alternative to those two options, although Mrs Willoughby wasn't flavour of the month when she failed to get the money on at Kelso. She only took her Switch card!' ■

WHILE OTHER LESS SPORTY SHEPHERDS watched their flocks over Christmas, Tim Reed was reminding us all just how to ride winners. A victory at Ayr on Boxing Day, his first of the season, and two more there last Monday prompted the elderly – and I use that word in its most relative sense – jockey to suggest that you can get a fine tune out of an old fiddle. We just hope we don't have to wait until Easter before he rides another.

Tim, 38, is one of my all-time sporting heroes, mainly because of the sheer (excuse the pun) hard work he has put into it, his good humour, the fact that he should weight at least twelve stone, a touch of madness and a wonderfully indecipherable Geordie accent. Though he has enjoyed great success as a professional jockey – roughly 350 winners – he remains very much an amateur at heart, and at most times has run another job concurrently with the riding: either looking after his father's sheep on their farm by Hadrian's Wall, having a crack at becoming a butcher, or, as he does now, running a bed-and-breakfast business to supplement income from the farming and riding.

As an amateur, he was second in the championship to Tim Thomson Jones. 'Every time I rode a winner, his mother went out and bought him another horse to ride,' Tim reflects on the slightly one-sided financial battle going on behind the scenes. 'Then at the other end of the season the Jockey Club told me I was riding too much and that I had to turn professional. I wish they'd ring up now and tell me I'm riding so little I should turn amateur so I could ride in point-to-points.' Go back to point-to-points? That's the touch of madness I mentioned.

In the early 1990s, on a jump jockeys' team visit to Russia, the locals christened him the 'Mountain Goat' for his ability to climb steep slopes as if they didn't exist, and they understood his accent better than his English colleagues.

One of his biggest winners was Ken Oliver's High Edge Grey in Wetherby's Charlie Hall Chase. At the time, the fences there had just been rebuilt and were controversially stiff; a chaser had only to flick the top to be brought crashing down to earth. There were many complaints. When Tim weighed out and the clerk of the scales asked him if there were any extras (such as a breastplate), he replied in the affirmative and produced a loo roll.

His worst injury was caused not, as you might expect, by half a ton of flying horse falling on him, but by a couple of pounds of newborn lamb: Tim slipped a disc trying to catch it.

His B&B business is in a good spot for rambler types. It is situated ten miles from Hexham, near the Pennine Way and the largest fort on Hadrian's Wall. With his wife Emma still working, the cooking was initially left to Tim. His only experience had been a one-day session with several other jockeys and the *Two Fat Ladies* on television. He admits the only thing he learnt during that stint was how to drink while cooking. But all was going well with the sausages, bacon and eggs until one guest rang up requesting an evening meal. In a panic, he asked Emma to scribble down a recipe, and he has since perfected this one meal. 'So far,' he says with relief, 'no one has stopped two nights running.'

YOU PROBABLY WON'T NOTICE IT, but there is a major hand-holding exercise going on at Cheltenham this season as outgoing clerk of the course Philip Arkwright guides his protégé, assistant, apprentice, sidekick, successor – call it what you will – Simon Claisse through the minefield that is this job.

A clerk of the course, as Simon will no doubt find out when he takes over in May, is happy at the end of a day's racing if the only mention he gets is on the racecard. This beast is rarely praised; just cussed when things go wrong or if his description of good ground doesn't match David Nicholson's (stop press: make that Alan King's).

When I caught up with Simon on Thursday evening to find out whether or not he had a Claisse to answer, he had just lost a cheque.

'How much for?' I asked, thinking he had lost Cheltenham's pre-Murphy's Craic takings.

'No, a Czech,' he explained. 'A Czech jockey wanted a sauna, I've switched it on, and now I can't find him. If he doesn't want it, I'll have to switch it off, lock up the weighing room and go home.'

Sounds as if Major Arkwright, who was probably relaxed in front of the fire with a Scotch at this time, knows a good job to delegate when he sees one.

It is no wonder Simon, 39, got the position for which 75 applied. He has the prerequisite selection of tweed suits, a degree from Reading University in farm management, had managed a farm for seven years and has spent the last ten with the Jockey Club. He has also ridden 27 point-to-point winners. When he managed a farm near Winchester, he restructured the running of it so well that the one person no longer required was, er, the manager. But – and this somewhat compensates for that misfortune – when he ran the point-to-point and racecourse offices at the Jockey Club, he put in place the training programme for 'wannabe' clerks and set the 'exam' they have to take after nine months of training. In the spring, he will, therefore, have to answer his own questions on the subject. We're expecting nothing less than an A grade.

Simon has two major claims to fame. One was after a fancy dress party when he turned his car over into a ditch eight miles from home. Wearing a blonde wig and a blue skirt (having gone as Goldilocks), he was somewhat surprised when he couldn't get anyone to give him a lift home, but not half as surprised as the police when they arrived. The other occasion was during this year's point-to-point season when riding his own horse, the flying Forest Musk. Simon found himself riding a Members' race winner up against the top-class Struggles Glory at Charing. After Simon had pulled up, the stewards 'did' him for not being off. That was slightly unfortunate, not to say embarrassing, for as big chief in charge of point-to-pointing, Simon had taught the stewards what to look for in a non-trier. Some people would say that was a resignation offence in his position. This column would say it showed character. ■

THE FURORE SURROUNDING GOLF'S RYDER CUP is rumbling on and Britain, as a team, remain among the tennis 'elite' – not my word – having slain that well-known Goliath with a cat-gut racket, South Africa in the Davis Cup.

Unlike football, these are two predominantly individual sports which, when used sparingly, turn into very exciting team competitions. The thought occurred to me, though, that the one predominantly individual sport we might be very good at as a team is horse racing. A Rider Cup, as it were. After all, two of our strongest suits in Olympics past have been the equestrian team events, show jumping and eventing.

In May we had the inaugural Shergar Cup at Goodwood, a contest between Europe and the Middle East with each team represented by five runners in each race. As competitions go, it was a nail-biter. The Europeans needed the first three home plus a fifth in the last race to win, and they did just that to win 126–120. From small acorns either mighty oaks grow or squirrels have a modest meal. It will benefit from the experience and some tweaking, but it lacked the tradition – something that will come if it lasts that long – and passion of either the Ryder Cup or Davis Cup.

That is not to say there haven't been jockeys' teams, and I can safely say I was a member of both the most stunningly successful and the most disastrously unsuccessful jockeys' teams of all time.

The victorious team was the one that represented the jockeys on not one of the greatest TV quiz shows ever designed, *Busman's Holiday*, when we beat a team of hairdressers and AA patrol men – dressing hair and mending cars also being predominantly individual sports. The prize for winning was a week – in our case riding horses, but had it been the AA patrol men it would have been changing spark plugs – somewhere in Europe. If you won the head-to-head with Sarah Kennedy it was a fortnight somewhere in the world. At the time I told my editor there was no chance of the team winning and therefore no chance of us needing a holiday during one of the busiest weeks of the year, because we would make damn sure we didn't win. Apparently being jockeys we're damn good at making sure we don't win. But having answered one of Sarah's questions on hairdressing – 'Who is the celebrity crimper John Freida married to?' (answer: Lulu) – which in a golfing context was like holing a 60-footer, we were on a roll. However, one of our team, Simon Cowley, was one of the few professional jockeys to have studied Classics at Oxford University and we hadn't properly briefed him about making sure we finished second. Needless to say, when he answered the impossible tie-breaker correctly you have never seen such a disappointed winning team – even though Budapest didn't turn out so bad.

The most disastrous team was the one that went to Pyatigorsk, southern Russia, in 1993, which comprised Carl Llewellyn (two Grand Nationals), Luke Harvey (Welsh National), Steve Smith-Eccles (three Champion Hurdles) and me. The three previous British teams to visit had all expressed worries about an obstacle, a wall, which was so small that there was a strong likelihood the horses would not see it in the long grass and would trip over it. This time the Russians had proudly placed a small tree trunk on top of it, but at about three feet it still looked pretty innocuous. In the race, seven horses out of ten runners fell individually (none was brought down by any others) at the fence. It was as if someone was sat a hundred yards up the course with a machine gun. Percentage-wise I think there were fewer casualties during the Charge of the Light Brigade.

Luke Harvey broke his collarbone and I cracked my knee. Forgetting that fridges were virtually unheard of in the area, my request for some ice was met with the unsympathetic reply that I'd have to wait for winter. Steve Smith-Eccles, one of the bravest jockeys ever to have sat on a horse, sensibly cried like a child, even though he was fine, so that he wouldn't have to ride in the next race. Having been comprehensively rolled on, Carl Llewellyn's body descended into shock and began, gradually, to shut down on him. By evening, when he was virtually pulseless, we were seriously worried about him. The Russian doctors were summoned, and after stabilising him they took him to hospital – or would have done had the ambulance not had a flat battery. I don't know if you can imagine the scene: an ambulance, with a not-quite-dead jockey in the back, being pushed by two doctors, a nurse, one jockey with his arm in a sling, another with his knee in a splint and the only healthy one at the controls trying to jump-start it. We can, with some clarity. We haven't been back since.

I have shaky, homemade video footage of those seven fallers going down like skittles. I was going to send it in to *You've Been Framed*, on account of the £250 prize, but then the memory of *Busman's Holiday* cured me of any such thought. ◼

AS SPORTSMEN GO, they don't come any more sporting than Philip Pritchard, a 42-year-old Wotton-under-Edge doctor.

In the days when being an amateur meant it cost you, the doctor devoted himself to rugby, often travelling from Guildford, where he was working as an anaesthetist, to Gloucester four nights a week for training – for not even petrol money. He played schoolboy internationals, was awarded his county cap and peaked playing for Gloucester in a John Player Cup final. Wow, cigarette sponsorship – that's showing his age. He once broke his ankle but failed to diagnose it for three weeks. By then it required an operation, but, in his own words – and if you're due to go under the knife soon, look away now – 'Being an anaesthetist, I was too frightened to have an anaesthetic.'

Due entirely to injury, he gave up rugby for something safer. Chess? Safe it may be, but if you're dealing with anaesthesia every day you don't want it as your hobby as well. No, he took up the pansy's sport of amateur race-riding over jumps where, at worst, a horse travelling at 35mph with iron shoes can roll on you or act as a catapult.

So far, apart from his enthusiasm and a few winners, including a 25–1 shot at Newton Abbot yesterday, his biggest contribution to the sport has been as the course doctor at the Cheltenham Festival. His quick diagnoses there – he has whittled it down from three weeks – have been a revelation.

In a crowded room on Saturday night, Tony McCoy, the champion jump jockey, told me he was going to Tralee the following day. Due to the combination of his Irish accent and the noise (but not due to the drink I'd taken), I thought he said 'Chile', which would have been as exotic as the doctor, who heads for Madagascar with his wife tomorrow.

Now I don't pretend to be a traveller in the Columbus mould, more of the London Transport one-day travelcard type, but I once rode in Madagascar. The racecourse was called L'Hippodrome Fandresena Ambohimandroso (by the time the commentator had told you where the racing was from, the contest was over). The first thing we had to do on arrival was clear the course, about the size of a football pitch, of cattle. Our horses, or rather ponies, were little pot-bellied things that we found tied up in bushes. They hadn't had a square bowl of oats for, um, for ever, so were damned if they were going to oblige by putting any effort into our sport. In the first race a Dutch colleague was actually lapped by the winner.

In the second race, I discovered that my mount, a mare called Tollichka, was also the mother of a colt in the same race. She ran like she was due to give birth to its brother. I am not saying the race was bent, but the local hero was a jockey called Eddy and the draw for the mounts was supposed to be out of a hat. The few Europeans among us were looking as miserable as our mounts in the paddock when, from behind a shed, appeared Eddy's mount. It looked like Mill Reef reincarnated. Oats? It must have been on two bowls three times a day plus cod liver oil. It had a gleaming coat, a sheepskin noseband so big, bright and fluffy it must have been made from the hides of at least two sheep, and was two hands taller than our ponies. Crucially, its most impressive muscles were in its legs, unlike our ponies, whose best muscles were the ones straining to contain their bellies. My granny doesn't get about too well these days, but I'd have been confident of its chances with her on board. It duly romped home.

I've tried a thousand times since to picture the events which went on in the paddock beforehand ever happening at Royal Ascot. Maybe my imagination isn't up to much, because I've failed. For into the paddock determinedly strode a local man, dressed in rags. Whether he was expressing an opinion about horse racing or nature was just taking its course, he – how shall I say this? – unzipped himself, extracted his equipment and started to pee on the hoof, advancing forward like a fireman dousing an imaginary bush fire. The crowd, about 500 strong, apparently used to such behaviour, didn't flinch. Had Kenneth Wolstenholme been commentating on my expression, he might have said, 'He thinks he's seen it all … he has now.'

Yesterday the doctor rang up asking for advice about Madagascar. I've told him to pack his mackintosh breeches. ▣

DR PHILIP PRITCHARD, who was last seen heading off to Madagascar to ride for ten days, is back, unscathed. The trip was successful but, as predicted, not without incident. The 'doc' became the first British jockey to win there since Tim Thomson Jones when he won a race at Antsirabe on an animal called Diamond Eyes after three false starts had eliminated the first and second favourites (one ran away and the other lost its jockey).

However, a former winger for Gloucester, the doc's athletic prowess came into its own away from the racecourse. Madagascar may be tenth in the international list of how much of a return an owner can expect from his horse – Britain languishes in 42nd place – but any savings you make are likely to be picked from your pocket. And to prove it the doc's wife, Teresa, was the victim of three attempted muggings in 24 hours.

The first time, in Antananarivo, the capital, a local tried, and failed, to grab the gold chain around her neck. Half an hour later, another grabbed her purse. This time the ever-ready doc was prepared for it, handed Teresa his camera, and legged it after the villain. In a scene reminiscent of a James Bond movie he had, after 600 yards, got to within a flying tackle of his quarry. At this point, knowing that the game was up, the thief threw the purse into a crowded market place. 'Do I go after him or get the purse back? was my first thought,' says the doc. He chose the second option.

By now they were what you might call street-wise, walking around without watches, little in the way of jewellery, one hand on their hat and the other in their pocket.

When, the following day, another suspicious-looking local got too close for comfort the doc took a leaf out of his medical journal and dispensed his own brand of rough justice. He thumped the poor punter before he even had a chance to see what these two tourists had to offer. 'It's about prevention being better than the cure,' says the doc. ■

YOU MAY THINK that with Guineas trials taking place daily, the jump season is over. Far from it. One of our most charming 'Festivals' takes place at Perth during next week. Perth is a thriving country track run by former jockey Sam Morshead and his wife Anthea, who now takes over as clerk of the course on race days. She hopes her big week will kick off with victory for her father Peter Beaumont's Young Kenny in today's Scottish National.

Morshead retired from riding in 1997, having ridden over 400 winners, and was a lovely mix of cavalier jockey and naughty schoolboy. My abiding memory of him is from the changing room. When he changed, his vest, shirt, tie, jumper and jacket would come off as one garment and it would go back on as one garment, usually while he held a sandwich in one hand and a cup of tea in the other. The snack often failed to complete its journey intact.

You couldn't get away with it now, but one day in a Chepstow novice chase run in thick fog the only fences the field jumped were the last two on the first circuit and the last on the second circuit. Sam finished second, and when asked why he hadn't won he replied that he was laughing too much to ride a finish.

Remarkably, Sam was down to the last three for a job as stewards' secretary when a job at Ayr racecourse came up. He only went for the interview because he thought it was a good excuse for a day's salmon fishing. Having fiddled around with Ayr and Musselburgh he has now, living five minutes from salmon, grouse and stag, what he considers the perfect job.

The clerk of the course's present nightmare seems to be dolling off fences at which there has been a faller. 'We had one occasion,' he recalls, 'when the bollards were in the right place but the arrows were put in the fence back-to-front and were directing the runners into a ploughed field. Everyone could see this unfolding but luckily the lines of communication to the fence worked and it was rectified.'

THE NUMBER OF JOCKEYS WITH A DEGREE riding at the Cheltenham Festival can probably be counted on one hand, possibly on the two fingers that most riders gave to their school. If you want to get on in what is essentially a young man's business, then you don't havetime to go to university. If you did spend three years swotting, you would emerge into the daylight at the end of it about 500 winners behind Tony McCoy. Alternatively, if you tried to combine the two you would have missed so many lectures you would, in all probability, have failed your finals.

Although paper certificates of scholastic achievement count for the square root of zero in the saddle, we have managed (and it wasn't easy) to track down the weighing room's answer to Carol Vorderman. Despite protestations from racing's very own Bachelor of Science that she fluked her exams in 'land management' at Reading University, Fiona Needham will partner her father Robin Tate's Last Option in the Christies Foxhunters' Cup on Thursday. She will also be one of the few girls involved at the Festival in a riding capacity.

Last Option he may be, but he is also the last horse to beat Double Thriller. He may have slightly let the form down so far this season – his bridle came off after a mistake first time out, and he hated the heavy ground last time – but a great deal more can be expected, especially if the going dries up.

Described by a friend as 'Liz Hurleyesque', Fiona was the leading female rider over jumps last season and spends as much time at her parents' home in Thirsk looking after the horses as she does in

Newmarket looking after her husband Kevin, the British Bloodstock Agency's shipping manager. 'He's dieting to ride in point-to-points,' said Fiona dismissively. 'He doesn't need anyone to do the cooking at the moment.'

She has been luckier with horses than she was with cars. At Reading, she went through them with regularity. She jumped a hedge into a field in one and, much like you might on a horse, thought the best way out was to try and jump back. To this day her rescuers wonder why the car was stuck in the hedge facing out of the field. Another one burnt out, a tree fell on another, though she lived in a treeless area of Reading – her parents found out only last year that the car had been parked outside Kevin's woodland home near Newmarket at the time – and in Tattersalls car park she managed to write off her car doing 5mph.

Within days of leaving Reading, Fiona was involved in an amicable divorce from land management. She is now a part-time bloodstock agent, and an ostrich feather in her mortar-board was the purchase of Owington, who went on to win the July Cup.

Her father, the second most legendary Robin after the one who used to live in Sherwood Forest, finally retired from riding in point-to-points at the age of 60. There were occasions when father rode against daughter, and one time when father rode against daughter and son-in-law. In her first season, Fiona tried creeping up her father's inside in a point-to-point. He, and I quote, 'pinned her on a corner and told her afterwards it was lesson number one'. Did she take the lesson on board? 'Oh yes, very much so,' said Robin.

According to the hungry Kevin, his wife has ridden some good horses and a lot of awful ones. The Tates have successfully managed to produce a killer breed of horse, all from the same mare, which are named accordingly, such as Another Hooligan. The offspring after Kevin and Fiona became engaged was called Shock Engagement, and in the spring before they were married the beast took off with the bride-to-be during a race at Witton Castle and cleared a barbed-wire fence. After that, Cheltenham should be a doddle. ▩

RACEGOERS WHO ENJOY VISITING EXETER may, this week, be forgiven for thinking there has been a good old-fashioned *coup d'état* at the top of Haldon Hill. According to one newspaper, Commodore Geoffrey Billson, formerly captain of the destroyer HMS *Exeter*, has taken over as clerk of the course.

The former naval officer has, in fact, taken over from Richard Merton as general manager. Major General Nick Ansell remains, as he has been for the last four years, clerk of the course. If he didn't get mentioned in too many dispatches during his military career he gets plenty in this Diary to make up for it. It was he who was riding a mare on an Indian safari when it lay down during the stop for lunch and gave birth. 'When I took over here I was given two pieces of advice,' recalls Ansell, a veteran of many Grand Military Gold Cup campaigns. 'Philip Arkwright, clerk of the course at Cheltenham, said I should keep my name off the front page of the racing papers because you only get there if there has been a calamity. Tim Forster said there were three things in this world, liars, damn liars and clerks of the course, and pleaded that in giving going reports I might be one of the few exceptions. I hope it is not tempting providence, but I seem to have observed Philip's advice to the letter in that the Racing Post don't think I even exist.'

In these politically correct times, however, the pair prefer to be known simply as 'the boys Nick and Geoff'. 'I think this makes us more approachable,' says Ansell. Billson's riding career is not quite as distinguished as Ansell's and amounts to a mounted patrol of the Falkland Islands, as a guest of that well-known cavalry regiment the Grenadiers. 'The captain could ride well but his soldiers had no experience. When they fell off, which was frequently, they would be hit on the head by their packs, then by their rifles. They would then salute and jump back on.' On one occasion he was run away with along a beach but was not unduly worried by the experience because he knew the pony would have to stop at the foot of the almost vertical cliff at the end. Little did he realise that the Falkland Island pony was a relation of the mountain goat, and when it was halfway up the cliff face, discretion became the better part of valour and Billson sensibly baled out.

Ansell is swift to point out, however, that a major general does, in fact, trump a commodore. Billson accepts that, but is equally swift to reply that the navy is, of course, the senior service.

As Exeter is sometimes run in conditions of zero visibility, low cloud and fog of the pea-soup variety, I can't think of anyone better to run the show than the boys from the army and navy.

JIMMY FROST, weighing-room antique, winner of the Grand National and Champion Hurdle, is enjoying something of a purple patch. The winners have been trickling out of his father's small Buckfastleigh yard at the rate of one or two a week, most of them partnered by Jimmy.

Having started with Billy Williams, Ian Williams' father, at sixteen, Jimmy rode his 400th winner, on a horse belonging to the Queen Mother, five seasons ago and promptly stopped counting. He also rode 86 point-to-point winners before he decided to turn professional. Jimmy is 40 now but clearly remembers an afternoon's pointing at Tiverton when he had three rides for Oliver Carter. The first one dropped him five times before the start and fell in the race. The second did him three times and, again, fell in the race. The third, the good one, just fell. 'That was eleven falls from three rides,' he recalls, before adding with the benefit of hindsight and the wisdom of old age, 'I was a bit of an idiot for getting back on them.'

Jimmy rarely takes outside rides these days but occasionally helps out Robert Alner and old boss Toby Balding, for whom he rode Little Polveir and Morley Street, on bank holidays. Balding's Fyfield yard is like an officers' mess before the Grand Military meeting, and with the Royal Artillery Gold Cup being run this Tuesday, Jimmy was prompted to recall a March schooling session which was attended by a soldier who, invariably, was keener than he was able. The soldier fell off and injured his elbow. During breakfast, Toby asked Jimmy to go to Andover Hospital and pick him up.

'What do I want to do that for, boss?' asked Jimmy.

'Well,' said Balding, 'he's also a steward at Newbury, and it doesn't harm to have them on your side.'

Jimmy arrived, found a doctor and, although he wasn't entirely sure of name or rank, asked for the soldier.

'We've no one here by that name,' said the doctor. 'What's he done?'

'He fell off his horse and hurt his elbow,' answered Jimmy.

'I know the man you mean,' replied the doctor. 'Fell off his horse, but it's not his elbow. He's got piles.'

'Oh,' said Jimmy, who can now expect a lengthy ban the next time he sets foot in Newbury, 'stewards never did know their arses from their elbows.'

THE CAREER OF EIGHTEEN-YEAR-OLD AMATEUR RIDER Frank Windsor Clive appears to be heading in the right direction. He is great value for his 7lb claim and is demonstrating the suspicion of a brain.

Since he was a child, he has had only one thought on that brain – becoming a jockey. To that end, he has worked for Venetia Williams since leaving school two years ago. Lovely as she may come across on television, don't imagine for a minute that working for her is any soft option. The key to this grounding is the old adage that 'good horses make good jockeys', and she is beginning to put him on a few, such as Royale de Vassy, on whom he won at Cheltenham in November.

That's all stuff you could probably have worked out for yourself. What you probably don't know is that until the age of eight, Frank didn't speak a word of English. Eight? I hear you thinking. That's considerably earlier than some Irish jockeys who don't appear to begin to pick it up until they have been riding here for ten years. However, Frank is a little more exotic than that. He was brought up by his father Bob and his Venezuelan mother on a stud in South America, speaking Spanish and learning to ride bareback.

The Windsor Clives are a well-known hunting family from Herefordshire. When other people had second horses halfway through a day's hunting, the Windsor Clives tended to have second jockeys. Frank's grandfather, also Frank, has a glass eye. Now, this can't be true – like a lot that passes for fact in this column – but I'm going to tell it anyway. Grandfather Frank was, so the story goes, knocked unconscious out hunting one day. The doctor sent to attend him looked in his eye, saw not a flicker of life in it, and had him dispatched to the mortuary where he came to on a slab several hours later. He's still going strong, aged 79.

Bob Windsor Clive's first job in racing was with my father, who was training at East Ilsley, and there's a strong chance Bob baby-sat the two-year-old me. The (other) not altogether pleasant experience of living in a 1960s lads' hostel, especially Dad's, which boasted the foremost cockroach-breeding colony outside the Gorbals, very nearly meant it was his last job in racing.

His career as a professional jockey, riding for Michael Scudamore, was one of the shortest on record – a year and a half – on account of his weight. This was despite regular trips to a famous Dublin dietician who told you to eat less and less and take pills that made you high. Bob then became what might be loosely termed a 'fortune hunter'. One or two moments resembled *Raiders of The Lost Ark* rather too closely for comfort. After two years of training with great success in Tehran for a group of owners that included the Shah, there arrived Ayatollah Khomeini, who was less than impressed by horse racing. His incoming flight was passed in mid-air by Bob going in the opposite direction. Iran, as it were, became 'I ran.' He moved to a stud in Venezuela and became a private trainer. Out there, he married a native and, probably more challengingly, persuaded 65 staff with 'iffy' work ethics that *pronto* was preferable to *mañana*. Now it's Frank's turn to do the fortune hunting. ▣

HAVING SURVIVED 'GERM WARFARE', the cavalry's big day out at Sandown Park yesterday succumbed to the weather. But a bit of rain has never stopped the army, and, like some great battles in the past, action will just be delayed by a day.

However, therein lies a problem. With three races restricted to military types, some of our boys with three rides – which is normally what they have in a good year – might be looking a little ragged by the third. One of those whose style is unlikely to be greatly altered by the small matter of exhaustion is Milo Watson, 42, the future Lord Manton but only by a few minutes, as he is a triplet. A veteran of nine Sandown campaigns, he partners Simply Dashing, Returning and Flat Top, all of whom are likely to start as favourite. Talk of trebles is tempting fate.

Milo's CV is long and varied. He's a director of a soft furnishings manufacturing company, the wearer of Biggles-style baggy breeches, and was in the Life Guards for fifteen years – and by that I don't mean he sat in a high chair on a hot beach waiting for swimmers to drown. He was virtually unbeaten as a boxer in the army, despite rarely training (Milo was usually good enough to wrap it up in two rounds, and if his opponent got to the third, he was usually so scared that advancing was the last thing on his mind). Besides riding broncos in Canada, he played polo for Prince Charles. Once, a week after having been so late for the final of a low goal competition with the Prince that he missed the first chukka, he was, quite understandably, posted to the Falkland Islands for six months.

He is, according to Johnny Greenall – which is a bit rich because *he* fulfilled a similar role to Arthur Stephenson – Mick Easterby's 'adopted son'. But it was when riding for Mick's brother Peter at Sandown that he surpassed himself. Fellow officer Jack Wingfield-Digby had forgotten his helmet so, having a similarly small head size, he borrowed Milo's for an earlier race. That was fine until Jack took a purler and was carted off to hospital. Milo chased the ambulance, without success, to retrieve his helmet. Of course, as luck would have it, no one else's fitted, so he had to borrow a helmet two sizes too big.

It was quite obvious when it fell over his eyes on the way to the start that things weren't going to be easy. The only way he could see was to stand up in the irons and tilt his head backwards. Even making allowance for a few wild and whacky styles, no one has ridden in that position at speed since Luke Harvey retired. However, you don't get to be a major in the army without initiative, and Milo worked out that if he held his stick halfway down the shaft he could use the top of it to push his helmet up whenever a hurdle was approaching, or at least whenever he thought a hurdle was approaching. And thus he rode.

Meanwhile, imagine the scene in the Easterby sitting room in Yorkshire, where the great man was watching television. He'd seen it all, or so he thought. 'What's that bloody Milo doin' now?' he asked, becoming ever more incandescent. 'What's t'bugger playing at?'

CHAPTER SIX

IN THE LINE OF DUTY

Hanging in the closing stages

THIS WEEK I DREAMT THAT THINGS HAD TAKEN A TURN FOR THE WORSE on the Lambourn barbecue scene. When I awoke, that well-known phrase 'a horse in a china shop' came to mind. It's a long story, but the ingredients include sweet revenge mixed liberally with one injured jockey and two carthorses. Simmer for a while, add wine to taste, and serve on best broken china.

Earlier this summer Naunton trainer Nigel Twiston-Davies hosted a barbecue during which day merged into night, which then merged into early morning. Nigel has a coloured horse – you won't find it in his ten-to-follow, but it is the most outstanding horse in his yard – called Brian, a bombproof gypsy pony whose prime quality is that he can find his own way home from the pub. When the barbecue moved from outside to inside, Simon Sherwood – who won nine out of ten races on Desert Orchid – decided to bring Brian into the house. Although Brian is most things, he is not well versed in household manners. I don't have to tell you what he did on the kitchen floor in a minor backfiring – backfiring being the operative word – of the practical joke.

This week, the Sherwoods hosted the home match. With the Twiston-Davies family and their yes-man first jockey Carl Llewellyn on the guest list, they should have known better and removed their carthorse, Beavis, and Jack Sherwood's pony, Strawberry, from the area. Shortly after midnight Strawberry, with Cathy Twiston-Davies (7lb) up, and Beavis, with Llewellyn on back to front (no change there then), arrived in the Sherwood kitchen. Strawberry was tied up to the television while they reckoned they could make a pretty good racecourse out for Beavis, starting in the kitchen, through the dining room, on to the sitting room, back through into the kitchen again and across the start–finish line – a bit like Plumpton only bigger.

Llewellyn struggled to maintain the partnership through the doors, which he obviously couldn't see coming, and was pole-axed on entering the sitting room. Forgetting for a moment the old racing maxim 'There are fools, bloody fools and those who remount', Twiston-Davies instructed the squeaky-clean Welshman to remount and offered him a leg-up. However, Llewellyn, who thought he'd been offered a leg-over for remounting, eyed up a glass coffee table as a mounting block. The subsequent tinkle of breaking glass spooked the otherwise placid Beavis, who proceeded at speed around the rest of the course. Nine out of ten Sherwood china trinkets went for a shattering burton, but luckily the *pièce de résistance*, the Sherwood Ming, fell into a safe pair of hands.

On waking up I rang Lucy Sherwood to check that it was just a dream and that the dents in Llewellyn's head and his black eye were, in fact, caused by his stepping in front of someone on the golf course. 'No, no. We ran out of wine,' she said innocently, 'and everyone went home at midnight.'

IN THE WEIGHING ROOM (UNLESS YOU WERE AT HEREFORD), last weekend – the Bomb Scare Grand National – has gone down as one of the greatest, most amusing and longest in the careers of a generation of jump jockeys. Aintree 1997 – you can bet that they will all tell the grandchildren about it. It also restored my faith in the human race, and I would like to take this chance, on behalf of jockeys and press, to thank the residents of the Melling Road, whose sitting rooms became instant press and changing rooms, complete with cups of coffee, sandwiches and sausage rolls.

The situation was set up for one-liners. As the jockeys were being evacuated from the weighing room, Simon McNeill grabbed a few notes from his wallet and the complimentary bottle of Martell brandy that each rider had been given (it did not see out the afternoon, as you can imagine). Outside, as 60,000 people began to leave, McNeill met Jockeys' Association secretary Michael Caulfield. 'Secretary,' he said with a dead-pan face, 'can you ask them to hurry up and get the race on? My video runs out at five o'clock.'

In a race of 1,000 exits, McNeill managed to find the 1,001st when the National was eventually run on Monday. He discovered a unique way of departing from the action when he was, of all things, bucked off by Glemot after being hampered at the seventh.

WANT TO KNOW ABOUT BENTS AND FESCUES (types of grass, not types of character you might find in a seedy Soho nightclub)? Then just ask Kelso and Carlisle clerk of the course Jonnie Fenwick-Clennell.

Until now you only had to attain the rank of captain in the army (which makes Major General Nick Ansell a bit over-qualified), be a jockey (the only time they look at the grass is when they are deposited, head-first, on to it – which just goes to show how rarely Bob Davies hit the deck) or be immensely charming (like Hugo Bevan) to qualify as a clerk of the course.

To make the job pay you need to look after three courses. So when Jonnie lost Hamilton last summer he was worried about what he might do. After walking Carlisle with Mike Harbridge, a leading sports turf consultant, he decided to keep one step ahead of the field by enrolling in a Turf Science and Golf Course Management course at Myerscough College, near Lancaster.

If the *Guinness Book of Records* was an on-the-ball publication, Jonnie would have a mention under the section 'most weight ever carried'. He had two rides before retiring, both on an 18-hands-2-inch steed called William, whom he had traded for twenty Cheviot lambs, in the West Percy Hunt Members race at Alnwick. 'One year I went to the scale at nineteen stone six pounds,' says Jonnie. 'A year later it was eighteen stone six pounds.' ▩

EVER WONDERED WHY SOME BOYS BECAME FLAT JOCKEYS instead of rocket scientists? It's all to do with size. Size, that is, of the brain. Recently, a Flat jockey rushed out of the weighing room to the car park at Wolverhampton to catch a lift home with his trainer (like all trainers he was in a hurry to get home).

'You were hard on that horse,' said the slightly disgruntled trainer, who had just seen his unplaced horse given a hiding.

'I wouldn't know,' replied the jockey. 'I haven't had time to see the replay yet.' ▩

A BROKEN LEG forced Tom Jenks to miss what would have been a big pay day on Earth Summit in the 1998 Grand National. Until he starts riding again in August he is trying to widen his horizons by spending the first half of summer working for Midland's stockbrokers Harris, Allday, Lea & Brooks. 'There's so much to take on board,' exclaimed

Jenks yesterday. 'It's like getting instructions in the paddock from Jeff King. After you've had them you have to shut off for five minutes and let the steam out.'

ONE OF THE MOST ENDURING MEMORIES of Earth Summit's Grand National was the camera shot of Simon McNeill and Paul Carberry deep in conversation as they led the runners back on to the racecourse towards the end of the first circuit. Some 11.3 million viewers and up to 500 million around the world must have been wondering what they were talking about. Tactics, the way the race was going, the testing nature of the ground? Not a bit of it.

'Are you going to Mark Dwyer's retirement party tonight?' asked Carberry, who is a stone better jockey when he hasn't been to bed before six in the morning.

'Damn right,' replied McNeill, who had been wasting hard to do ten stone. 'I'm gagging for a beer.'

After more general chit-chat about what they would get up to at the party, Carberry began to drift away to the left going to The Chair.

McNeill: 'What are you doing over there? Don't leave me on my own going into The Chair. I want some help.'

Little French Voice (of Thierry Doumen): 'Don't worry, I'm here.'

After the water, Doumen, in his first National, asked McNeill the way. 'A droit,' said McNeill, who is not known for his command of foreign languages. That instruction, of course, is to go right. Bearing in mind Aintree is a left-handed course, McNeill suddenly corrected himself in English. 'Go left, go left,' he said. He has since reflected that it is a good job Doumen's English is better than his own French.

CHAMPAGNE DOESN'T OFTEN FIND ITS WAY INTO THE TACK ROOM, but I suspect it might at Kingsclere today when Bill Palmer, Ian Balding's head lad from 1970 to 1998, retires. He was 65 yesterday and has spent the last 50 years in racing. He is one of the few people to have sat on both a Derby and a Grand National winner, having ridden out Mill Reef and partnered Highland Wedding in a race. It was Bill who nursed Mill Reef through the worst days when he broke his leg, and such was his dedication that he would share his bacon sandwiches with the great horse. He is, according to Balding, the 'best horseman I've ever come across'.

As a jump jockey he rode over 100 winners, but it was a race he lost that sticks in his mind. Going extremely well down the far side at Taunton, he was upsides Owen McNally, whose mount was tired, going nowhere and kept trying to run out at each obstacle. 'Lend us your whip,' pleaded McNally, and, unable to see how he could possibly get beaten, Bill did just that. He turned into the straight, let out a little bit of rein and began to go clear. It was only at the last that he heard another horse thundering after him, McNally's mount, and it got up to beat him a neck.

IF YOU LIVE IN KNIGHTSBRIDGE BARRACKS you will be forgiven for thinking that the Gold Cup is run next Friday, as opposed to the following Thursday. The Tote Cheltenham Gold Cup may be celebrating 75 years but it is a mere babe-in-arms compared to Sandown's Horse and Hound Grand Military Gold Cup, which was first run in 1841. Obviously it was difficult to stage the race while the Light Brigade were charging, and during the First and Second World Wars, but when runners go to post it will be for the 133rd time.

Memories of his great victory aboard Threapwood in 1964 came flooding back to Major General Nick Ansell, now clerk of the course at Exeter, on a recent horse-trekking holiday in Rajasthan (where the jodhpur came from). What was amazing about his victory was that he managed to train the horse yet still turn up for work often enough to get promoted to the very top of the 5th Inniskilling Dragoon Guards.

However, on this holiday with his wife and some friends, Ansell drew a little skewbald horse. As you can imagine, in northern India there was more meat on a butcher's pencil than on most of the horses, except for Ansell's, which carried a little more condition.

Everything went well until, after a third morning of light cantering, Ansell's mount started to go 'stickily' and tried to lie down with him. As you do in such situations, he kicked her in the belly and on they went. 'The second time she tried to lie down I treated it as a warning signal,' recalls Ansell, 'and on dismounting I noticed a small hoof protruding from her back end. We dragged her over to a shaded tree and within a few minutes she had produced a topping little colt foal.'

The man in charge apologised profusely, a substitute horse completed the remaining four days of the trek without further mishap, and the only question that remains is whether the foal is called The General or Nick. ▩

THE FOLLOWING CONVERSATION, which took place at a tube station last Sunday, has little to do with racing except that a lot of racing people went to the Countryside March and the Turf Club did a good lunchtime trade.

Little Boy: 'Where are we going, Dad?'

Father (farming type not too familiar with London): 'I'm not sure. We'll follow the masses.'

Little Boy (excitedly): 'What, the Massey Fergusons?' ▩

DAVID NICHOLSON has won Tuesday's Fulke Walwyn Kim Muir Chase three times in the last six years with Tug of Gold, Strong Beau and King Lucifer. The only change has been the jockey (me, Tom Jenks and Robert Thornton). This year's amateur-in-the-hot-saddle is Ollie McPhail, who rides Baronet. He will also ride Coole Hill in the four-miler for the Duke.

The name 'Dobbin' and its slow-horse implications has never held back the Grand National-winning career of the jockey of the same name. 'McPhail' doesn't seem to be holding back our boy either, although 'McSucceed' might have a better ring to it. Ollie, 21, with fourteen winners this season, is quite a character. He once went the wrong way at Ludlow and another time dropped (and retrieved) his mobile phone in a Portaloo at a point-to-point. He has no weight problems, but a colleague in the yard did. 'Tony McCoy has a magic potion,' suggested McPhail and fellow practical joker Thornton. 'He takes a drop in his tea, morning and night. If you take some your weight will be fine.' They filled a Lucozade bottle with calamine lotion and the point-to-point rider dutifully followed instructions. By Friday, because it wasn't working, he became desperate, and instead of taking a drop drank the whole bottle at breakfast. Halfway through second lot he was taken ill complaining of headaches and a nosebleed, which put the wind up the jokers who had visions of themselves up on an imminent manslaughter charge. The lad recovered though, and much to McPhail's surprise he had lost 6lb. 'It works, but is not to be recommended,' says McPhail. ■

I SAT NEXT TO SOMEONE IN A RESTAURANT RECENTLY who sent their steak tartare back because it wasn't cooked enough, and I was reminded of a story about a bloodstock agent in the days when trips to the Keeneland and Saratoga sales were still something of a novelty. After his long and exhausting flight, the elderly agent was asked, on his arrival, whether he would like a Jacuzzi to help him wind down. 'Yes, please,' he replied. 'Not too strong and plenty of ice.' ■

ONE OF THE JOCKEY CLUB'S BEST-KEPT SECRETS is its Newmarket shoot. Back in the 1920s, when pheasants hadn't been invented and stable lads were still fair game, the Jockey Club shoot was one of the biggest in the country. Amazing when you consider that in those days most Jockey Club members would have had a dozen gamekeepers on their own estate payroll anyway. Now, according to Christopher Foster, Keeper of the Match Book, it is more of an excuse to have a sleep-over party in the Jockey Club Rooms at Newmarket one evening followed by a morning's cobweb-clearing and shooting on the Hamilton Road Stud. 'It's very small,' said Foster, who doubles as keeper of the Game Book. 'We only have five drives and the bag is well under a hundred. It's a chance to give some hospitality and have some fun among racing people.' One presumes that under Instruction H9, guests are allowed only six hits per drive otherwise they can be banned for excessive use of lead.

THERE HAS, I'M AFRAID, BEEN SOME CONFUSION. People in jump racing, usually known for their intelligence, are struggling to come to terms with the fact that there are two jockeys called Brennan.

They are Martin Brennan and Mickey Brennan, collectively known as 'M. Brennan' but otherwise no more related to each other than my colleague on this newspaper and BBC commentator Jim McGrath is to *Channel 4 Racing* pundit Jim McGrath. It doesn't happen with the Callaghans (Jason and Eddie), the Johnsons (Richard and Kenny), the three Smiths (Vince, Adie or the other one) or the brothers Supple (Robbie or Gerry), which tends to support the theory that the problem lies in that all-important first initial.

When Martin was the sole Brennan riding the Midlands circuit, mainly for his father Owen, it was simple. Then, four seasons ago, along from Carlow came Michael, a successful conditional attached to John O'Shea's yard and also riding the Midlands circuit. One of them rides Miss Roberto at Newbury today. It got so bad that one day Frank Jordan booked M. Brennan to ride his horse expecting Michael to turn up, only to be greeted by Martin in the paddock. Luckily for Frank, he wasn't too bothered who rode that particular horse.

During this summer, however, to help clear up the confusion, Michael asked the Press Association news agency, who send out the runners and riders to the national newspapers every day, to change his name on the racecard from Michael to Mickey, the name by which everyone knows him. End of confusion? Er, no. More, in fact. On Channel 4's *The Morning Line* last Saturday, one of their 'Turf Trivia' questions asked viewers to name the three Brennans currently licensed to ride over jumps. The answer – according to Derek 'Tommo' Thompson it had been confirmed by that safe pair of hands when it comes to trivial matters of the turf, the car park attendant at Southwell – was: Martin, Michael and Mickey. 'Actually,' confesses Mickey, 'I am Michael and Mickey. I'm one and the same. Someone really is taking the Mickey now. Or do I mean the Michael?'

Yesterday, the Jockey Club confirmed the existence of only two Brennans. It hasn't all been bad for either Brennan, though. Martin says, 'When Mickey rode a treble at Southwell one day a lot of people rang up and congratulated me. "Thank you very much," I replied. "It was a great day." I didn't have to buy a drink all night either.' But when Mickey rode a finish a circuit early at Fakenham one afternoon a few seasons back, Martin was booed by punters later in the day. 'I rode a finish a circuit early, and so did Rupert Wakley and Xavier Aizpuru,' recalls Mickey. 'I was so far in front they had time to cop on to it, but I'd already stopped to a walk.'

I hope that clears it up.

THE NEW YEAR HAS BEGUN AUSPICIOUSLY BADLY for Eastbury trainer Alastair Lidderdale. He is in hospital nursing a sore head and broken vertebra.

Alastair was, until recently, private trainer in Compton to George Ward, but is now going it alone in his own yard at Eastbury, Berks. On Sunday he was out with the Berks & Bucks Draghounds when his mount flew a hedge but forgot the landing gear. Alastair landed away from the horse but wrong end up. It is a measure of the goodwill and community spirit within racing that within a few hours a friend had 'temporarily' taken over the running of his yard, while volunteers were appearing out of the woodwork to help with the riding out as his wife Alison works in London.

When Alastair arrived at the hospital, doctors were initially more worried about his head than his back. However, while he may have lost a few hours, it appears he had not lost his sense of humour – although, granted, in his condition it may not have been intentional.

'Where does it hurt?' asked the doctor.

'All over,' moaned Alastair.

'Now come on, Alastair, you can do better than that,' replied the doctor, probing for a modicum of self-diagnosis from his patient.

'It hurts all over,' replied woozy Alastair again.

'Can you be a little bit more specific?' asked the doc, trying to coax out an answer.

'Yes,' replied Alastair. 'From my head to my feet.'

THE CESAREWITCH CAN MEAN ONLY ONE THING: an outing for some of the nation's top lightweight jockeys, especially as only nine of this year's 32 runners have eight stone or more. King among them is Gary Bardwell, who rides lively outsider Jamaican Flight.

Bardwell, 31, has put his size, or to be more precise lack of it, to good use. Extremely hard-working (he has eight rides in Germany tomorrow), he has won several big handicaps like the Chester Cup, Ayr Gold Cup and Royal Hunt Cup, plus the Winter Derby. This year alone he has ridden in nearly 500 races, though he has won only fifteen of them. That's a strike-rate marginally worse than Arthur Scargill's, but it's excusable. Most of the horses he rides are out of the Handicap – or, to put it more succinctly, just plain slow.

When he came into racing he tipped the scales at a massive six stone, and his mentor, Mick Ryan, nicknamed him the 'Angry Ant'. The 'Ant' bit may be right, but he has rarely been known to get angry. He is also quiet, so much so that a jockeys' meeting one day was brought to a halt with laughter when a colleague, subsequently found guilty of excessive use of irony, piped up, 'For God's sake, Gary, shut up.'

Following the BBC's *Newsnight* programme on bulimic jockeys popping 'pee pills' and living off Ex-Lax chocolate, there were calls for the minimum weight to go up to eight stone. Gary's voice was not among them, for he's that rare animal among jockeys – a four-meals-a-day man, and more if he can find time for it. While Richard Hughes puts on 2lb just driving past a fast-food outlet, Gary often parades in front of his parched and panting colleagues, scratching at the window of the sauna while eating a Big Mac, shortly before he has to ride at 7st 10lb. 'I do have a weight problem,' confirms Gary. 'I can't eat enough. I'm non-stop eating all day, and I don't put on an ounce.'

As a result, the other jockeys often get their own back by making Gary the butt of their jokes. 'I was driving back from the races with Philip Robinson and my backside was on fire,' he recalls. 'I asked Philip if the seat heater was on and he replied that it wasn't. About ten minutes later I was on the point of combusting and asked him again if the seat was on, and it transpired they'd lined my underpants with Deep Heat.'

The most original practical joke played on him was at Leicester one day when he was last to leave after the final race. Michael Tebbutt, who along with Richard Hughes is one of the tallest Flat jockeys riding, decided to take Gary's suit (bought from the 'C' of C&A) and leave his own 5ft 10in clothes. Consequently, when Gary stepped out of the shower the only clothes left were a foot too long in every direction. He had no option but to roll up his trousers and sleeves and make the rest of his way home, looking much as Ronnie Corbett would have done in Ronnie Barker's clothes. ◙

ON THE BASIS that racing is part of the entertainment industry, it's a pity that apprentice Alan Daly, also known as 'Arfer', isn't riding Ramruma in today's St Leger at Doncaster. The thought may not have entertained the filly's trainer Henry Cecil, but the post-race interviews would fit the criteria.

Daly, 24, 5ft 7in and weighing in at 7st 12lb, is on the lean side of Kate Moss. Don't be deceived, though: he is twice a stable lads boxing champion and lost on points to his fellow jockey Francis Norton when going for the hat-trick. Attached to David Elsworth, the Irishman is now three winners short of losing his claim.

It is his eagerness to please, he'd admit, which has landed him in the sort of trouble this column thrives upon. His first job in England was as an apprentice to Jack Berry. One morning he was sent to tack up a Salse filly but was given the wrong directions and tacked up the filly in the next box. He was duly legged up and had no sooner landed in the saddle than the horse took off across the yard bucking for all it was worth. 'You fool!' screamed the head lad. 'That one's not broken in yet!'

The first time he arrived in Lambourn he asked a lad in the street where Bryan Smart trained. The lad got his names confused and gave him directions to Brian Meehan's yard, where, as it happened, they were expecting an Irish lad who was already half an hour late. Daly was given a frosty reception, a sack and fork, and ordered to muck out the horses. As he was tipping the muck from the third horse he remarked to a girl that it seemed a bit unfair to be asked to ride work and then be told to muck out first.

'We all have to muck out before riding out here,' she replied.

'But Mr Smart never mentioned that,' said Daly.

'But you're not at Mr Smart's . . .'

Mr Smart reckoned it was the best excuse he'd ever heard when

Daly turned up half an hour late, but he had an even better one after the jockey was delayed en route to Warwick races. Daly was driving up the M40 when a car roared up behind him and was temporarily held up. The other driver, who was having the sort of breakdown the AA can't repair, began suffering from symptoms associated with road rage, and once past Daly he tried to stop him in the middle of the motorway. When Daly got off the motorway at Warwick, the other driver followed him to the racecourse car park whereupon he pinned him down on the ground. Did his boxing come in handy? 'It doesn't matter how good you are at boxing,' he points out, 'when you're eight stone and the opposition is sixteen stone.' The situation was saved by a little old lady who had seen what was going on. 'Pick on someone your own size, you big bully,' she said. With that the driver withdrew, weeping. Strange days. ■

GEOFF LEWIS RETIRED LAST WEEK and hopes before long to have his feet up in the Costa del Sol. He will investigate the possibility of looking after a few horses at Mijas, the new racecourse near Malaga, and will keep his eye in, buying yearlings for some of his old owners.

Of course, Lewis will be remembered when he is long gone – in fact, when we're all long gone – for his partnership with the great Mill Reef as a jockey, but he also trained a champion: Lake Coniston, the top sprinter of his generation. Few are they that both ride and train champions. Less well publicised is the fact that Lewis is a great practical joker.

It was in Hong Kong, when the working day was often over by seven a.m., that the jockeys had to have their wits about them. Lewis came in one morning to be greeted by Dennis Elliot wearing a Stetson hat and with a large chocolate cake on the table in front of him. Lewis was followed in by Bill Hartack, an intensely private person who had ridden five Kentucky Derby winners, including Northern Dancer in 1964.

'Want some cake?' asked Elliot.

'Yep, thanks,' said Hartack, adding, 'I've got a cake just like this in my hotel room. And I've also got a Stetson like that. Hang on a minute.

That is my cake, and that is my hat. You bastards. You'll never get into my room again.'

There was nothing like a challenge for Lewis and his colleagues, and they decided to wager £1,000 with Hartack – the loser having to pay the cheque to a children's home in Deep Water Bay – that they would be able to get into his hotel room.

'How are we going to do it?' asked Elliot when Hartack had gone.

'Easy,' said Lewis. 'I can imitate him over the phone, ring the manager, tell him I'm Bill, tell him I'm having some antiques delivered in a box and that I don't want them hanging around downstairs. We just need someone to go in the box and someone else to get Bill down to the bar for a drink.'

'Since it was your idea, Geoff,' said Elliot, 'you're in the box.'

So a couple of Chinese jockeys, who were also in the delivery business, had the box dropped off with the diminutive Lewis inside. The danger, of course, was being rumbled by trigger-happy security officers to whom Hartack had paid a hefty tip not to let anyone into his room. Holding the lid shut with a rope on the inside, Lewis resisted all security's attempts to open the box. 'What's more, they hit the box on every f***ing corner on the way up,' he remembers of his less-than-glamorous ride.

Once in the room, he stood up, only to be greeted by security officers. 'Don't worry,' said one of them, restraining his friends from firing, 'it's only Geoffrey, Mr Hartack's friend.' And they let him stay. He helped himself to a glass of champagne from Hartack's fridge and waited.

'I've never seen anyone so annoyed in all my life. Being posted as a special antique was one of the greatest coups of all time, and although we'd stuck a limit of Christmas on the wager we'd done it within 24 hours of the bet being struck.'

ED JAMES, THE FORMER TRAINER, is fourteen days into his sponsored walk of six of the country's national trails – make that 'trials'. His intention of sleeping rough in a waterproof sleeping bag lasted precisely 24 hours, and his dog (vet's certificate) has already left him. A torrential thunderstorm and 40mph winds on the first night, which prevented him from getting to sleep until 4.30, have persuaded him that his next career move will almost certainly not be SAS-related. He's now staying in B&Bs along the way.

Day two brought better fortune. He was striding into North Newbold in the pouring rain when a car pulled up alongside.

'Are you trainer what's doing fokkin' stupid walk?' asked the driver.

'I am,' replied Ed.

'Well,' said t' driver, 'I'll see you int' pub in five minutes.'

The stranger bought him lunch.

THIS WEEK I HAVE ROMANTIC NEWS from the most unlikely source. The form book has been completely shredded on this one because Anthony Stroud, former racing manager to Sheikh Mohammed and successful bloodstock agent, has become engaged. Until now he has, for years, been second top-rated confirmed bachelor in racing after Sir Mark Prescott. However, neither he nor onlookers – in this case a herd of gazelle – was totally sure he'd got the nod from his girlfriend, Camilla Courage, when he popped the question.

On the last day of a riding safari in Kenya, he and Camilla had dropped off the main string when he pointed out that her horse looked lame. Gallantly, and despite the horse being as sound as a bell, he said he would see if it had a stone in its foot. While looking for the non-existent stone he got down on bended knee and took off his hat – he burns easily, I seem to remember – and proposed. With that Camilla uttered an 'Oh my God!' and galloped off, leaving him on his knee in a cloud of dust. Surrounded by giraffe, zebra and God knows what else lurking in the bush, he was unsure whether that exclamation and manoeuvre was a yes or a no. His uncertainty was prolonged because his own mount wouldn't, having been left on its own, stand still long enough for him to remount. When he finally caught up he was given the thumbs up.

That was last Thursday. Back on duty at the sales in Kentucky yesterday Anthony was receiving calls of congratulations from around the world. 'But I'm expecting a wreath from Sir Mark,' he added.

THESE ARE SUSPICIOUS TIMES IN WHICH WE LIVE. In the current climate everyone's a bit jumpy from the Prime Minister downwards, but we're in good hands. The eagle-eyed British public, it seems, doesn't miss a trick.

Last week, much to the surprise of Lynne Kent, Betfair's northern racecourse representative, two policemen called round to her house in York and asked her to identify herself. 'Are you Mrs Kent?' they enquired. Mrs Kent, who had but an hour before waved goodbye to her husband, Hardy, and her two children as they left in the car not unnaturally feared something unspeakable had happened to her family and her heart skipped a beat as she steeled herself for tragic news. That notion was quickly dismissed, however, when the two policemen began reading out her rights. 'Mrs Kent,' they said, 'anything you say may be taken down and used in evidence against you in court …'

Having waded through the legal formalities, they got down to the crux of their visit. 'We have reason to believe, madam, that you have illegal weapons on your premises. Would you like to declare them now? It would, madam, make life much easier for you in court, and more than likely lessen your spell at, er, probably Holloway.'

'What do you mean, illegal weapons?' asked Lynne.

'Don't ask frivolous questions, madam,' said the policeman. 'You know what we mean. Could you show us to your garage, please.'

At this stage Lynne was still baffled. What if old Hardy Eustace had indeed secreted away a shipment of illegal arms in the garage roof? And then, gradually, like the sun rising over the distant Yorkshire Wolds of a morning, it began to dawn upon her. Among the clutter of the garage was a job lot, several dozen in fact, of Betfair 'bookmaker' umbrellas. You know the sort: long, the Betfair logo obscured by cellophane wrappers to keep them pristine, with shiny, pointy ends, the type that when fully opened keep the rain off a bookmaker, his pitch and his clients. But, it would seem, when seen through net curtains at 40 yards, unmistakably similar to a neatly stacked arsenal of semi-automatic weaponry. The police scratched their heads, put it down to 'sharp-minded' local residents, and apologised. 'Only doing our job, madam.'

Their apologies were, of course, graciously accepted by the woman who is now known at Betfair headquarters in London as Osama Bin Lynne. ■

AS WE SEEM TO BE STRUGGLING FOR MEDALS IN ATHENS, it will be of interest that the world high jump record has just fallen – to a racehorse trainer. Year in, year out, Richard Hannon sends out big winners, but until now his own athletic prowess had been open to question. No longer.

One of the animals at East Everleigh which he has been less successful at training is his lurcher, Blue. The recalcitrant long-dog had a habit of buggering off, so the situation was rectified, much to Blue's displeasure, by the installation of 'invisible fencing' around the Hannon property. A collar was fitted so that every time he crossed the 'fence' an electronic system delivered a shock. One morning recently Richard decided to take Blue with him up on the gallops at six a.m., so to get him over the boundary he took his collar off. Some mornings even racehorse trainers can still be a bit sleepy, and without thinking Richard strode purposefully across the 'invisible' fence, Blue's collar in his hand, towards his Land Rover.

Having given you all this background, it won't take a genius to work out how the high jump record was broken. On receipt of the shock Richard did a passable impression of the space shuttle on take-off, but, crucially, his mind was elsewhere and he didn't immediately connect the shock with the dog collar, so it kept shocking him. So much so that he wondered whether what was happening to him wasn't heart-related.

At this stage one of his triplets, Henry, awoke to the commotion and rushed over to his window where he could see his father dancing and yelling on the lawn as if he had just stuck his hand – or, worse, some other extremity – in a bee hive. 'I knew exactly what was happening,' says Henry. 'I told him that the key to it was to drop the collar.'

Richard has his own take on the incident. 'It certainly wakes you up at that time of the morning,' he reflected.

THE SOMETIMES PRECARIOUS LIFE OF A JUMP JOCKEY might be classified in the 'dangerous' category, as might that of a racing driver, or even a member of the Tactical Firearms Squad. But you would have thought that when it came to dangerous jobs, being a horse race commentator would not figure too highly on the list.

As I see it, apart from a sore throat, there are three possible dangerous scenarios for the racecourse commentator. One is vertigo, which is all in the mind so does not really count anyway. The second would be an unusually strong gust of wind catching the commentator while he is on his way across the grandstand roof to his position (rare, as far as I know, and most unfortunate if it did happen). Thirdly, there is always the chance during a desperate finish of the commentator – Peter Bromley comes to mind for some reason – blowing a gasket.

However, it cannot be that dangerous, can it? How else could Sir Peter O'Sullevan have kept going almost into his eighties? Although Jim McGrath, the BBC's race caller since Sir Peter hung up his mike, has pleaded with me not to put ideas in people's minds, news comes from Australia about Albion Park's unfortunate on-course broadcaster.

David Fowler was mid-race and concentrating hard when he felt a hand patting him on the head. Fowler is a complete professional and did not flinch. There was not even a squeak in his voice. Realising that patting him on the head was not significant enough to disrupt Fowler's commentary, the intruder, a serial call-disrupter, stuck the poor commentator in a headlock. Suddenly it was I Can't Breathe in the lead from Gedoffmate, disputing second place with Call the Police, and For F**k's Sake in fourth. 'I had to keep concentrating on the call but became worried when I was grabbed round the neck in a headlock and half choked,' Fowler said afterwards. The intruder was arrested by police and removed from the broadcasting box. It turns out he had tried to disrupt broadcasts before. 'But it was too late, the damage was done,' added Fowler, who was so upset he stood down from commentating on the last race.

Mission impossible for the disrupter would be to shut Derek Thompson up. An attempt might get him back in people's favour, though. ■

HERE'S A QUESTION. Who has walked from winning post to winner's enclosure backwards with every Classic winner over the last five years carrying a 60lb pack on his back and with another man's hand up his sweaty shirt? You're probably asking yourself two supplementary questions at this stage: why hasn't this lunatic been locked up, and why haven't we seen him on television? That's the point, though – he is the television.

Adrian Camm is the freelance cameraman who has done much to revolutionise the way racing is viewed from the nation's armchairs. On course, he is becoming as much a celebrity as the little men he films. And no wonder. Carrying a 60lb pack for four hours on a sweltering afternoon is a sporting feat in itself. Duke of Edinburgh Gold Award? Forget it. Herculean efforts like this earn soldiers automatic selection to the SAS.

The 'steadycam' is £20,000 worth of hydraulic framework and camera that allows the cameraman to shoot pictures from ankle height to head height without it appearing – as it does on even the latest video camera – that the operator is suffering from the advanced stages of Parkinson's Disease. His are the worm's-eye views of horses walking in the paddock or a jockey raising his whip to signify that he has just passed the post in first place.

Today, 'Big Adrian' is at Newmarket for Channel 4. Next week it's York where, if it's hot, he can expect to lose 5lb, mainly in fluids. Pedigree and conformation experts agree that the seventeen-stone Yorkshireman is ideally bred for the job. One grandfather, Jack Hanson, fought a world heavyweight championship eliminator. Don Cockle, his opponent, who cut him in the eighth round, went on to fight 'Rocky' Marciano. ('Two punches away from being world champion,' as Big Adrian says proudly.) The other was a gambler who was banned from all betting shops in his area – for being too successful. (One punch away from hitting his bookmaker, I should think).

It was recently reported that Frankie Dettori gave Big Adrian a hearty crack with the stick every time he walked past because the big man can't exactly run after him. Now all the jockeys are doing it. The other day, Sheikh Mohammed felt his biceps, nodded appreciatively and commented, 'Still strong.' Even David Nicholson, who has an allergy to photographers, likes him.

Of course, it has not all been plain sailing. Dettori clipped him during a flying dismount once – the nearest we've come to a much-awaited flying fall – and once, when the Italian flamboyantly kissed the lens, the whole apparatus collapsed. Another time, after Cape Verdi won the 1,000 Guineas, Big Adrian was following Dettori back, causing Michael 'Mouse' Roberts's mount, which had trailed in last, to do something at speed. It spooked, and now with his own worm's-eye view from the grass the South African jockey was not at his happiest. He was about to give Big Adrian a mouthful when the victorious Dettori rode to the rescue. 'Tell me, Mouse,' he said, 'what's the going like today?' ▩

JOCKEYS OCCASIONALLY GET HURT IN SCHOOLING ACCIDENTS. Limbs are broken and bruised, and brains concussed. In Jenny Pitman's day, compound fractures to the ego were a not uncommon occurrence. However, news comes from Lambourn of a doubly unique schooling injury. I say 'doubly' because, for starters, it involved the trainer, or more correctly her husband, who wasn't on a horse; and secondly, it involves a lost finger, and that must be a first. And by 'lost' I don't mean like a mutt that strays and might well turn up at a dog pound later in the day. There is, it seems for John Taylor, no coming back for the top inch and a half of his tickling finger.

Having chronicled in previous editions of this Diary how John managed to get an ocean-going racing yacht stuck in Uplands Lane and how he managed, one Punchestown meeting, to wedge his horsebox under an arch at Rathsallagh Hotel, news of this accident may not altogether come as surprise. I also stood back once and admired him felling a large elm tree. A man of great practicality, he had, by means of Pythagoras, worked out where it would fall and cleared the space accordingly. But when the moment came it pivoted vindictively, narrowly missed him and chose for its landing site a hen house. The consequence of this miscalculation was a lot of clucking, enough stuffing for several feather duvets, and scrambled eggs for breakfast.

John's schooling fences have been designed by himself, by a means of hydraulics to swing on and off the all-weather gallop at the press of a button. It works on the same principles as the fences at Clairfontaine. That this is not an altogether trustworthy system was evident at the Normandy course recently when the hydraulics controversially failed, on the last circuit, to remove the fence from the course just before the winning post. Heads down in a terrific drive for the finish, the leading three horses turned somersaults upon meeting this unexpected obstacle just short of the line.

John's hydraulics also failed, with equally drastic consequences. When it jammed he sought to unjam it manually – a manoeuvre, it seems, he achieved with only partial success. The steel frame of the fence landed on a steel block and, crucially, the Taylor digit. He then had an Arun Ralston moment (Ralston, you'll remember, sawed off his arm with a blunt knife after a climbing accident in Colorado). John didn't wait five days to be rescued though. He tied some baler-twine round his arm as a tourniquet, pulled what remained of his finger out, recovered a few bits of flesh and drove home in the tractor.

The stump is now mending, one presumes, under a rather filthy-looking plaster. 'If you're stupid enough to stick your finger in an unsafe place there's a good chance you might lose it,' says John, seeking no sympathy, with the moral of the story. ◼

DURING A RECENT LIBEL CASE, Ian Botham, replying to a question from the defence, said, 'Ah well, he's Australian.' His answer seemed a satisfactory reason why England's greatest all-rounder had not sued the former Australian cricket captain Allan Border for what seemed a far more damaging slur against his character than anything Imran Khan had written.

General delight, it seems, is taken in this country when an Australian sportsman goes home with his tail between his legs having been beaten by us – mainly because it doesn't happen very often. However, far from being happy about the imminent departure of jockey Brent Thomson, I am rather sad. Maybe it's because he was actually born in New Zealand. That sort of sets him apart from other 'stralians.

Having only really come to know him over the past couple of months, I feel I am missing out. A good jockey (brilliant at Chester), legendary with one-liners, known to book restaurants in the name of Sir Lunchalot, and a man who seems to take everything in his stride, he feels, at 38, that opportunities back in Queensland will be greater than they presently are here. 'If I were a young man, I might view it differently,' reflected Thomson at Goodwood.

His first stint here, in the mid-1980s, lasted four years. This present spell, now in its third season, was not going too badly until he broke an ankle last autumn. To get fit he took a few rides in Queensland before returning, and success there opened a few doors. His bad run here, according to his best mates, has had something to do with drink: he has hardly had a winner since he went teetotal nine months ago, and those same best mates would prefer he returned to the old 'amber nectar' rather than to Australia.

My favourite Brent Thomson story concerns a journey he was undertaking in his car late at night through Wood Ditton, a one-bend village near Newmarket, with a couple of eminent trainers (at least they are now; they weren't then). He failed to make the bend and ploughed through a hedge into someone's cabbage patch. The distraught old lady who owned the property rang the police to say that a car had crashed into her garden. She then peered through her window, saw Thomson running across the lawn, and redialled the police to tell them that there was also a dwarf amok among her roses.

FRANKIE DETTORI HAS COME IN FOR SOME FLAK THIS WEEK after his mount, Cape Pigeon, was beaten fairly and squarely at Windsor by Walter Swinburn's comeback mount Talahath. Mid-August is traditionally a quiet time for British racing. If owner Eric Gadsden had complained about it at any other time of the year it would hardly have got a mention. Instead, it made headlines.

What they say about the best jockey being the one who makes the fewest mistakes is not far off the truth. 'To err,' wrote Alexander Pope, 'is human, to forgive is divine.' It says something about jockeys, and also confirms my opinion of owners who complain publicly about them. 'Jockeys are only human,' said Carl Llewellyn while discussing the subject on Thursday. 'They're bound to make mistakes. If an owner wants total reliability he should buy a Scalextric set instead of a horse.'

The art of riding a bad race and getting away with it is, I believe, to say something that cuts the trainer (or owner) so dead that he is rendered incapable of delivering a rollicking. Sammy Milbank once gave an appalling ride to a Flat horse trained by Fulke Walwyn. Milbank timed his delivery to perfection. 'Sorry, guv,' he said before a thunderous-looking Walwyn could begin, 'you caught me on an off-day.' Another variation on this theme was the jockey who got off saying, 'Sorry, guv, I can't always be brilliant.'

But Kieren Fallon, who has gone from relative obscurity to an establishment figure with the job of first jockey to Henry Cecil in eighteen months, tackles the same subject in a slightly off-the-wall manner which Cecil will, no doubt, enjoy. After the Irishman had given his mount an uncharacteristically lacklustre ride, the young southern-based lady trainer of the horse stood there open-mouthed in disgust. Fallon hopped off the horse and, showing a slight lack of the usual deference shown on such occasions by jockeys to trainers, delivered a *coup de grâce* which really did ensure he would never ride for her again.

'All right, luv?' he said. To the best of my knowledge the trainer is still standing there, aghast. ■

SOMETIMES I WONDER how the medical profession regard us racing folk, particularly jockeys, who are about the only breed of people who would sooner go back to work risking what has scarcely mended than be given a sick note.

Last year, you may recall that we featured amateur rider Alice Plunkett, whose ear had been severed in a riding accident. Just to remind you, her biggest worry was that her terrier would find her ear first and run off with it. However, as a news item it came into its own when leeches were attached to her ear to aid the healing process and to persuade blood to flow again through the once-severed blood vessels. A good job they did too. Now you wouldn't know Alice's ear had ever parted company with Alice, and last week the eventing-amateur rider's career took another turn when she commentated on the Blenheim horse trials for a local radio station.

The postscript to all this is that doctors have returned to the Dark Ages, using what might loosely be termed 'creepy crawlies' on their patients. In search of a remedy for a leg injury to Lambourn's finest, trainer Peter Walwyn, they have resorted to 'larva therapy biosurgery', which is a long-winded and probably American way of saying they slapped a couple of maggots on the wound.

Walwyn is not accident-prone, but when he does injure himself he doesn't do it in half measures. For instance, when he was once kicked on the arm by a horse, he needed four operations and a court case before it was right again. This time, in mid-August, his hack slipped up on the road and trod on his left leg in the shin area. It left a gash too wide to stitch. After its point-blank refusal to heal in ten days, the doctor called up a pair of maggots – all the way from Bridgend, Wales. The maggots were attached to the injury under some netting to stop them falling off. 'When they arrived they were that big,' said a proud Walwyn holding his thumb and forefinger about half a centimetre apart. 'When they came out two days later they were this big.' There was now a gap of about two inches. 'There was some wriggling and a bit of tickling going on,' he added.

Those of you (me) who thought maggots were only good for fishing and the disposal of animal carcasses might think twice now before swatting a greenbottle. It may have had a more interesting past than you think. The beauty, though, of the greenbottle maggot is that it feeds only on dead flesh (unlike the bluebottle, which prefers live flesh), and is therefore ideal for cleaning up wounds.

How did Mrs Walwyn cope with sharing a bed with Peter and two maggots? 'I told her she mustn't complain,' said the trainer. 'What's a husband with maggots when you also share the bed with a dog that has fleas?' ▩

IF YOU WERE WATCHING HAYDOCK A FORTNIGHT AGO you would have seen Keen Leader, a faller at Cheltenham two days previously, being given an exhibition schooling round by Ron Flavin. Now with Jonjo O'Neill, Ron has a bright future, especially now that he's worked out the British motorway system – get a lift to the races. One of the first questions he asked his landlady when he arrived in Lambourn from Limerick was, 'The M4. When you get on it, how do you know if you're going east or west?'

Up until last month, Ron had been riding for about a year and a half with something of a handicap. In May 2001 he was brought down and got what all males dread – a kick in the testicles. Nothing happened immediately, but one morning he woke up and in the tidy package that is sometimes described as 'meat and two veg' he found some fruit – a grapefruit, to be precise. And that, as you can imagine, is one swollen ball. Not being shy, you only had to ask and he'd show. Sometimes you didn't even have to ask. As freak shows go he was right up there with the Bearded Lady, though in his case it wasn't pay per view. In October, though, he had a second operation to reduce the swelling. After three weeks off it seems to have worked, though things are still sensitive in that region. ▩

IF THE END OF THE WORLD WAS NIGH, how would you cope? Vic Strauffer, an American commentator and the self-styled 'goof on the roof', coped rather magnificently, I think you'll agree.

He was recently calling a race from Hollywood Park – which is, one imagines, one of the courses closest to the notorious San Andreas fault, if not actually on it. When the runners were midway down the back stretch during a fillies' race the ground began to rumble. His eyrie on top of the grandstand also started, one assumes, to wobble, and in the back of his mind he must have reckoned this was the big one, that California was about to be rent asunder and chief among the fatalities would be the 'Goof'.

He first drew attention to the earthquake with a very matter-of-fact statement. 'We are in the middle of an earthquake here in southern Califonia,' he said, before returning to his call. The enormity of what he had just said then hit him. 'Lady Lucayan tries to slow it down. She leads by two and a half lengths. By the way, folks, I'd like you to know I love you all and that horseracing was my first love.' He then returned to his call.

Turning into the home straight, Pleasant Thunder began making a move through the six-runner field, which only served to remind him of his impending doom. 'That wasn't thunder you heard, that was an earthquake,' he said. 'I've got to make this my greatest ever call.' Up front it was now ding-dong, Lady Lucayan being caught in the dying strides by the fast-finishing Pleasant Thunder, who had 'come to win in a shaker'. By this stage Strauffer was clearly warming to his theme, and as they flashed past the post together he reported that it was a photo. 'And I don't know or care who won the photo,' he concluded his great call.

Wouldn't it be good if all commentators were so glad to be alive? ▣

PETER BURRELL, Frankie Dettori's erstwhile ginger-haired manager, now manages the business affairs of footballer-turned-actor and part-time gamekeeper Vinnie Jones. During a trip to the Dubai World Cup with both, Pete was persuaded to alter his hairstyle to be more in keeping with the boys. I can hear you thinking: Vinnie Jones plus altered hair state equals US Marines-style short back and sides. Not at all. Possibly because of the proximity to oil wells out there, Pete has gone for the slicked-back look. 'Just like Robert De Niro,' says an admiring wife, Lucinda. 'Some days oil, some days gel.'

Jones may have minced the occasional footballer, but he doesn't mince his words. 'I was sick and tired of that fox asleep on his head,' he explained yesterday. 'It's taken about seven years off him – a pity it wasn't seven pounds. We can't do nothing about his luncheon area though. But if we'd left it as it was, we'd have had the hounds after us when I take him shooting.' ▩

PETER BURRELL, Frankie Dettori's easily influenced manager, is mixing with one too many footballers, it seems. He has returned from a trip to America with a tattoo of a racehorse on his right ankle. The jockey on it is wearing red, white and blue colours – symbolising the Union Jack, according to Pete – and it carries a number seven on the number cloth to signify the magnificent seven winners Dettori rode at Ascot's September meeting in 1996. One hopes, unlike men who get 'I Love Sharon' tattooed on their arms and then get divorced from Sharon, that Pete has a long and happy association with Frankie.

The artwork was carried out by Tattoo Mania on Sunset Boulevard – one of the more upmarket tattoo parlours in the world – watched by a queue of twenty increasingly impatient Hell's Angels, who kept telling brave Pete there was no need to cry.

'It's scabbing over nicely,' said Pete yesterday. 'The other thing I've found out is that you know that any girl who says it looks OK on you has one herself, but keeps it covered up.' ▩

SUE BRAMALL, who used to train in Yorkshire but emigrated to Ireland a couple of years ago, is becoming used to the way some things work over there. She advertised for a travelling head lad/horsebox driver. It did not take long to fill the vacancy. The new man proved to be a big success. With him at the wheel, Tipperary wasn't such a long way away after all. One day, though, he failed to turn up for work.

'Where's Paddy?' asked Mrs Bramall.

'He's gone for his driving test,' said her assistant. ▩

THE MOST TALKED-ABOUT BRITISH SPORTSMAN in Norway this week is not David Beckham. No, sir. Or, as the whale fisherman might say to the reindeer herder, '*Nei dessverre*.' The man cropping up most in conversation is Robert Bellamy, little known in his own country outside Stow-on-the-Wold, little known outside National Hunt racing and, prematurely balding, completely unknown by his local hairdresser. But – get this – in Lapland at the moment, he is second only in popularity to Father Christmas.

Some might even argue that 'Bells' isn't that well known within National Hunt circles, but a week today he will partner the Norwegian-trained Trinitro in the 1999 Martell Grand National and, quite rightly, he is enjoying his fortnight of fame in the fjords. Chris Broad, his agent, jokes, 'He thinks he's Omar Sharif – albeit with less hair.' It's probably not as bad a comparison as it seems. Working Trinitro through the snow this week, he did look like an extra from *Dr Zhivago*.

The 33-year-old jockey's visit to ride the nine-year-old near the horse's Bergen base was given blanket coverage, even though duvet coverage might have been more appropriate given the temperature. Bellamy's every move was followed by three television crews, including the BBC, and a bevy of journalists. They have obviously taken him to their hearts because they took him to the top of Norway's tallest ski jump and didn't push him off. He says, 'People who think jump jockeys are mad should have come with me. Eddie the Eagle went up in my estimation considerably.'

Much of Trinitro's training has been conducted in the snow by Rune Haugen, also 33. The horse, Scandinavia's first runner in the Grand National, is already a 'National' winner, having won the Norwegian version over two and a half miles last time out in September – beating Ashwell Boy – though Norway's National and Liverpool's are, without wishing to be rude, about as alike as Norway's 1980s pop phenomenon A-ha and the Beatles.

My lasting memory of riding in Scandinavia is the mixed-sex saunas, the only place in the world where a jockey set to carry two stone of lead in his saddle makes out beforehand that it is essential for him to sweat off 4lb.

Haugen's base is, according to Bells, the finest training establishment he has ever seen. 'Jackdaw's Castle with a decent house' is how he summed it up. Quite a compliment from a man who has seen some of this country's finest training centres from the inside: Martin Pipe's Nicholashayne, where he spent eighteen months as an assistant; David Nicholson's Condicote; Jackdaw's Castle, where he was first a conditional and then a fully fledged professional; and before all that, the Royal Agricultural College at Cirencester, where he studied agriculture for a year on the aptly named 'gin and tonic' course.

So, down to the crux of the matter. Any chance of Robert Bellamy being granted the freedom of Bergen? 'He's a good, agile jumper so has a good chance of getting round,' prophesies Bells, whose only previous ride in the race, in 1992, came to a grinding halt going into the nineteenth fence. 'If he gets round, like any other horse getting round he could finish twentieth and he could finish fourth.' There you have it.

(Alas, the extremely bold and very keen Trinitro led the field to the first fence in the 2000 Grand National, but when he got there he took the unwise decision to head-butt the obstacle.) ▪

THE FOLLOWING WAS OVERHEARD among the tweed suits at Sandown's Royal Artillery Gold Cup meeting this week.

Senior Officer in the King's Troop: 'You know you need an SAS certificate to guarantee promotion in this regiment?'

Junior Officer (his attention suddenly turned to cold nights, long marches and interrogation on the Brecon Beacons): 'An SAS certificate? That sounds a bit stiff.'

Senior Officer: 'Yes, Seen at Sandown. The regiment's still run by the horsey lot, you know.' ▪

THERE'S A POST-AINTREE STORY about a jockey who turned up at this hotel in the small hours. He was slightly the worse for wear and had with him three local girls he had met in a nightclub. Although they were less than attractive, to him, in his inebriated state, they were first, second and third respectively in the 1999 Miss World Contest.

At the hotel there was an avuncular doorman. 'Come in, sir,' he said, 'but I'm afraid you can't bring your friends.'

The jockey pleaded with the doorman for a full five minutes before demanding to know why his new friends weren't allowed in.

'Because, sir,' said the doorman, 'you'll regret it in the morning.' ◙

AT LAST SUNDAY'S 'LESTERS', where jockeys get to vote for their colleagues, one of the most deserved presentations was a Special Recognition Award to Gary Lyons.

Earlier this season you might remember that Rodney 'Pigeon' Farrant retired and then proceeded to whinge about the lack of opportunities (even though he had ridden Martha's Son and Princeful), the disloyalty of trainers and the fact that jockey's agents are running the show. He was also lucky to be light enough never to have to sit in a sauna, other than to warm up. Gary is at the other end of the attitude scale. He never complains. He's the first to help youngsters and would be delighted just to ride in a race against a Martha's Son, let alone partner something that good. Having spent twelve years with Reg Hollinshead, he's also earned the loyalty of several small trainers, including Willie Jenks, who could easily put his son Tom up.

Lyons is about the only jump jockey not to have an agent and spends more time in the sauna than Tony McCoy without a tenth of the incentive. Many of his rides don't have form figures in front of their names; instead they have what looks more like a disastrous hand at Scrabble. How many words can you make from three Ps, a couple of Fs, a U and an R? Occasionally one of them clicks, like the front-running Jemaro who once hung so badly right-handed at Uttoxeter that his rider had visions of coming up the adjacent railway track rather than the home straight. This year, Gary guided Jemaro around Aintree's 90-degree Canal Turn on the way to a clear round in the John Hughes.

Gary is, of course, from the 'have saddle – will travel' school of grafters. And he will travel by whatever means. One day, he and Adie Smith were trying to do two meetings, Haydock and Warwick, with little margin for error. The first setback was when Adie had to attend a stewards' inquiry. Halfway there and behind schedule, Adie, in what couldn't be construed as the greatest moment in the history of forward planning, announced that they would probably need petrol. 'Well, if we stop for petrol we're done,' suggested Gary. 'Better chance it.' About fifteen miles from Warwick the car spluttered thirstily to a stop on the hard shoulder of the M40. The only option was to thumb it, in full riding kit, which is exactly what they did, eventually being dropped off at the track with seconds to spare. Was it worth it? 'He pulled up and I fell,' said Gary.

With anyone else you'd say that was a definite no, but with Gary Lyons I wouldn't be so sure. ▣

AS ONE OF THE FEW JOCKEYS to have been carried from the course on a stretcher with a bloody nose, I'm not sure whether I regard fellow amateur Chris Bonner with admiration or pity. Now assisting Michael Bell in Newmarket, it took him a week and a half and a whole bottle of painkillers to realise he had broken his leg in a first-fence fall in the Aintree Foxhunters. He was getting on his hack first thing last Monday when his lower leg finally gave way. He is now in plaster and off work. ▣

FORMER TRAINER JACK BERRY was presented with a memento for his achievements by Goodwood clerk of the course Rod Fabricius at a dinner on Tuesday night. 'When I sat down next to Debbie Fabricius [Rod's wife] at dinner,' said Berry at the start of his impromptu speech, 'I immediately smelt a rat.' Realising that he had dug himself a Lord Oaksey-sized hole, he added, once his audience had finally settled down, 'I mean that in the nicest possible way.' Is that possible? ▣

IT IS TEN YEARS TO THE WEEK that three jump jockeys, including me, were invited to ride in two steeplechases in Russia. Who could refuse the offer to drink fermented mare's milk one evening (we all did, actually – it's filthy) and ride its offspring the next day?

In that decade a lot has changed in Russia. Communism was in the process of being dismantled by Mikhail Gorbachev at the time, and we rode at Pyatigorsk, a country course in southern Russia. The situation at the capital's Hippodrome was so bad that not enough hay and food could be got there to feed the horses in training. This summer the Ministry of Agriculture has resurfaced the track, built 80 new boxes, and racing has returned to Moscow. This Sunday the Derby will be run there for the first time in nine years, and though the facility remains incredibly poor by western European standards the move back to Moscow should encourage the foreign investment that is now being sought.

It is now Pyatigorsk's turn to suffer. An invitation to a team of British jockeys last spring was strongly advised against by the Foreign Office because of the town's proximity to Chechnya and the threat of kidnappings. The hint was taken. One of the leading studs in the area, the Stavropol, where we were taken in 1990, was turned into one of the main Russian army supply camps for the war against Chechnya. Kalashnikovs, previously kept under car seats by racehorse trainers on our visits, are now more openly brandished, and one of our hosts, called Kaietov, who fed us on caviar and had photos of himself out hunting with Gorbachev on the walls, has since been assassinated. I believe it had more to do with the mafia than our visit.

The war in Chechnya has not been bad for everyone though. One of the most successful jockeys in Moscow since it was reopened in June is Alim Kulik. He is now retained by leading owner Said Zakaev. Kulik was riding work on his horse one day when Russian planes started bombing nearby. While everyone else legged it for cover Kulik shook his fist at the planes, screamed in defiance and continued to gallop his horse – presumably at some speed. Zakaev was so impressed he signed him up. It's not quite how Kieren Fallon got the job with Sir Michael Stoute.

Of course our own trip and the three subsequent visits by British teams were not short of incident or accident. Race-riding was only a small part of it. You may remember the Diary's report on that last trip to Russia in 1993, when the Russians rebuilt a wall that had hitherto been so small it barely showed above the long grass, and the entire British team fell at it. Lunching on boiled mutton and vodka in a fly-blown shepherd's hut halfway up a mountain on one stud is just one other experience that sticks firmly in the memory – and throat.

CHAPTER SEVEN

YOU COULDN'T MAKE IT UP – THE MEDIA

Not following instructions

IT IS GOOD TO KNOW that the great and the good are still superstitious about sitting thirteen round a table for dinner.

With that in mind, Claude Duval, my esteemed colleague at the *Sun*, was asked by the Countess of Halifax at York last week to dine at Garrowby, a stunning house at the end of a very long drive which, one assumes, is on a shortlist of one for the Queen's digs for Royal Ascot at York next year.

Lest you be worried about the Earl of Halifax's breakfast reading, let me assure you the *Telegraph* was already there in the shape of Richard Evans. When he approached the gates of Garrowby slightly ahead of schedule, he turned to his taxi driver.

'Can you slow down a bit?' he asked. 'We're a little bit early.'

'Sir,' replied the taxi driver, 'I think you'll find we're by no means there yet.'

The countess had explained to Claude that the late invitation was to make the numbers up to fourteen, ribbing the Punters' Pal with the words, 'We'd rather have you than a teddy.'

'I think you'll find, m'lady,' said Claude, 'I'll drink a lot more than your teddy bear would.'

Having thus earned the sobriquet 'Teddy' for the night, there was complete confusion at dinner whenever the countess asked, 'More Chablis, Teddy?' Both Claude and Lord 'Teddy' Grimthorpe held their glasses out for more at the same time. ◆

TRAINERS ARE WELL KNOWN FOR THEIR INSULARITY. At a party on Wednesday night, Gary Stevens, the top American jockey but, as yet, winnerless at Royal Ascot, got on the drums (he has often stated that if he had an alternative career, it would be as a musician). 'I know who the drummer is,' said Richmond trainer Bill Watts, 'but who are the other two with him in the band?' They were former Small Face Rod Stewart and Rolling Stone Ronnie Wood. ◆

HUMBLE APOLOGIES, BUT THE OLD ONES ARE THE BEST. In the days before dope testing, the old Duke of Norfolk saw a successful trainer giving his horse a 'sugar lump' in the paddock.

'Caught you at last,' roared the duke. 'I've had my eye on you for years.'

'No, no, Your Grace,' replied the trainer, putting his hand in his pocket. 'It's only a sugar lump. Look, you have one and I'll have one.'

A minute or two later, their jockey came into the paddock.

'Make all,' the trainer instructed, 'and when you turn into the straight and hear the bell, kick for home. If anything passes you it will be either me or the Duke of Norfolk.' ▣

HOW THE OTHER HALF LIVE. The inner sanctum of the Royal Enclosure is the Jockey Club Luncheon Room, where members of the Jockey Club and their guests can go for a sumptuous buffet scoff-up at lunchtime. In fact, it is the final destination for half the lobsters landed on the Western Isles.

One senior member, clearly more used to having his lobster delivered to his dining-room table by his butler, was not enamoured with having to queue for his lunch. 'My God,' he was overheard to complain, 'this is like the YMCA.' ▣

IT'S TEARS FOR PIERS. This is Sir Piers Bengough's last royal meeting in the role of Queen's Representative. He retires in October after fifteen years in the job and will be succeeded by the Marquess of Hartington. Before taking up the less risky hobby of owning racehorses – his Charles Dickens was third in the 1974 Grand National and Cabochon won the 1991 Ascot Stakes – Sir Piers was an accomplished owner-rider. Indeed, he finished eleventh on April Rose in the 1965 National. One day, so the story goes, he was riding out for the trainer Alec Kilpatrick. Out of the long grass sprang a chicken, startling his mount, which promptly dumped him. Major Bengough, as he was then, dusted himself off and started legging it across the field.

'The horse went the other way,' pointed out the trainer.

'I'm not worried about the horse,' retorted the major. 'It's the f***ing chicken I'm after.' ▣

NATIONAL HUNT TRAINER CHARLIE BROOKS hosted a big post-race drinks party in the car park last night. He recalled that as a schoolboy at Eton a good friend of his absconded to Royal Ascot during 'games'. As the boy was going to the paddock he bumped into his housemaster. Seeing himself in something of a predicament he decided his only chance was to make a pre-emptive strike.

'Hello, sir,' he said. 'I believe you are tutor to my twin brother Robert at Eton.'

That night his housemaster was on his rounds when he met his pupil again. 'Now then, Wobert,' he said. 'I met your twin brother William at Woyal Ascot today. I never want to see him there again.'

THERE WERE ONLY TWO LEGENDS AT ROYAL ASCOT: Bosra Sham and Australian George Hanlon, thrice winner of the Melbourne Cup. Old George, after a liquid lunch with Geoff Lewis on Wednesday, was not in much of a position even to scratch himself. But this is the man who has had such a wonderful life as a Melbourne trainer that whenever he sees a racehorse he doffs his cap.

Every Australian racegoer has their own Hanlon story. Once, when an owner criticised him after a race, Hanlon took the bridle off the heaving horse. 'My bridle, your horse,' he said before walking off.

Hanlon is capable of amazing feats. Once, he was due to fly to Tasmania for the Hobart Cup. A little late, he had to run for his plane, passing through two security checks on the way. On the flight he slept, and woke up as they landed.

'Welcome to Canberra,' said the captain.

'Where the f**k?' was Hanlon's understandable first utterance.

He has never regarded jockeys as anything more than a necessary evil. When he trained for Jim (J. A.) McGrath's father Brian, he was exercising the McGraths' good filly Bellition in the sea one day. It was a cold Melbourne day and the little lad riding Bellition was soaking wet and shivering.

'Are you cold, boy?' asked McGrath Sr.

'Yup, I'm sure freezing,' said the lad.

'What d'you say that for?' asked Hanlon of McGrath Sr. 'You only reminded him that he was cold. If you hadn't told him, he would never have known.' ■

MULLIGAN, the all-singing, all-dancing and apparently literate favourite for today's Arkle Chase, is an inconsiderate individual. After his fifth smooth win out of five at Warwick his trainer, David Nicholson, told reporters that for the unfazed horse's previous outing he 'went to Ireland and didn't leave an oat'. This, when an unhorsey copytaker at one newspaper had finished with it, read 'went to Ireland and didn't leave a note'. ■

THERE ARE PRIZES FOR MOST THINGS AT CHELTENHAM, from best-turned-out horse to leading jockey. However, there's nothing for the best-named horse, which goes to one of Mulligan's opponents, Celibate. He is by Shy Groom out of Dance Alone, and just to ensure he lives up to his name, he's a gelding. Flagship of Charlie Mann's stable, the horse was featured on the trainer's Christmas cards last year. On the front, beside some holly, the question is begged, 'What is the difference between Tom Cruise, Richard Dunwoody, Liz Hurley and Celibate?' Inside, underneath a picture of the horse jumping, is the answer: 'No one wants to be Celibate. Have a very happy Christmas.' ■

THE FIRST HUMAN CASUALTY OF THE MEETING ... Ruby Walsh, the seventeen-year-old son of Channel 4's eloquent and unmissable Irishman Ted Walsh. A leading Irish amateur like his father, Ruby was taken to Cheltenham General yesterday morning after a clash of heads with Triumph Hurdle hope Commanche Court, whose bandage he was taking off. The first bang unsteadied him so much that he fell back against the wall, banging his head for a second time, which just about finished him off. After a few tests he was back, none the worse, for racing during the afternoon. ■

STEWARDS' INQUIRY. Of all the jockeys in all the world. Yesterday's Cheltenham Festival racecard featured, on the front cover, the former cavalier Brod Munro-Wilson on his Christies Foxhunters' winner of yesteryear, The Drunken Duck. More recently 'Brod' earned notoriety when a judge described him as a cad.

Before leaving racing Brod rode his own horses as an amateur. He possessed an interesting style, turned the art of calling a cab over a fence into a science, and rode a finish as if he were conducting the Royal Philharmonic. To make it to the front cover of 50,000 racecards at jumping's premier meeting must be regarded as one of the great comebacks of all time. ▩

IRISH CHEERS TURNED TO BOOS (and probably booze) after Istabraq's win in the Royal SunAlliance Novices' Hurdle. Determined to keep everyone out of the winner's enclosure but the owner, trainer and stable lad, a security-minded Edward Gillespie failed to recognise the horse's trainer and schoolboy-lookalike Aidan O'Brien, who, after vaulting a rail, was arrested on touchdown. Presumably Gillespie thought the Irish Champion trainer was playing truant. ▩

AFTER HIS BIGGEST EVER VICTORY, in the Queen Mother Chase, jockey Rodney Farrant planted a big kiss on Lesley Graham as she was interviewing him, on horseback, for Channel 4. Back in the changing room where his colleagues were watching on a monitor, weighing-room wag Luke Harvey piped up, 'He'll remember this day for ever. That's only the second girl he's ever kissed.'

Farrant is universally known as 'Pigeon'. It stems back to when he rode a giant novice chaser for a farmer who, on seeing the diminutive Farrant on board, likened him to a pigeon-dropping on his horse. ▩

LOSERS OF THE WEEK. One owner booked into Cheltenham's 'in' hotel, the King's Head at Bledington, having pre-paid a £700 deposit for himself and his entourage. Or so he thought. In a bit of a mix-up he had booked into another slightly less 'in' inn of the same name in a nearby town. There, after one night, he was more than happy to forfeit his hefty deposit. On hearing of the poor man's plight, the King's Head in Bledington, who were suffering this week from a severe case of 'no room at the inn', found accommodation locally for the party but undertook to hay and water them.

The other loser was an Irishman called Leo from Co. Monaghan. He claimed he had won the deposit for his house on Metastasio at Naas in January, and so, as you do, staked the house, which he owed to the horse, on Metastasio in Wednesday's Coral Cup. Metastasio was prominent until three out. 'Ahghgh,' said Leo, shrugging off the loss. 'It was only a small house to be sure.' ■

JOCKEY CLUB TOP BRASS, including an officiating steward, a senior handicapper, the clerk of the course and the director of the drinks cabinet, missed the second race which was won by Karshi, owned by one of their own, Lord Vestey. They were all stuck in a lift. 'It was beginning to get a bit sweaty,' said one. 'Just like *The Poseidon Adventure*,' said another. 'We could hear the tapping getting closer.' ■

DAVID WALSH, who gave Barton Bank a heroic ride in the Gold Cup to finish second, is getting a reputation as something of a test pilot. Got a dodgy jumper? Call up Walsh, attached to the Nigel Twiston-Davies yard – he'll get it round. Before the Gold Cup, it's alleged he was told that he'd been backed to be champion by the millennium. 'When's that then?' he replied. ■

ONE IRISH PUNTER ARRIVED IN THE JOCKEY'S MEDICAL ROOM in the firm belief that the pins and needles he was suffering all over his body and the breathlessness were the early stages of a stroke.

'Have you had anything to drink, and/or is there anything that might be stressing you?' asked Dr Philip Pritchard.

'Well,' he said, 'I've had 40 pints in 24 hours and just lost £1,000 on the first race.'

The diagnosis: a nasty case of hyperventilation. ■

IT HAS BEEN a financially productive week for Cheltenham's hundreds of construction workers. Apart from building the three-tier hospitality town and tented village, there was only one horse to back this week, which they were on to a man – Make a Stand in the Champion Hurdle. ■

MOBILE PHONES HAVE, alas, pervaded even the Royal Enclosure. One side of a conversation on the airwaves was heard yesterday.

Gentleman in Full Royal Ascot Regalia: 'I'll meet you in the Mill Reef bar after the third. I'll be wearing a black hat.' ▩

WHO AMONG THE TRAINERS gets to ride in the Royal Procession is always of interest. Yesterday it was Lord Huntingdon. No surprises there as he is 'family', but to be fair he was sitting in the first carriage with the Queen, Prince Philip and Prince Charles, which is an 'upsides' of some note. Some fifteen lengths behind him in the third carriage was Ian Farquhar, Master of the Duke of Beaufort's Hounds and a former ADC to the Queen Mother. One morning, after a particularly heavy night while ADC, he completely missed an engagement with the Queen Mother. The following morning he received a parcel in the post – an alarm clock from Ma'am. ▩

ONE OF THE WORLD'S GREATEST LIVING HORSE VETS IS MEXICAN. A small, round bachelor who adores women and speaks only moderate pidgin English, he was asked over to Royal Ascot by a friend this year. When he declined, his friend asked him to come over for Glorious Goodwood instead. 'Gloria Woodward?' asked the vet. 'You think she like me?' ▩

APART FROM THE LADY IN CHARGE OF THE CHAMPAGNE BAR, there are very few people working behind the scenes at Ascot who are indispensable.

One of them, however, is Grahame Welcome – 'as in the door mat' – who supplies the number-cloths for the horses. He supplies 40 courses and has done so for 40 years. Having worked at Fontwell on the number board during the school holidays, he progressed to handing out number-cloths at Windsor. When he complained that they were appalling, Windsor agreed, but said they didn't know where else they could get them. 'I'll make them,' said Grahame, and so began a business that now supports a perma-tan and a cigar habit.

Originally they were black numbers on a white background, but they were a nightmare to keep clean, and now it's white on black for the BBC, white on red for Channel 4 and white on blue for Sky. The highest number-cloth he ever produced was 126 for the fourth division of a novice hurdle at Sandown in the days when numbers were taken from the then four-day declaration stage. 'I've still got it,' he said yesterday. ■

THE THREE BBC TV COMMENTATORS Jim McGrath, John Hanmer and Tony O'Hehir are now known as the 'Royal Family'. They were travelling back to their hotel near Liverpool last Friday on the eve of the National when they were involved in what the aviation world call a 'near-miss' with a large bus on a roundabout.

'If that had hit it would have wiped out the whole National commentary team,' pointed out the driver, McGrath.

'That is why the Royal Family never travel together,' piped up Hanmer from the back. 'And I think, perhaps, we shouldn't either.' ■

WHAT IS IT WITH CHARLIE BROOKS AND AINTREE? Last year he was reprimanded by the chief constable of the Merseyside Police, who had seen him wearing a policeman's jacket – primarily to keep warm during the evacuation – when highlights of the meeting were shown on *Match of the Day*. How unlucky can you get? Well, unluckier, apparently. It seems the jockeys' valet, whose briefcase was blown up in a controlled explosion in the weighing room, was not the only one to lose out.

Having travelled up to Aintree last Thursday with fellow Lambourn trainer Oliver Sherwood, Brooks decided to leave his case in Sherwood's car and collect it after racing. When he failed to materialise, Sherwood, who was fed up with waiting, eventually drove off. On the following evening in the car park, Brooks eventually turned up to collect the case and, lest he forget again, carefully placed it on the ground while he and a few others enjoyed a drink from an owner's car boot. Shortly afterwards, Kim Bailey was about to leave and asked his driver, Rupert Wakley, to bring the car over. Wakley, who rode Hillwalk in the National the following day, promptly reversed over Brooks's case and the car became so wedged on it that it eventually took five trainers to lift it off. ■

THERE'S ONE THING THAT REFUSES TO LIE DOWN AND DIE – the Ramsdens' successful Top Cees libel case against terminally ill (weeks to live) *Sporting Life*. On Thursday at Newmarket, Lynda Ramsden came within a whisker of winning the Swaffham Handicap, the race at the centre of that case, with Noble Demand cutting down the winner with every stride but just failing. Doing the rounds at Newmarket, where it finally reached the stewards' room, was the following joke. What is the difference between Luciano Pavarotti and Kieren Fallon? The answer is, of course, that Pavarotti can hit top Cs.

Also getting in on the fun this week was the race reader Alan Amies, one of the *Sporting Life*'s expert witnesses. You'll remember in the case that barrister Patrick Milmo asked him a lot of questions to which he already knew the answers. Had Amies ridden? Of course not; Alan was the first to admit he was the wrong shape. Had he trained? Of course not. Had he done a lot of other things? Of course not. 'Mr Amies,' concluded Milmo, scenting victory, 'you know nothing.' Trainer Mick Easterby had his fun by naming a two-year-old after his great friend, calling it 'AA-Youknownothing'. Well, at Musselburgh just over a week ago, the colt, which seemed unlikely to be anything other than first in alphabetical lists, came first in a race. The *Raceform* Form Book comment about AA-Youknownothing's win reads, 'Wearing a tongue strap for the first time, as he had previously choked, he proved, like his namesake, that he is both game and honest, and is progressing.' At the bottom of the Musselburgh results are, like all *Raceform* returns, the initials of that day's race reader – 'AA'. ▩

ONE TO CHEER THE BOOKMAKERS AT THE END OF A BAD WEEK. The following was doing the rounds in the weighing room at Cheltenham.

A school teacher asked three boys in her class what their father did for a living.

'My dad's a baker,' replied the first boy.

'My dad's a turf accountant,' replied the second.

'My father's a chiropodist,' replied the third and smallest of the trio.

'Well, for your homework,' explained the teacher, 'I'd like you all to come back tomorrow being able to spell your father's job and prove it.'

The following day the first boy got up from his desk, wrote B-A-K-E-R on the blackboard and produced a loaf of bread. He was followed by the second boy, who got up, spelt out T-U-R-F A-C-C-O-U-N-T-A-N-T and then produced a betting slip, on which was written, '6–4 the little fella can't spell chiropodist'.

OWEN BRENNAN WAS ASKED if the going would effect Strath Royal in the Gold Cup. 'It's not the going I'm worried about,' he replied, 'it's the coming back.' He was right: Strath Royal was ninth of the eleven finishers.

THE FIRST 'CASUALTY' OF THE 1998 CHELTENHAM FESTIVAL was reportedly Radio 5 Live's racing correspondent Cornelius Lysaght. When you come to Cheltenham you hope your luck's in, and Lysaght was fairly sure his was when his Monday nap and his next-best selection both obliged at rewarding odds. It all went horribly wrong shortly afterwards though when he arrived in Cheltenham town centre and promptly wrote off his BMW by driving into another car. The hire firm – who, not surprisingly, have hired out most of their cars to visiting Irishmen this week – tried to fob him off with a Lada. They eventually agreed to meet him about halfway and he's now a roving reporter in a Rover.

Lysaght was swiftly followed by Jim Wordsworth, boss of Anglo-Hibernian Bloodstock Insurance. Taking a short-cut the wiggly way over Cleeve Hill, he ran into a green Rolls Royce driven by one of his clients. 'We don't need to exchange addresses then,' was their greeting.

TONY DOBBIN WAS THE FIRST JOCKEY TO BE HURT when Direct Route fell in the Arkle and broke the rider's thumb. He missed the winning ride on Unguided Missile and also misses One Man today in the Champion Chase. However, Dr Philip Pritchard reported that five jockeys were hurt in the crush to get out of the tea room in order to ask Gordon Richards for the ride when it was announced that 'Dobbin' had been hurt.

THE CAREER OF AMATEUR RIDER, Racing Channel interviewer and one of mishap's many mistresses, Alice Plunkett, is spiralling out of control – upwards.

She made her debut in this column a few years back when she had her ear severed in a fall. Since then Alice has had to give up race-riding, not because of the ear – which thanks to a couple of thirsty leeches is now in perfect working order again – but for much better reasons. Her eventing career has shown so much promise that Racing Green, the smart mail-order clothes producers, have decided to sponsor her to the tune of three horses – on the condition that she doesn't get smashed up in a point-to-point. And there's only one way to guarantee that – to quit.

However, her racecourse reports on the Racing Channel are beginning to attract a cult following (well, she's had one fan letter asking for a photo so far). Obviously as a 'cub' on live television she's entitled to make, and indeed has made, the occasional *faux pas,* like being at Bangor and saying she was at Hereford. 'A complete stranger came up to me at Haydock a couple of days later,' she recalls, 'and said, "Alice, you're at Haydock today," and then walked away without saying another word.'

When she was first employed by the Racing Channel she was told that for her first two reports she would have to accompany old hand Robert Cooper – for £75 a day. On the way to the races she told Cooper that it was a bit steep.

'What's a bit steep?' asked Cooper.

'Having to pay £75 to do these two reports,' replied Alice.

'No,' said the avuncular Cooper, 'I think they mean they'll be paying you £75 for these two reports.'

On the same journey to that November Flat meeting at Nottingham, Cooper announced that Alice must meet Mr and Mrs Lovelace. In the belief that they were the most important owners going to the meeting she searched the newspapers in vain to see which horse they owned. It turned out that they were the couple who sell Cooper cut-price mushy peas.

But it is her attempt to get an interview with Tim Forster that is one of television's best ongoing sagas. She has been refused three times so far and each time has dutifully reported back to viewers the reason for failure. 'When I tried on a Wednesday,' she says 'he told me that Wednesday's girl should be finding bargains in the supermarket and making the beds. When I tried on a Monday he said Monday's girl should be doing the washing and hanging it out to dry. When I tried on a Saturday he said Saturday's girl should be cooking and filling up the freezer for Christmas. I'll get him eventually.'

At Leicester on New Year's Day, she was wearing a floppy hat to cover a graze to her forehead sustained during her latest mishap. The injury occurred in a head-on car crash near her home. Both cars were totalled. The other was driven by a close relation, her father, and the crash took place on the bend in the farm drive.

CHRISTOPHER POOLE, former deputy racing editor of the *Daily Telegraph*, writer of fourteen racing books, the voice behind 4,000 Saturday-afternoon racing round-ups for BBC World Service, staunch supporter of the persecuted cigarette smoker, and racing correspondent of the *Evening Standard* for the last eighteen years, retires from everything except the fags this weekend.

'You know that 38 million people listen to World Service on a Saturday afternoon?' he once told the *Sun*'s Claude Duval, intimating that he might possibly be the best-known racing journalist in the world.

'Yes,' agreed Duval, before the inevitable Punters' Pal put-down, 'but most of them don't understand English.'

Having attended every Breeders' Cup, his retirement is timely now that you're likely to be banged up for smoking in public places in America. Once, when sat in front of a large 'no smoking' sign at Churchill Downs, he was politely asked to put out his cigarette. He replied, 'I don't know about the laws in your country, but in mine, unless this is a munitions dump or arms factory, I'm allowed to smoke.' ▪

TIME MOVES ON. Geoff Lester, doyen of the *Sporting Life* reporters, was previewing the Coventry Stakes yesterday for Ascot's closed-circuit television with his co-presenter Alice Plunkett, 26.

'Were you born when Mill Reef won the Coventry in 1970?' asked Geoff, 51, who remembers it like yesterday.

'Well, not exactly, no,' explained Alice. 'My parents weren't even married in 1970.'

IN ORDER TO GET ON TO THEIR PART OF THE GRANDSTAND, trainers are given a triangular cardboard badge with their name on it. They are also given, of course, a complimentary one for the wife. Having been given one of these badges to cover all four days of the meeting for himself, one trainer asked why his wife couldn't also have one that covered the meeting rather than having to pick a new one up daily. 'Some trainers,' explained the man behind the desk, 'like to bring a different lady every day of the week, sir.'

PETER BROMLEY, commentating at his 40th Cheltenham Festival, had just called home the most storming of all his Champion Hurdles. He had just brought Istabraq's emphatic victory vividly into the nation's kitchens and rattled the speakers of a million radios tuned to BBC Radio Five Live. Even by his own high standards this was an outstanding call, an equal to Istabraq himself. 'Nine to four on. Thank you very much. Go and collect,' he rounded off.

When the field had pulled up and the adrenalin had begun to subside, Bromley mopped his brow, handed back to John Inverdale and, feathers ever so slightly puffed up after this marvellous execution, walked from the balcony back into the BBC technicians' room where he was expecting a mild pat on the back. There, somewhat deflatingly, he found his sound engineer, the man closest to the great commentary, asleep.

JUMP TRAINERS REGARD A TRIP TO ROYAL ASCOT as an exercise in public relations – to see and be seen. Kim Bailey, who has won a National, a Cheltenham Gold Cup and a Champion Hurdle, is there all week nursing bruised fingers.

He was recently watching Australia versus India at the Oval when Mark Waugh hit one of the hardest sixes ever seen. Rather than going high in the air before being retrieved by gravity, this one travelled like a bullet towards Bailey, who was sitting halfway up the Bedser Stand with a drink in his hand. He stuck his hand in the air at the appropriate moment, but the ball was travelling so fast his attempted catch only slowed it down to the speed of light. Bailey's fingers are still stinging. The attempted catch was caught on television and within a second Bailey's mobile phone rang and his former assistant Eddie Hales, watching the game on television in Ireland, castigated the trainer for dropping the ball. 'I may have spilled the catch,' admits Bailey, 'but I didn't spill my drink.'

SOME EXPERTS LOOK AT THE FORM, others look at the horses in the paddock, and some combine the two. One hospitality chalet, hosted by Piers Pottinger of Bell Pottinger Communications, selected their tips in some novel ways. On Tuesday the emphasis was on silly names, which netted them Flagship Uberalles at 11–1. On Wednesday they went for horses with a 'Q' in their name, which resulted in Call Equiname winning at 7–2. But with not a single Q among the 30 runners for the Coral Cup they had to go for the Queen Mother's (the biggest Q of all) Easter Ross, an early faller. Presumably because they were having too much success, yesterday's *modus operandi* was to go for horses with no chance. This proved most successful with Anzum at 40–1in the Stayers' Hurdle and Go Ballistic at 66–1 each way in the Gold Cup. ▩

YESTERDAY, according to the experts and racecourse executive Edward Gillespie, was the day for conceiving the millennium baby. A little-known offer from the racecourse – now obviously 24 hours too late, for which I apologise – was free tickets and a maternity facility at the course at the 1 January 2000 meeting for anyone who could prove that conception took place within the grounds of the racecourse. The rumour had clearly reached the Courage Enclosure, where one couple were apprehended, according to Gillespie, in an 'advanced stage of foreplay'. ▩

THE TROPHY FOR THE SMURFIT CHAMPION HURDLE is an ornate Victorian number which looks something like a cross between a christening font and a bird bath. In fact, it looks so like a christening font that it was borrowed once for that very purpose, although efforts to track down the culprits resulted in what most horses who ran behind Istabraq yesterday felt – failure.

The Irishman saddled with the task of returning it to Cheltenham on behalf of last year's winning owner, J. P. McManus, is a man of astonishing foresight. A month ago, he rang Nigel Dimmer, who looks after all the Cheltenham trophies. 'Wouldn't it save everyone the bother,' he said, confident that Istabraq would do it again, 'if I just gave it a polish and put it back on JP's mantelpiece?' ▩

CHRIS MAUDE was asked before the Champion Hurdle if his mount Upgrade, winner of last season's Triumph Hurdle, had any chance of beating 4–9 shot Istabraq. 'Only if my horse kicks him at the start,' he replied. ▪

TONY MCCOY DIDN'T TAKE LONG to get into the winner's enclosure, landing the first race on Hors La Loi III. When he got into the paddock beforehand, he reported to trainer Martin Pipe that Cardinal Hill, the Irish favourite who eventually unseated his jockey while in vain pursuit at the second-last, was catching pigeons at home. 'That's nothing,' replied a confident Pipe. 'Our fellow can catch 'em, cook 'em and eat' em.' ▪

THERE WAS A DECENT-SIZED QUEUE outside Lloyds Pharmacy yesterday – the first chemist to open on a British racecourse. Not surprisingly, after reports earlier this week in the tabloids suggesting that everyone gets frisky during the Festival, their number one bestseller was a morning-after pill. Not *the* morning-after pill, you'll understand, but Nurofen – painkiller, hangover cure and general panacea for the morning-after-the-night-before. Lip salve was their number two bestseller, but the chap who asked for something to ease the burnt hole in his wallet got short shrift. ▪

ANNA MOORE, daughter of Irish trainer Arthur, spent most of Tuesday looking for car keys. Cheering on cousin Paul Carberry in the opener, she punched the air as he crossed the line on Sausalito Bay, launching her friend Caroline Norris's keys into the Cotswold countryside. Caroline, the Irish photographer for the *Racing Post*, was working and therefore oblivious to the situation until Anna ushered her into a taxi after racing. The keys, which Anna had spent the remaining five races looking for – no easy task under 100,000 feet – were handed in at 7.30 in the evening. ▪

IT IS HALF A CENTURY since Cottage Rake, owned by Frank Vickerman, trained by Vincent O'Brien and ridden by Aubrey

Brabazon, won his three Gold Cups. Two of those elegant gold trophies were on display yesterday, as was the next generation of owner, trainer and jockey: Brenda Norris (Frank's daughter), Jane Myerscough (Vincent's daughter) and Dick Brabazon.

Dick brought his father's diary for the year 1949. Short and to the point, it makes interesting reading. The only entry for 8 March, in pencil, was 'won Champion Hurdle', which he did on Hatton's Grace. The Gold Cup that year was postponed until 11 April, when his entry was 'won Gold Cup', which he did on Cottage Rake. In between the great double he got married. The entry for 30 March reads: 'My wedding day (I must turn up).' 'I think,' said Dick, 'the bit in brackets is in my mother's handwriting.' In case you were thinking that the meeting was held up so that 'Brab' could get married, I'm afraid you're wrong. It was snow. ▩

WHO'S BEEN SLEEPING IN MY BED? Beds are few and far between in Cheltenham this week, so one worse-for-wear but far-sighted punter took himself off to the jockeys' hospital beside the weighing room and kipped there for the night. True? 'Yes,' said clerk of the course Philip Arkwright with a grin. 'I met him at six o'clock this morning, coming out of the jockeys' loos. He most definitely wasn't a jockey, and one of the beds had been slept in.' ▩

WITH 4,000 STAFF BROUGHT IN, the occasional catering blunder is to be expected. On Tuesday, horse breeder Peter McCalmont was having a drink in the 'big white', one of the many marquees.

'Excuse me,' he protested, 'this wine is corked.'

'Of course it's corked,' came the rather smart reply. 'How else do you think we keep it in the bottle?'

At this point, McCalmont sought a supervisor, who turned out to be not a day over seventeen. Realising the word 'corked' was obviously the cause of confusion, he sought this time to avoid it.

'Excuse me,' he said, 'this wine's off.'

'How can it be?' replied the supervisor. 'It was only delivered yesterday.'

All this is reminiscent of the occasion three years ago when a wine waiter was ordered to put 100 bottles of champagne in 50 ice buckets, to cool them down. He was stopped after he'd emptied in his 40th bottle.

BUY OR SELL. Tote turnover was up for the week, but what about tout turnover? All shades of shady, and a majority of them unshaven – at least 200 touts, an increase on previous years – were plying their trade outside the entrance to the racecourse yesterday. The Diary's advice? Shop around. Tickets for the Members' Enclosure, face value £50, ranged from £50 in some places to £120 just a few yards up the pavement.

There was a general reluctance to talk to the press. 'What are you, asking all these questions, a rozzer?' asked one. The oldest tout on parade reckoned he'd been coming since 1928, which makes him a short head behind the Queen Mother in the age stakes. Had it been a good meeting for him? 'It's a winner every time you wake up in the morning at my age,' he said, before revealing that before tickets he used to bring in bars of chocolate under his coat and sell them on the course. Another explained how it all works. 'I bought ante-post, you know what I mean like? You buy for £50, sell for £70. That's a £20 profit. It ain't diggin' roads, is it?' Quite. ▩

THERE ARE TWENTY RACES AT THE FESTIVAL and course records were broken in half of them. There are several possible reasons. Either the course has shrunk or, after 200 years of trying, horses have suddenly been bred to run faster. Most likely, though, it is all down to what has come to be called the 'trampoline' effect. Underneath a good-to-firm crust there is a deep moist layer with plenty of juice in it. Perhaps it should be called the egg sandwich effect. Either way, horses have been bouncing off it. ▩

ON WEDNESDAY, tensions were high among the bookmakers after they had been constantly hit during the first two days. One Victor Chandler representative was sent down to their rails representative to pick up more cash from the kitty. His request was not greeted with great joy. 'We can't bloody print the stuff down here, you know!' ▩

ON THURSDAY, a woman was asked how the Gala Royal Party at Windsor Castle had been the previous evening. 'It was great fun,' she confirmed, 'and they've got a lovely house.' ▩

CERTAIN PRIMITIVE FORMS OF LIFE thrive in warm, moist conditions, and Ascot obviously provides a perfect environment for the multiplication of that simple soul the press man.

Five years ago, 450 people from around the world were given press accreditation; this year, the figure topped 1,200. Ascot supremo Douglas Erskine-Crum says, 'It needs an overhaul. The big increase is mainly from journalists outside Britain.'

Are half of them on a freebie? 'No, not many. We turn quite a few away, and if we're at all unsure we'll ask to see their work afterwards.' On my reckoning he's going to be busier than the Oxford & Cambridge Examinations Board over the next few weeks. ▪

I'M NOT SAYING WE'RE EASILY BOUGHT, but the best-attended press conference of 2000 was the one on Monday announcing the sponsorship of the Thomas Pink Gold Cup at Cheltenham. Why? On the invitation there was a note stating that all those attending would receive a gift from the sponsor. Clearly it doesn't take a journalistic genius to work out what that gift might be – £60 worth of shirt. In a cock-up of 1993 Grand National proportions, I was on holiday. ▪

YOU SEE SOME STRANGE SIGHTS IN RACECOURSE PARADE RINGS. There was a case once, at Newbury I believe, of a lady being asked to stop breast-feeding her baby on the basis, obviously, that no children under the age of sixteen are allowed in the paddock.

You may recall the time in Madagascar when a local 'gentleman' got caught short at the very moment he entered the (slightly undefined) paddock and let nature take its course on the hoof, as it were, without stopping. At Kempton recently we had a slightly different scenario when a guest of the race sponsor, City Index, judging the best-turned-out horse competition, slipped quietly out of the paddock and returned with a plate of sandwiches. Nick Boyd, the racing public relations guru looking after the City Index account, and partial to the occasional sandwich, was promptly offered one from the plate.

'I hope, er, you don't mind me mentioning it,' said Nick, not unlike Herbert Pocket in *Great Expectations*, 'but it's, well, er, it's not normally considered very good form to take afternoon tea in the paddock, old chap.' Not wanting to see the City Index account go missing, Nick tried to lessen the impact. 'It could be dangerous for the horses,' he added, thinking along the lines that if the plate were to drop and shatter that would, indeed, be dangerous.

'Oh,' said the guest, carefully inspecting the sandwiches. 'They're not that bad. I don't think one of these would kill a horse.'

READERS OF ONE OF THE NATION'S OTHER BROADSHEETS last Monday (don't tell anyone, but it wasn't the *Telegraph*, *Times* or *Independent*) could be forgiven for thinking they were experiencing déjà vu.

I know it's dangerous for those living in glass houses to throw stones, especially with my spelling, grammar and tipping, but while the rest of the paper's esteemed sports section reported on last Sunday's action its racing page took us back in time – to Monday, 5 June. The year, 2000, was at least right. Philip Robinson had won the previous day's French Derby on Holding Court, Chris McCarron was about to step into Frankie Dettori's shoes at Epsom, and the racecards were printed for Leicester, Thirsk, Carlisle and Windsor. So, I hear you asking, how did the tipping go, given that they had the benefit of hindsight? I'm afraid they still only managed nine winners from a possible 24.

WE ARE NOW IN THE THICK OF THE SALES SEASON. You might have noticed earlier this week a yearling by Sadler's Wells sold at Tattersalls Houghton Sales for a record 3.4 million guineas. Last year, Tattersalls turned over 121,903,350 guineas (the gross national product of several small nations) at their sales, and 116,500,000 guineas of it was in the three months between now and Christmas.

Of course, to all but one of the human race it is an impossible task to keep up with all the facts and figures. That human – well, at least I think he is – is Jimmy George, 36, a modern marketing phenomenon. In the past racing has imported its marketing men, and on the whole they've arrived up to the eyeballs in qualifications, been very good at pie charts, baffled us with gobbledygook but known the square root of nothing about racing. Jimmy, on the other hand, was born for this job. A bit shaky on pie charts maybe, but he'd talk to a brick wall (and frequently does), he's verging on anorak status when it comes to pedigrees, and, crucially, he remembers a face.

Consequently, if, for example, Ping Pong, the extremely little-known Chinese bloodstock agent, turns up at Tatts, Jimmy can not only tell him apart from his identical twin Pong Ping, he greets him like a long-lost friend, he congratulates him on his 1,000 guineas purchase from last year's Horses-in-Training Sales winning the Shanghai St Leger, tells him that the horse's three-parts brother is coming up for sale this December, and takes him out to lunch. He has yet, I discovered, to buy John Magnier a drink, but then again it doesn't seem to have adversely affected the Irishman's total annual spend at Tatts.

It all started when Jimmy was at Exeter University and heard there might be a teaboy's job going at Tatts. He contacted Martin Mitchell, a director, who said that if he was passing he should call in. Of course, Exeter to Newmarket was a five-hour drive and it was long odds against him 'passing', but miraculously he said he would be in ten days' time.

'Travelled far?' asked Martin when he arrived.

'No, no, just passing,' replied Jimmy.

Martin likes to throw in an awkward question to interviewees. What trip, he asked Jimmy, would he expect the progeny of Dragonara Palace to get (the answer to which I'm not sure even the owners of Dragonara Palace would have known)? Jimmy's honesty – 'Sorry, I haven't a clue' – got him the job, and he remained at wastepaper basket level for three years.

The prospect of living in abject poverty for the rest of his life prompted him to leave and join *Pacemaker* magazine, firstly selling ads, then editing. He sold his house in Newmarket, bought a flat in London, and the day after moving was summoned into the office of *Pacemaker*'s big cheese Nick Robinson.

'Jimmy,' he said, 'good news. We're going to relocate to Newmarket.'

'You do realise what I was doing yesterday, don't you?' said Jimmy.

Relocate he did with *Pacemaker*, but in 1994 he rejoined Tatts as marketing manager and has been there ever since. Tatts have some 5,500 horses to sell by Christmas, by which time Jimmy will be on his knees and 'boring not just others but even myself'. 'It's not a hardship,' he adds cheerfully, 'it's fascinating.' How many people can say that about their jobs? ▩

FORGET ROYAL REBEL. Showing a lot more form than the majority of horses at the meeting was Colonel Douglas Gray, late of the Skinner's Horse (the Indian Cavalry), a week before he gets married in the chapel at Sandhurst – at the age of 91. His bride-to-be, Helene Wilson, is 82.

Apart from probably being the most senior racegoer this week, with the exception of the Queen Mother, he's sharper than a hat pin and one of the finest horsemen to grace the meeting, this or any year. In 1934, in India, he won the Kadir Cup – 'Pronounced "carder",' he said, 'as I once had to tell the Duke of Edinburgh' – which was to pig-sticking as the Gold Cup is to horse racing. The ancient art of pig-sticking, for those of you who don't know, required a little more skill than prodding a sedentary Gloucester Old Spot with a pitchfork: it meant a rider on a galloping horse lancing a jinking wild boar which had been flushed from the bush. Wild? They were furious, so it was no job for Flat jockeys. In 1938 he rode in Battleship's Grand National. He was knocked off his mount, Emancipater, at Becher's. After the war he managed the Haydon Stud, the National Stud, and when the British Racing School looked like going pear-shaped before it had even been built he was brought along to 'ginger it up', which he must have done as it's flourishing.

Like the Queen Mother, who was given a corgi pup for her 100th birthday and still buys store horses which have no hope of seeing a racecourse for several years, the colonel is still making long-term plans for the future. Marriage apart, he plans to lead an expedition of old soldiers back to India in 2003 to celebrate the bicentenary of the founding of Skinner's Horse. ▩

A ONCE-A-YEAR RACEGOER was introduced to Stan Mellor, the first jump jockey ever to ride 1,000 winners, in the No. 1 Car Park. 'Have you any interest in racing?' he asked. ▩

SPEND-A-PENNY I. 'Royal Ascot's a right carry-on,' mused shrewd Yorkshire-born-and-bred Tim Easterby, Pipalong's trainer, yesterday. 'You go to Beverley and a cup of coffee costs you a pound. You come to Ascot and it costs 85p.' ▧

SPEND-A-PENNY II. You'll remember the sewers below the main grandstand, flooded and then, for want of a better term, backed up, which requires more than a man with just a plunger to come and unblock them. Obviously, when the stand is replaced a few years hence, so will the antiquated tunnel system. In the meantime cameras have been set up underground to make sure any blockage is spotted early. So while we watch racing on television, some poor soul watches another, entirely different programme – *Bog Watch*. It doesn't bear thinking about.

The first blockage of this meeting came up by Clubland, where Buck's, Cavalry and Guards, White's and The Turf Club are situated beside the pre-parade ring. A pipe outside the racecourse's curtilage spilled over. Ground-floor White's was in danger of looking like the lower deck of the *Titanic* until the water board came to the rescue. 'At least,' remarked one passer-by of the freely flowing effluent, 'it's quality stuff.' ▧

GEOFFREY GIBBS, senior Handicapper until 1997 and the bane of any trainer trying to set one up for a handicap, was standing on the top of the weighing-room steps wearing new bifocal spectacles with which he has as yet to come to terms. He tripped and was about to go base over apex when caught by that well-known cricketer Sir Michael Stoute.

'Thank you, Michael,' said Geoffrey, his dignity just about restored.

'Not at all,' replied Sir Michael. 'But I wouldn't have done it four years ago.' ▧

NEVER LET IT BE SAID THAT DEREK THOMPSON ISN'T SHARP. Last Saturday, John Francome, suffering from a raging cold, cried off *The Morning Line* but said he would be fine to do Channel 4's afternoon programme.

Before going on air, John was due to speak in a hospitality box at 12.15 p.m. and give a few tips for a small remuneration. When he arrived, Thommo was just emerging from the box, having turned up at noon as a self-appointed substitute for the 'ill John Francome'. Good work, Thommo – the list of people to have put one past John Francome is very short.

John's cold was still with him at Chester, where a chemist asked a fortune for six small tablets. 'If I wanted to be robbed,' he said to the girl behind the till, 'I'd have gone to Liverpool.'

WHEN THE WORDS 'ASSISTANT TRAINER' AND 'SCHOLAR' are used in the same sentence, one of the intervening words should be fairly negative – like 'not'. Now, though, the opportunity to link the two more positively doesn't knock any louder than with the Alex Scott Memorial Scholarship, the winner of which will be given an all-organised, expenses-paid busman's holiday to any racing centre in the world for up to a month.

All the winner has to do is pass an 'interview' with Julia Scott and Sir Mark Prescott. Sir Mark is a master at producing 'assistants' who go on to greater things, such as Chris Wall, Pascal Bary, Simon Crisford, Julian Smyth-Osborne, William Haggas, Geoffrey Faber, David Loder, Dr Jon Scargill and Adrian Lee. He takes them on for two years at a time. 'If they haven't learnt all I know in two years they're never going to,' says Prescott, 'and if they have, then I get rid of them before they get too wise. The only advantage to working for a tyrant like me is that when potential employers know they've stuck me for two years they know they'll stick anything. As a general rule the more horrible I am, the better they turn out.'

Haggas still has the dented pan with which Prescott woke him one morning, and Adrian Lee, who now trains in the Middle East, fell into a carefully planned trap. Whenever Prescott had been away he felt things had been 'moved around' by Lee. When the trainer's birthday fell during an away trip, his birthday cards were left on the office desk. Three or four down was a heavily scented pink envelope which proved just too tempting for the inquisitive Lee, who wanted to see which female had sent it. He carefully steamed it open, and inside the message read: 'Adrian, why don't you mind your own f***ing business?'

Roddy Griffiths, last year's scholar, went to Australia. 'It was hard work,' recalls Griffiths, known by his original (as opposed to Aboriginal) colleagues as 'Skippy' after eating kangaroo steak on his first night. In fact it was such hard work that 'Skippy' was thrown out of a nightclub – for falling asleep at the bar.

A SCAM AMONG THE BRITISH VISITORS at last Sunday's Velka Pardubicka was to obtain press accreditation which allowed them carte-blanche access to most parts of the course. Several successful efforts deserve a mention, including three students who had spent five days – and hadn't shaved for as long – camping in the car park. They said they were covering the event for *Horse & Pony*. Another pair, Messrs Bell and Smith, told officials they were working for the *Daily Telegraph*. Possessive about getting my own accreditation before others helped themselves, I expressed some surprise at the arrival of my 'new' colleagues. Later that day, Bell and Smith returned to the press room where the lady official suggested that perhaps they didn't work for the *Daily Telegraph* after all. They had been rumbled. 'We don't,' they agreed quick-wittedly. 'We're from the *Derry Telegraph* – it's an Irish newspaper.'

THE SPIRIT OF FREE ENTERPRISE IS ALIVE AND WELL IN YORKSHIRE. A racegoer in a smart car blagged his way into one of the car parks closer to the action by dropping the gateman a crisp £50 note. 'Find this man a good spot,' yelled the gateman to his colleague across the car park. 'He's given me £20 and we'll split it between us.'

IT MAY NOT HAVE BEEN COOLMORE'S GREATEST ROYAL ASCOT (one winner) to date, but they have not lost their sense of humour judging by a practical joke played on the well-known bloodstock agent Adrian Nicholl, one of racing's smoothest operators (by his own admission).

Tom Magnier is a good mimic, and he rang 'the agent's agent' earlier in the week to invite him, as was fitting considering his importance within the bloodstock world, to take tea with the Queen on Ladies' Day. As you can imagine he was immensely proud. This was a secret to be shared so he told quite a lot of people, while in his mind's eye he had a pretty good idea of how his new business card 'Adrian Nicholl – by Royal Appointment' would look.

He was eventually saved the embarrassment of crashing the royal box and/or being arrested by the perpetrators of the prank, but not before he had spent the whole of lunch dry so that he would be totally sober for his command performance. 'You've got to knock his head off every now and then,' said Coolmore's answer to Rory Bremner.

CHAPTER EIGHT

YOUTH POLICY

Not making sufficient effort

FOR THE FIRST 200 YEARS racing's youth policy was to lend its would-be administrators to the armed forces for a career and, where possible, a couple of world wars. Once retired, these generals, colonels and captains would then be taken on either to run the show or train the horses. Now, of course, the British Horseracing Board runs a postgraduate course for bright young things interested in a career in the sport, and we have the British Racing School to bring on lads and jockeys. Now, trainers spend longer learning the ropes than either doctors or dentists.

Earlier this week Lisa Rowe, a product of one of the first postgraduate courses, was appointed managing director of Newmarket at the tender age of 28. It's a good lesson to learn: make the coffee well and you'll get another job; do that job well and before you know it you'll be running the business. Coffee-maker to managing director has taken Lisa only six years.

It is a big autumn for her. In September, a month before she clears her desk as Haydock's racing manager, she is getting married to Charlie Hancock, an estate manager from Suffolk (until the Newmarket job unexpectedly cropped up, the early part of their relationship – him in Suffolk, her on Merseyside – looked like a trial separation). Having ridden 67 winners, mainly point-to-points, she is unlikely to be intimidated by anything Newmarket can throw at her.

However, her meteoric rise nearly came to an ugly halt at Aintree a year after the Bomb Scare National. Security was tight, with guards told to shoot first and ask questions later. At the same time Lisa was trying to keep fit by jogging down to the Canal Turn every evening after work. One evening some new, eager guards were on duty and, though warned about the terrorist threat, hadn't been informed about the clerk of the course's jogging assistant. Naturally enough they took it upon themselves to unleash hell on our heroine in the shape of two Alsatians. On the plus side she was able to put some good sprint work into her keep-fit programme, but her 'Do you know who I am?', delivered with two dogs sitting on top of her, was not the most dignified speech she'll ever make.

LAST WEEK A VACANCY CROPPED UP for one of the sporting world's most coveted titles. On Thursday, Flat jockey Gary Bardwell, known to his mates in the weighing room as 'Trevor', to the racing public as 'The Angry Ant', and to racing historians as the last man to win the apprentice championship twice outright, hung up his boots, at the age of 35.

Well, that's a bit of a lie actually. At 4ft 10in he wouldn't be able to reach the peg on which to hang them, so technically Gary's not so much hung up his boots as put them on the bottom shelf and ridden off into retirement, thus vacating the title he was once given on a television show: Probably the World's Smallest Sportsman.

An old-fashioned lightweight, rarely a year passed without Gary winning a decent handicap on something that thought it was loose. His victories included a Royal Hunt Cup, an Ayr Gold Cup, a Bunbury Cup and a brace of Chester Cups. In racing as in life, size, or lack of it, can have its advantages. He could, for example, walk under a horse should he so wish. His car looked like it was being driven by the Invisible Man, and with a bit more finesse he might have got away with half-price public transport.

However, the day when he and Neil Gwilliams (who wasn't a lot bigger) arrived at Peterborough station on their way to Edinburgh and thought they'd try it on, he left his brain at home. With Gary just able to poke his nose above the counter, the ticketman duly issued him with two halves, pointed him in the direction of the shop selling comics and warned him about accepting sweets from old men. But, in a scene reminiscent of that in *The Great Escape* when the English escapees reply in English to a German officer who wishes them good morning, they were rumbled when Gary attempted to pay for the tickets with a credit card, the minimum age for which is eighteen. ▩

FRANKIE DETTORI BROKE ANOTHER RECORD LAST WEEK when he attracted 350 schoolboys to a meeting of Eton College's Rous (equestrian) Society. The 'Eq Soc' usually attracts a maximum of 40, but Dettori put an extra 300 on the gate – about 50 who were genuinely interested and another 250 who were looking for a tip – and the meeting had to be moved from its usual venue to the more spacious and historic Upper School. It was, says one insider, like the midday train to Bombay – boys hanging off every ledge. When one Etonian suggested that the great jockey might execute a flying dismount from a desk, Dettori said he could do better than that and, under the watchful gaze of a Winston Churchill bust, launched himself from the pulpit, which is a lot higher than your average horse.

Other recent guests have included David Loder, Punters' Pal Claude Duval of the *Sun*, our own Tony Stafford (total attendance of seven, if you include three masters) and Lord Wakeham. Compton Hellyer, the chairman of Sporting Index, who for the purposes of getting it past the headmaster was billed as the owner of Docklands Express, came along to explain the ins and outs of spreadbetting.

Betting, of course, is strictly off-limits at Eton, though I dare say the modern Etonian gets round it by use of his mobile phone. It is not so long ago that to be caught within 50 paces of Ladbrokes in Windsor earned an Etonian six of the best (and that is not a new type of bet), or a magnificent seven at the hands of the headmaster.

Things are altogether different in Ireland's foremost school for boys, Glenstall Abbey. Ireland is, after all, the country where one of the most celebrated tipsters is the priest Father Sean Breen. If I ever have a son, even if he's a Muslim, I'm going to put him down for this bastion of Catholic education. For at Glenstall, where old boys are known as Glenstallions, Father Basil, a keen racegoer before he joined the monastery ten years ago, thought it would be great for the boys 'to keep in touch with what many of their parents did and to teach them some life experience'. When he formed the Racing Club there was a little consternation from his brothers about the gambling aspect, so it was cloaked in the title the Glenstall Thoroughbred Society. It is now fully out of the closet as the Racing Club.

Annual membership numbers 80 out of 210 boys and Father Basil supervises about eight trips to the races every year, stable tours, and visits to studs and sales. One year they're being shown the finer points of a foal at Coolmore, the next they're seeing it sold at Goffs. Betting is not actively encouraged, but phone lines out of Glenstall on a Friday night are hot to Ballydoyle, the Curragh, Lambourn and Newmarket as members are invited to nap three horses every Saturday. Whoever tips the longest-priced winner wins £100 (a prize sponsored by parents). This term's ten-to-follow is just beginning to hot up, and last year the Racing Club sponsored a race at Tipperary. 'My aspiration for the club is to lease a chaser and run it in the school colours,' says Father Basil, who modestly credits the boys with the running of their own affairs. 'I just stand in the background.'

But for his incredible foresight, this year's trip to the Bomb Scare National at Aintree might have ended in an alternative (and probably preferable) script for the film *The Lost Boys*. He gave his nine pupils £20 each in case of an emergency (losing money to a bookie did not constitute an emergency). 'I told them if there was any problem to take a taxi to McDonald's in the centre of Liverpool and keep eating until I arrived,' recalled Father Basil. The plan worked considerably better than most professionally organised outings. ▩

CLAUDE DUVAL, the Punters' Pal of the *Sun* newspaper, spoke to the sons of owners at Eton College's Rous Society on Tuesday.

'Where are you staying?' asked the senior Etonian in charge.

'The Castle,' replied Duval.

'I didn't know *Sun* journalists were so well connected,' said the boy.

'They're not,' said Duval. 'The Castle Hotel, not Windsor Castle.' ▩

BLOODSTOCK AGENT CHARLIE GORDON-WATSON recently spoke to Eton College's Rous Society, a collection of youths who, when they grow up, will make up a large part of either the Jockey Club or Gamblers Anonymous – or both. Charlie carried out some research with major implications for two things: how certain trainers will be doing numbers-wise when the boys come into their inheritances, and, for fathers of Etonians, the destination of a few trust funds.

'If you had one horse in training on the Flat,' he asked, 'who would you have it with?'

The results were as follows: Henry Cecil 13, Sir Mark Prescott 8, Luca Cumani 8, John Gosden 3 (presumably one of those votes belonged to his son Sebastian), David Loder 2, and one each for Mark Johnston, James Fanshawe and James Toller, as well as quite a few 'don't knows'. Charlie went for Sir Michael Stoute. 'I felt sorry for him,' he said. 'He hadn't got a single vote.'

HUGHIE MORRISON, the East Ilsley trainer, runs Stop Out in the Weatherbys Super Sprint at Newbury today. The filly is expected to run well but is still a bit laid back. 'As I feel she's got a future, I haven't wound her up into a frenzy for this five-furlong sprint,' says the trainer, whose gelding Bellow won the July meeting's seller at 20–1 last week.

Morrison's three-year-old daughter Amber is already beginning to take an interest in her father's profession. What would you expect when your playground is a stable yard? Obviously, at that tender age some things are still quite confusing. When Amber's grandmother arrived for tea recently, she took it upon herself to explain that her whippet had just had an operation to prevent her having puppies – it had just been spayed. 'Oh yes,' said a knowing Amber. 'Daddy's got a horse called Bellow who has had a similar operation. He can't have puppies either.'

BECOMING A JOCKEY can be a long and at times testing process. Most of us went hunting, Pony Clubbing, showjumped or even, God forbid, when we thought we knew it all, had riding lessons for years before we were ever allowed near a thoroughbred racehorse. A Lambourn mum recently decided that her son, a bold, in-front-of-the-hounds type of jockey aged eleven, would benefit from proper jumping lessons. On his return, she asked him what he thought of his instructress. 'Ninety-five per cent mouth,' replied her son, 'three per cent wrinkles and two per cent bitch.'

NICK SMITH, ASCOT'S HEAD OF PUBLIC RELATIONS, has faced some tough questioning from the world's media since it was announced York would host this year's Royal Meeting. However, it took a nine-year-old called Leah on a 'press packers' assignment for the BBC's *Newsround* to stump him. 'What type of weaponry will you be employing to protect the Queen at York?' she asked innocently. 'I've given about fifteen interviews a day for about fifteen months of build-up,' said Nick, 'but never a question like that. We immediately took her to see Clare Balding in the BBC's outside broadcast unit.'

THE EIGHTEEN-YEAR-OLD SON OF A TRAINER recently rang his mother towards the end of his first holiday abroad with mates and without parents.

'Mum,' he asked from the Corfu phone box, 'could you tell Dad to pick me up from Gatwick on Tuesday morning?'

'Sorry, darling,' replied his mother, 'but your father will be on his way to York on Tuesday morning. You'll have to make your way back here by train or coach.'

'But Mum, I can't,' remonstrated the son.

'And why is that?' asked his mother.

'Because I've only got 70p left.'

THIS YEAR HAS BEEN A GOOD ONE FOR POPPIES. On Folly Hill at Faringdon in Oxfordshire one field, a blaze of red visible from miles around, has become something of a tourist attraction with cars parking up on the side of the A420, their occupants eager to photograph themselves knee-high among the flowers.

On Sunday the local hunt puppy show, something of an antidote to a busy week at Royal Ascot, was taking place on the opposite side of the road. However, the sign 'puppy show' seemed to be causing great confusion. 'Is this where we park for the poppy show?' demanded several 'flower tourists' before helping themselves to a slice of sponge cake which was ostensibly for those attending the hounds.

FRANKIE DETTORI IS TO BE A FATHER FOR THE FIFTH TIME, as you probably already know. On hearing the news, Liverpudlian Martin Dwyer, his weighing-room colleague, was stunned, probably thinking that if you had that many kids in Liverpool there would be a shortage of cars to nick.

'Blimey, Frankie, how many you going have?' he asked.

'Seven,' replied Frankie. 'And I'm gonna call the last one Ascot!'

IF THE PRECOCITY OF MODERN MAN was matched by horses then the Brocklesby Stakes, traditionally the first two-year-old race of the season at Doncaster in March, would be put back to some time around mid-December and the conditions changed to make it a yearling race.

Having been to male-only schools from the age of eight until eighteen, if I remember rightly I was about twenty before I spoke to a girl other than my own sister, let alone asked one out. In Yorkshire, it seems, you are considered slow out of the blocks if you haven't 'dated' by the time you're ten. No names no pack drill I'm afraid on this one, but a successful trainer's son (nine) recently rang the parents of an attractive daughter of similar age and politely asked whether he could take her racing at York last Wednesday.

'Certainly,' replied the mother. 'Would you like us to drop her off at the races?'

'No, no,' replied her young suitor. 'I've already booked a driver.'

'Well,' asked the ever-helpful mum, 'would you like directions to our house?'

'No, no,' he explained confidently, 'the car's got satellite navigation. We'll find you.'

So how did it go? Would Cilla have been pleased with the outcome? I think so. The satellite navigation worked with pinpoint accuracy, the pair lunched in the owners' and trainers' bar, he taught her to study form, and having made their selection for the first they encountered the only real hiccup – finding an adult willing to place their bet. That didn't take long however, and the good man duly placed their pocket-money on a 9–1 shot which romped up. 'I sent her with a tenner and she came back with £30,' says the girl's father, impressed, if anything, more than his daughter. 'It's going to be a hard act to follow. I mean, it's not quite going to be the same if another boy asks her out to a sweet shop, now is it?' ▣

IT IS A QUESTION I HAVE OFTEN WONDERED ABOUT but never been brave enough to ask. Simon Earle, the former jockey turned trainer, has never quite conformed to the stereotypical trainer look. Not for him a trilby and covert coat, more likely a wacky jacket made of recycled something, Nike footwear instead of brogues and an interesting hairstyle for which the word 'spiky' often doesn't do justice. 'Tell me, Simon,' asked the deadly serious eight-year-old son of a friend recently, 'are your horses frightened when they see your haircut first thing in the morning?' ▩

THE BOLLINGER CHAMPAGNE CHALLENGE SERIES, which last year gave us Angel Jacobs or Angel Monserrate or whatever he was called, kicks off at Newmarket today. The nineteen-runner field is the course's biggest of the day.

One of them, No Clichés, will be ridden by Nicky Tinkler, the third generation of his family to have race-ridden. He had his first ride on his sixteenth birthday recently and looked pretty tidy. Without wishing to give him any excuse to be cocky, it would not surprise me if he and his brother Andrew, fourteen, make an impact as jockeys during the next millennium.

Nicky, who leaves school in two weeks' time, is the grandson of Colin Tinkler Sr and son of Colin Tinkler Jr, the former jockey and former trainer. His uncle is Nigel Tinkler, for whom he rides today. Nicky has already been in more yards than the virus, and that is only taking holidays and mornings before school into account. Usually when they make a character like Colin Sr, or 'Geega' as he is called, they chuck the mould away, so in his sons Colin and Nigel and on through his grandsons I think we have the first positive proof that cloning has already taken place in Yorkshire.

Geega's place near Malton is called, naturally enough, Geega's Place. From a distance it has the most fantastic geranium displays in its window boxes. It's only when you see them close up or still blooming on Christmas Day that you realise they are fake. Geega had his first ride in a race, at Stratford, after just six hours of riding lessons. By his own admission he couldn't even bounce at the trot. His short and inglorious career came to an end when he was 'mangled' in a fall at Southwell not long after. He has since survived on punting (anything) and his telephone tipping lines.

His wife and Nicky's grandmother, Marie, was a very successful showjumper, and when she won the most prestigious ladies-only event, the Queen Elizabeth Cup at White City, she was pregnant with Colin Jr. As Geega points out, one of Colin Jr's great claims to fame is to be the only male ever to have won the Queen Elizabeth Cup. Marie also rode on the Flat and was champion lady rider aged 53. They subsequently divorced, and when Geega named a race after her, the Marie Tinkler Stakes, she complained that it sounded like a race named in her memory. Geega, in his own inimitable style, changed the title to the Very Much Alive Marie Tinkler Stakes.

Geega led the field in company ownership with Full Circle and was ahead of his time in the art of telephone tipping. So entertaining were his tipping lines that he could keep you hanging on, waiting for the all-important tip, at a premium rate while he made the tea, said good morning to all the lads, felt a horse's legs and cursed the dog.

His eldest son and Nicky's father, Colin Jr, rode and trained successfully but now prepares horses for the breeze-ups. One of his greatest legacies as a jockey was the result of an horrific accident at Newcastle when he shattered his leg on a concrete post. It proved the catalyst for having all concrete posts removed from British racecourses. ■

RACING HAS A FRUITY NEW DEFINITION for the word 'optimism', and it is retired maths teacher Fergus Wilson. He was hoping that his first ever Flat horse, Maidstone Majesty, would make his racecourse debut in next Saturday's Vodafone Derby. He'd even backed the colt to win £100,000 with a bookmaker who was prepared to offer him each way down to fifth place. Blimey, the risks some bookies are prepared to take.

To the relief of purists but to the tremendous disappointment of this column, and no doubt the town of Maidstone, where Fergus once applied chalk to blackboard, his Majesty is now a non-runner due to growing pains. No doubt that was also a common complaint among his pupils when faced with 45 minutes of algebra. According to Wilson, his trainer Martin Pipe is 'devastated'. Whether Pipe ever gets over this setback is open to question. 'It's very disappointing,' said Fergus, 52, yesterday. 'We've kept him a dark horse for two years. I'd only entered him in three races, the Derby, Irish Derby and Arc de Triomphe, but now he's got to have a month of light training which rules out Ireland. Realistically we're looking at the St Leger now. We will try to do the same with another horse in two years' time. The one thing I learnt from boxing was not to lie down at the first punch.'

For the past 35 years Fergus has been more interested in seeing the feathers fly than horses. 'Without wishing to boast about it I was pretty successful,' he said without boasting about his pigeon-racing exploits. 'I won the "National" with a pigeon called Maidstone Monarch, after whom I've named my next Grand National runner, and had another good pigeon called Maidstone Majesty, after whom the colt is named.'

While other owners have started at the bottom and worked upwards, Fergus has gone straight in at the top. His first jumps runner was Damas in the 1998 Grand National. The horse, lacking his owner's enthusiasm and the spirit the occasion warranted, refused at the eleventh. And while the Aga Khan's Derby ambition might have been inspired by his grandfather's five Derby victories, Fergus's ambition was inspired by Portuguese Lil who finished last – in his words 'only marginally last' – in the 1996 Derby. 'I worked out what it had cost them and thought I could afford that,' he explains. 'All in all, including what I bought him for, his training and his entry fees, it has cost me £10,000.'

Clear in his own mind, like any bloodstock agent, about the breeding, price and, importantly, colour (bay) of the animal, he wanted he set out on an odyssey to find Maidstone Majesty. Starting with Weatherby's Return of Mares he ended up offering a small profit to someone in Scotland for the Teenoso colt which, after spending a year with him in the Garden of England, went to Pipe. 'A lot of people ask me if I'm going to go into greyhounds next,' says Fergus. 'I haven't decided yet.' But we've had the bird and now the horse. Will Maidstone Majesty's next incarnation be as a dog? ◼

LOVE IS ALL AROUND US. Racing's established eligible bachelor club has suffered a couple of hits in the last week from which it may never fully recover. Only the unlikely event of Carl Llewellyn succumbing to an overriding wish to settle down would come as more of a surprise.

Tom Jenks, the former jump jockey, was the first to go when he announced his engagement to Kate Morgan. She is the sister of twin titans of the tartan turf brothers Ran and Luke Morgan, who, you may remember, both got done for use of the whip fighting out their first finish together last spring. Now farming 300 cattle and 1,000 sheep in New Zealand as well as shipping the odd store horse back home – Jonjo O'Neill has bought one, named Tommy Jay after him – Tom's engagement was not without complication. It being such a long way to fly, he had to ring up Kate's father, Captain Rupert, to ask his permission. Never having spoken to his father-in-law and understandably nervous as well as excited, he dialled Scotland. However, he failed to take into consideration the time difference, and in Dumfries, just as it was at Greenwich, it was five o'clock in the morning. When he was greeted by a gruff 'Hello?' the nerves doubled and his opening gambit was uniquely British. It was a question about the weather which, to the captain at that hour, was still very much on the other side of the curtains. 'When I did finally pop the question,' says Tom, 'there was such a silence I thought he'd either taken a bad fall or the phone had gone dead. I was tempted to put it down and pretend I'd been cut off.'

An added bonus for Tom, who shipped Kate out last January, is that she is a jewellery designer. 'It cuts the cost of an engagement and wedding ring dramatically,' he explained.

Tom was swiftly followed by Simon Sweeting, who now runs the Overbury Stud and oversees Kayf Tara's more passionate moments. He met his future wife, Lara, five months ago, and not only has he already popped the question, the wedding's booked for early February – a week before the conventional start of the breeding season, unless of course you're Juddmonte, when it starts in late December. In an unnatural burst of romanticism Simon took his bride-to-be to Rome to propose and gave himself three days in which to do so. He too had last-minute bottle failure, and having missed a glorious opportunity in the

Piazza Santa Maria he eventually came good in the less salubrious surrounds of Rome airport's departure lounge, just as 'last call for the flight to Birmingham' was sounded. ▩

HERE'S A SALUTARY LESSON FOR US ALL, indeed a couple. First off, if you name a horse after your nine-year-old son, don't run it in a claimer, win the race, lose the horse and then expect to return home to an ecstatic reception from said son.

That, in a nutshell, is what happened to Giles Bravery earlier in the week. Giles hit form with a double at Wolverhampton on Monday, where one of his winners was Harry B, who hadn't previously troubled the judge in eight outings. After the race he was claimed by Richard Price of Flakey Dove fame, and Harry B (the horse) has now swapped Hamilton Road, Newmarket for Criftage Farm, Ullingswick and a Herefordshire postcode. Giles was delighted to have sold the horse, but he was not flavour of the month with his son and heir when he returned home. Harry Bravery, one of the sharper crayons in the box, promptly suggested that Dad should have paid that nice Mr Price a £500 profit on the deal (which amounted to 10 per cent) so that he'd have Harry B back in the yard.

Meanwhile, back at Wolverhampton, Richard was dropping off a head collar for his new purchase at the racecourse stables when three opportunistic boys put in a not altogether friendly claim of their own – on his Rover 400. When he hopped out, briefly, leaving it running – something you might get away with at, say, Hexham, but not, apparently, in the Black Country – they hopped in and drove off in the direction of downtown Wolverhampton flicking V signs out of the window. In what must be regarded as a dramatic reversal of roles, they left him running. The car was later found abandoned, having been used in a robbery, but is now back at Criftage Farm with Harry B (the horse).

As I said, lessons all round. ▩

YOUR CHRISTMAS CARD FROM THE FANSHAWES could be a bit late this year, and possibly not quite what you were expecting.

The Newmarket trainer's card is not of Soviet Song with tinsel plaited into her mane but, as is the current fad, of his family, or in this case his seven-year-old son Tom, in a variety of poses. The photos were painstakingly taken, put into the computer and lined up to be printed with a suitable Christmas greeting by James's wife Jacko. Being of that generation, like a lot of us, whose second nature isn't computers, this took a not inconsiderable amount of time, but it was nevertheless worth it, or so Jacko reckoned.

All was going well and she had printed off a few when the printer ran out of card. Not wanting to go through the same process the next day she left the computer exactly as it was, set up to print multiples of Tom once she'd bought more card in town. In between her leaving her desk and her return the next day, however, young Arsenal fan Tom got on the computer for no more than a few seconds and, unbeknown to Jacko who'd spent all those hours lining everything up, played a game of Space Invaders, or whatever the current fad is, as well as changing his own picture for that of Freddie Ljungberg. 'It was a good job Tom was at school when Jacko started printing Christmas cards of Arsenal's number eight wishing you the season's greetings,' says James.

THE BRITISH HORSERACING BOARD has a Levy Board-funded pot of £10 million for a national marketing strategy. Handing out the loot, appropriately, will be someone by the name of Teresa Cash, who hopes to persuade people to go racing and, hopefully, become inveterate gamblers.

Notwithstanding the fact that most of my readers have probably fallen asleep because the dreaded 'BHB' and 'Levy Board' are both mentioned in the first paragraph, I reckon that the Racing and Betting Marketing Group's first strategy should be to grant Whitgift School and its head man, Dr Christopher Barnett, a sizeable portion of cash. The Croydon-based public school, founded 400 years ago this year, already has in training three horses owned by a combination of old boys, boys' parents, teachers and friends of the school: Whitgift Rose with Lady Herries, plus Quick Whitted and Phar Too Gifted with Richard Phillips. The first convert of the project, the headmaster's sixteen-year-old son Nathaniel, is about to join Phillips on a work-experience programme.

'Sir' has already had a polite enquiry from the Charities Commission to see who is paying for these horses and whether the cash is being embezzled from the school budget, government grants or being added on to the fees. The key to this is that the boys' involvement does not start and stop when they go to the racecourse. The horses have been to the school (and worked a stiff two furlongs over the cricket square) and after the Lord's Prayer at morning assembly there is a brief update on Whitgift Rose's progress. The horses run in the school colours of yellow and blue, and of course the names are pretty self-explanatory (Whitgift Rose is named after a pink rose created to mark the 400th anniversary), though not plain sailing.

'We've gone for mares and fillies,' says Dr Barnett. 'How could I go back and tell the boys that the horse we'd called Whitgift Boy had just been gelded because he was useless? When we were at the sales, our adviser from the British Bloodstock Agency liked a horse by Tragic Role. I could just about cope with that, but it was out of a mare called Pooh Wee. Schoolboy humour being what it is, there's no way I could have gone back and announced its breeding in front of 1,000 boys. We had to buy something else instead.'

Dr Barnett is keen to develop 'school packs' for racing on the basis of Whitgift's experience. Judging by the way Whitgift Rose ran at Kempton behind True Crystal on Wednesday night – 'nearest at finish' – the boys are also learning how to handicap a horse. Far from the next lesson being John, chapter 7, verses 1 to 12, I suspect it will be, in due time, 'How to get the pocket-money of 1,000 boys on without altering the price'. ■

IN THREE WEEKS' TIME we will probably have had enough of images of Ayres Rock, Sydney Opera House and possibly, though I doubt it, Australians themselves. So it's expedient to write about today's subject pre- rather than post-Olympics while we still have an appetite for all things antipodean.

But first some background. In March it was announced that two of

Australia's best jockeys would be making an impact here on working holidays. Melbourne Cup-winning jockeys Damien Oliver and Greg Hall, to be fair, put the emphasis on holiday rather than working and made more of a splash in the water hazards of Britain's golf courses than they did on our racecourses. Hardly worth a mention was a youngster coming with them, second jockey to Lee Freedman, who had never even ridden in, let alone won, the Melbourne Cup; who, if lucky, might have a few rides for Mick Channon. He didn't look old enough to fly halfway around the world unaccompanied, let alone ride in races.

So not really a factor then? Er, wrong. Today, 35 winners later, Craig Williams will be let loose in a British Classic for the first time when he partners Talaash ('a nice horse, but needs to improve') in the St Leger. Channon says he'd talk a glass eye to sleep, James Fanshawe says he could ride an absolute stinker, but he's so enthusiastic you'd find it impossible to bollock him, while Steve Drowne, injured first jockey at West Ilsley, must be wondering what the hell he did to upset the gods as he sees Craig kick yet another winner home.

The great thing about being Australian here is that the aggregate of four day-trips to Doncaster from West Ilsley are what, back home, you'd make to go to the cinema in one evening. Here it sends most people into early retirement. Of course, from Craig's point of view it just gives him more time for talking and an audience that, for three hours, can't escape. Unlike some of our younger jockeys who talk as if they're operated by a novice ventriloquist, mumbling monosyllabic sentences without apparently opening their mouths, it would surprise me if this guy shuts up when he's asleep. 'It's a great country this,' he said, surveying the damp, overcast day at Doncaster (force 10 on the Beaufort Scale) earlier this week, 'when you're flying above the clouds. Only joking. Like Mick says, if it wasn't for the weather so many people would want to come here they'd sink the place.'

Melbourne-born Craig, 23, comes from a family steeped in racing tradition. All of them, from his father to his second cousin twice removed, have worked in the business, and if they'd had a dog it would probably have been employed by Jockey Club security. He first came here following up on a 'love interest' (no happy ending I'm afraid) and spent a week riding out for Channon. It was an appalling piece of timing as Channon was on holiday. However, a mutual friend got the two together. A visa, the most difficult part of the whole trip, was arranged and almost immediately Skippy, as he has been imaginatively christened in the weighing room, started riding big-priced handicap winners. Indeed, if you'd backed each horse he'd ridden to a £1 stake, you'd be up to £58.

One of the things he discussed in the car with Channon this week was next summer. Providing a visa is forthcoming, he hopes to be back for a similar stint. 'Imagine that,' he says. 'For me that would be summer twelve months of the year – except yours only seems to last four days.'

SCHOOLS ARE TALKING ABOUT STAGING NON-COMPETITIVE SPORTS DAYS (and I'm not referring to British Olympic athletics trials), in line with the modern world's obscure notion that the vanquished shouldn't be mentally scarred for life by defeat. I'm still trying to work out whether the idea stems from our own sport's variation on the theme, Regional Racing.

Of course it won't work, for the simple reason that most children are naturally competitive. Take little Rose Dunlop, for example, daughter of multiple Classic-winning trainer Ed. Rose, five, turned up at school last Monday to find that her best friend and demon jockey Isabelle Upton had been to a local Pony Club show the previous day. Not only had she won a jumping class but she had brought the cup and her rosettes to school to show to her friends. The consequence was that Isabelle attained instant heroine status. About 80 per cent of Rose thought this was rather wonderful; 20 per cent was slightly jealous.

The following day, Tuesday, Ed was holding a press morning ahead of the Irish Oaks so there was plenty on, and Rose helpfully announced to her parents that she had packed her own 'break' (normally an apple and some juice) in her satchel. Shortly afterwards the au-pair came tripping into the kitchen, stubbed her toe on Rose's satchel, and proceeded to hop around the kitchen on one foot. It was instantly clear that there was something a little more substantial in Rose's satchel than an apple. Further inspection revealed it to be the bronze of a horse and jockey presented to Ed for Ouija Board's famous Oaks win. With it, Rose, in a masterstroke of toddler oneupmanship, had intended to trump her best friend's tin cup.

The fact that it takes a strong man to lift the bronze was neither here nor there. How Rose got it off the dining-room table into her satchel is to wonder how ancient Britons got Stonehenge up. But having been rumbled Rose was naturally a little upset, not to mention tearful. In the end a compromise was struck between daughter and father: he would substitute one of his own more portable Pony Club cups, and Mummy promised to bring Ouija Board's trophy to school on another, less hectic day for Rose to show to her friends.

CHAPTER NINE

HUMANELY DESTROYED

Suspended

APART FROM HIS GOD-GIVEN GIFT FOR RIDING DODGY NOVICE CHASERS, Luke Harvey, it seems, was also put on this earth for the amusement of others. Racing's quickest wit, who is unstinting in his quest to make sure the Dunwoodys of this world keep their feet on the ground, has received a shock of his own.

Getting up to make a cup of tea one Saturday morning, Harvey picked up the kettle not realising it was electrically live until he came into contact with his cooker. Unwittingly he became the missing link in an electrical circuit of mains strength and momentarily he assumed a zinging Don King hairstyle. Stuck to both metal objects by the voltage he took a good five-second dosage of electricity before he was dramatically knocked to the floor. 'They said that anyone with a weak heart wouldn't have survived,' said Harvey. It wasn't a practical joke, nor was it, as some have suggested, attempted murder. Instead the culprit was the plumber from a 'reputable' (reputable in this case means he took a cash payment) firm who had fitted a new shower in the Harvey house the day before. In the process he had drilled through an electric cable. 'I had a couple of novice chase rides that afternoon,' said Harvey, who felt unwell for four days, 'and I think people thought my bottle had gone because I was shaking so much.' ▣

IT IS RUMOURED, not without foundation, that Tim Easterby will take over from his father Peter at the start of February. Peter, first and foremost a very successful farmer, has won the Champion Hurdle five times and the Gold Cup twice. The great Great Habton trainer's son has applied to the Jockey Club for a licence to train, and, though Peter politely denies it, you wouldn't have to be a forensic scientist to regard such a request as evidence.

Does it mean an end to stories like this though? Easterby Sr was rollicking his travelling head man, known throughout racing as 'Granger', for letting a horse out by mistake one day.

'What do you think I am,' asked Granger of his boss, 'clairvoyant?'

'Who the f**k is she?' replied Easterby. 'Did she used to work for me?' ▣

JUMP JOCKEY LUKE HARVEY'S future post-racing looks assured. His humour, previously confined to the weighing room, can now be found on the sports pages of the *Newbury Weekly News* and at the end of a Racing Channel microphone. He has not forgotten his origins and he is still the quickest wit in silks.

Just before a recent race, an owner asked him when he had last ridden a winner. 'Listen,' said Harvey, who is often the butt of his own jokes, 'I'm a jockey, not a memory-man.' ■

RICHARD DUNWOODY'S NEED FOR SPEED is well chronicled. Horses just aren't fast enough. Scottish National today, round two of the Formula First Championship tomorrow. Next week Punchestown races in the afternoon, but testing at Mondellow, conveniently close to Naas, in the mornings. Walking the course, as it were, for a later round in the series.

Well, it seems Dunwoody isn't the only jump jockey with a passion for dashin'. One corner of the weighing room at Stratford this summer might look more like the Warwickshire chapter of the Hell's Angels as Carl Llewellyn, Tom Jenks, Martin Brennan and Barry Fenton arrive on their new boy's toys – 600cc worth of motorbike. It is a worrying new trend – for other road users at any rate. Until now jump jockeys, most of whose travel takes place in the wet and ice of winter, have restricted their biking activities to moped hire in the Greek isles.

Llewellyn has just invested some of his Aintree earnings from Martha's Son and Grand National third Camelot Knight on a metallic gold Suzuki 600. According to Jenks, he arrived to pick it up looking more moped-owner than mean-machine menace in jodhpur boots, corduroys and a jumper knitted by his mum. 'I plan to put my riding kit in the horsebox and drive myself to summer meetings. Although it says in the bumf it goes from 0 to 60 in five seconds, it's taking me two wobbly minutes,' says Llewellyn.

Jenks, according to Llewellyn, rides his Honda CBR 600 (top speed 150mph) in a tweed suit. 'No, I'm fully leathered up,' says Jenks, who is also fully lathered up at the prospect of a hot summer. Though it hasn't improved his winners-to-rides ratio on the horses, the bike has, he boasts, done wonders for his nocturnal strike-rate.

However, none of them is quite as hard as he thinks. Last autumn, when Jenks was travelling a little faster than he should have been, an old granny pulled out in front of him and it was only practice at swerving on horseback to avoid fallers that the occasion became a near-miss as opposed to a hit. 'When I got round the corner, I pulled up and sat on the verge shaking for ten minutes,' he admits.

None of them is on a par with David Bridgwater yet. He used to be the proud possessor of a 1,000cc Harley Davidson. When his wife, Lucy, refused to ride pillion because she was pregnant, he swapped it for a more sedate quad-bike – slightly more practical on his Gloucestershire smallholding. Were it not for a badly broken arm, he could now take the wife, child and dog biking round the farm.

Bike ownership for 'Bridgy', though, was not without incident either. He once pulled up at the traffic lights in Stow-on-the-Wold as a group of Hell's Angels arrived at the opposite set of lights. 'Yup,' thought Bridgy, 'I've got one of those as well.' To stamp his masculinity upon the situation he tweaked the throttle. However, as the lights turned green – perhaps concentrating a little too hard on the tune he was getting from his exhaust – he dropped the bike. The consequences: a north-bound traffic jam, the south-bound Hell's Angels making 'some sort of gesture' as they passed, and Bridgy having to persuade a lorry driver to help him lift the heavy Harley back upright. The moral: The Bridgwater bark is not louder than his bike. ▣

THE MODERN TRAINER IS, on the whole, a responsible person. If he or she is off out for a meal or a drink, it is now commonplace for him or her to employ the services of a chauffeur for the evening.

Consequently, Paul Cole recently had a driver to take him and his wife Vanessa to a party and pick them up afterwards. The Coles were blissfully asleep in the back of the car when they were woken up by a police siren in the centre of Reading. The police promptly pulled the car over, breathalysed their driver, arrested him for being twice over the limit and hauled him off to the cells for the night. Not quite the idea, you will agree, of having a driver.

The real irony of this little tale, however, was that the trainer had remained stone-cold sober during the evening and, after passing a voluntary breathalyser test to satisfy the policeman, drove the car back to Whatcombe – a somewhat better option than kipping in the back of a freezing car outside Reading police station.

THE ONE THING THE COUNTRY HAS NOT BEEN SHORT OF so far this winter, we're all agreed on, is water. Trout have been seen in the River Lambourn, which had been dry for most of the 1990s. Pinker's Pond on Middleham Moor is attracting a variety of wildfowl instead of mud-wallowing cattle, and soft ground has even been spotted at Ludlow. So there's water everywhere, isn't there?

Well, actually, not quite everywhere. Middleham's new £380,000, all-singing, 80,000-gallon, all-dancing equine pool, completed in September, remains singularly lacking in this country's currently most abundant natural resource. It is so dry you could not take a water louse for a therapeutic lap at the moment. Ironically, of course, had it been an open-air pool it would probably have been full by now.

There is a lot of finger-pointing in Middleham, but it seems, like a lot of humans who win the lottery, winning a £1 million European grant for the town has done nothing except make the town council miserable. The council refused to allow a water pipe across a 30-yard strip of it's land but has now, reluctantly, given the go-ahead after a lot of foot-stamping, and the pool should at least be damp by Christmas. Until then, trainers will have to continue to make do with the River Ure. ▣

SEVEN OF THE JOCKEYS riding at Ayr yesterday had hired a plane from Oxford, so talk in the sauna was, not surprisingly, of those magnificent men in their flying machines.

'We often get gliders landing in our fields,' said Herefordshire farmer's son and country boy Richard Johnson, 'and in return they offer you a free flight.'

'We often have balloons landing in our paddocks,' said Peter Niven, who lives near popular ballooning spot Castle Howard. 'In return they give you a bottle of Scotch.'

At this stage Adie Smith, who lives in the less rural Pontefract, piped up, 'We tend to get stolen cars in our garden, and they give us trouble.' ▧

MICK CULLEN, one of the best-known lads in Lambourn, died recently. Travelling head lad to Fred Winter for eighteen years, and for twelve years with Oliver Sherwood, he was, there's no doubt, a character, and a thirsty one at that. He was also a stable lad boxing champion and an excellent breaker of horses, and had you set him the twelve Labours of Hercules – which his colleagues frequently did, over and above mucking out the stables of King Augeas – he'd have completed them in half the time. The bigger the challenge you set Mick, the more determined he set about it. Consequently, on a wet Monday morning when the hay lorry arrived, someone would suggest he wouldn't be able to unload the lorry single-handed. 'You weak load of bastards,' he'd mutter as he set off to complete the task.

After an evening in the Malt Shovel the landlord would attach Mick to his dog, which waited outside the pub, and the dog would lead Mick the 200 yards home. This worked fine until one night a local bitch came into season and the dog hurried to Upper Lambourn – some way past Mick's house. History doesn't relate where Mick slept that night, but we assume it was outside a kennel. ▧

OVERHEARD AT CHELTENHAM'S COUNTRYSIDE DAY towards the end of the foot and mouth crisis.

Mother: 'It looks like we will be able to start hunting soon.'

Young Son (clearly from the Henderson school of thought which reckons animals need a run or two before they reach peak): 'That won't be much fun, will it? The foxes won't be very fit.' ▧

TONY MCCOY WAS BEST MAN to fellow jockey and former lodger Brian Clifford last weekend. McCoy may be talented on a horse, but according to guests, give the champion a microphone and, oh dear, it all goes to pot.

In the long history of best-man speeches, his was not one of the all-time greats. As he is teetotal he cannot even blame it on drink. Reading out a telegram, McCoy said, 'To our son and new daughter-in-law, wishing you a very happy day.' Then, leaving his script (always dangerous) for a moment, he added in all seriousness, 'Now, then, let's see who this one's from.' ▩

YOU KNOW WHEN YOUR LUCK'S OUT. On Wednesday a coach carrying racegoers to Goodwood crashed on a bridge in Petworth and was left teetering on the parapet. Potentially it was a serious accident because the only thing preventing the coach from taking a 40ft drop down an embankment was a flimsy young tree. Like the closing scene in *The Italian Job*, the coach rocked a little closer to the edge any time somebody moved. Not surprisingly, having seen their lives pass before them, its 35 occupants were, to quote Elvis Presley, 'all shook up'.

And although it is politically correct nowadays to go and get some therapy after such an incident, these were racegoers, made of sterner stuff, who know there is nothing like a drink to calm the nerves in such a situation. So as soon as they had been rescued and the couple with cuts had been patched up, they all headed, ashen-faced and still shaking, on foot for the nearest pub. 'Sorry,' they were told on their arrival. 'We don't serve coach parties.' Unlucky. ▩

REGULAR READERS, if there are any, should know to take most things published in this column with a sizeable handful of salt. I try not to let the truth get in the way of a good story, and consequently last week I dropped Steve, landlord of 'Badgers' pub, in it from a not inconsiderable height.

You'll remember about the Goodwood-bound coach that crashed on a Petworth bridge. The walking wounded turned up at the nearest pub to be told that because they were a coach party they would not be served. I thought it was amusing, and so would Steve had it been about someone else's pub. Though we didn't name it, you wouldn't have to be a champion on the Petworth pub quiz circuit to recognise 'Badgers'. Steve, I'm glad to say, took blankets to the injured and not only had the passengers back but entertained them on such a scale that their sore heads the next day were nothing to do with the accident. Last Saturday he would happily have taken a blanket to smother me, but we're good mates now. ▣

TOMORROW THE BIG SPORTING EVENT IS, of course, Sunday racing at Newbury. This is preceded between 11 a.m. and 12.30 by an open day at Ian Balding's Kingsclere yard. This is an opportunity to see plenty of horses and look around Park House's famous 'colours' room. Formerly a Catholic chapel, it was converted into an operating theatre and recovery box when Mill Reef broke a leg. It is now like a little working museum, housing colours, racing trophies and memorabilia, and a mechanical horse. It becomes the gym if anyone ever gets through the first round of the stable lads' boxing.

Secondary to Newbury is football's World Cup final, and the Diary could not let it go without a football story about the BBC's pundit Jimmy Hill from his days as a keen horseman.

Riding to the meet of the Heythrop Hounds, he was trotting down the road beside a very smartly turned-out lady. All was going well for Jimmy until his mount, rather loudly, passed wind.

'I do beg your pardon,' said the ever polite Jimmy.

'Oh,' replied the lady, rather stunned. 'I had presumed it was your horse.' ▣

HERE'S A STORY TO WARM THE HEART THIS EASTER, and one that suggests the Good Lord is punter friendly. Stan Moore, as you know, is the increasingly successful East Garston trainer. Last Saturday there was a big tip in his Parsonage Farm Stables and among his owners for locally trained Lord Protector, at 12–1 the considerably more fancied of David Arbuthnot's two runners in the Lincoln.

While Stan was at Doncaster supervising his own runners, one of his owners, and the source of the tip, was at Newbury making the most of someone's generous hospitality. Shortly before the Lincoln – and, so the story goes, considerably worse for wear – our hero stumbled down to the Newbury bookies and asked for £1,000 each way 'on Arbuthnot's in the Lincoln'. Now history doesn't quite relate whether the bookie, with an eye for an opportunity, stuck our man on Arbo's no-hoper Zucchero at 33–1 or whether Zucchero, number 8 on the card as opposed to Lord Protector's 15, just leapt off the page at our well-oiled friend first. However, the consequence was that when Zucchero squeaked home by a nostril, Stan's owner was up on the day to the tune of £40,000.

'That,' says Stan, 'is something we'd all dream about. He rang me at Doncaster shortly afterwards and said, "What a result!" I asked him what he meant. Lord Protector, his tip, had been beaten. Then he told me he'd been on Zucchero. Hopefully he'll have an order for the breeze-ups after that.' ▣

GILES BRAVERY, one of Newmarket's great characters, employed the services of Mick Kinane for the first time at this week's July meeting. 'I usually use an unheard-of 7lb-claimer at Wolverhampton on a Saturday night – he knows what I look like but I have no idea what he looks like,' Bravery said to Ed Dunlop before picking up the saddle. 'This time, I think it's the jockey who is going to have no idea what the trainer looks like.'

Sure enough, Kinane weighed out and stood next to Bravery clearly looking for someone completely different to pick up the saddle. 'Will you tell him or shall I?' said Bravery, nudging his younger colleague. Dunlop duly introduced the pair. ▣

NOT LONG AFTER GRUNDY HAD WON THE 1975 DERBY, Peter Walwyn, his enthusiastic trainer, was asked to open a local village fête. At the time, 'Big Pete' was training at Seven Barrows, a wonderful establishment just outside Lambourn, boasting hundreds of acres of gallops, a big house with a swimming pool, 180 stables and about half a dozen cottages for staff.

'Be delighted, be delighted,' said Big Pete at the request.

'Well,' said the vicar, 'I'll send you the details. Can I have your address?'

'Seven Barrows,' began the trainer.

'Is that spelt "seven" or seven the figure?' asked the vicar.

'What do you think this is,' ranted Walwyn, 'a bloody council house?'

BLOODSTOCK AUCTIONEER NICK NUGENT made sure when he planned his wedding to Alice Player, whose father Peter is chairman of Newmarket, that he would be back from the honeymoon in time for Ascot – if not to be there at least to watch on television.

Nick may be one of the most entertaining auctioneers in the world – he is frequently flown around the globe from his base in Ireland for charity dinners – but it could never be argued that he is one of the tallest. At weddings, as you know, it is traditional for the ushers to ask guests as they enter the church whether they are with the bride or groom before directing them to the correct side of the aisle. At Nick's wedding to Alice a few weeks ago, his ushers came up with a variation on that theme. 'Are you with Snow White or the Dwarf?' they asked.

THERE ARE THOSE (NOT ME) who believe the new, enlightened, democratic people's committee for running racing, the British Horseracing Board, has been acting like the Politburo at the height of Soviet communism.

The jockeys, trainers, lads, Tote, Levy Board, bookmakers and the Racecourse Association have all had recent run-ins with the BHB. One of these trade associations (which did not want to be named for fear of reprisals) sent an email to another which had recently been involved in a scrape with racing's rulers. 'Welcome to the "I've been shafted by the BHB" club,' it read. 'As this club is no longer exclusive, we think we should have an annual get-together.' The reply was swift and to the point: 'Good idea, but the way things are going we'll need to hire the Albert Hall.'

BE CAREFUL WHERE YOU EAT YOUR SANDWICHES at Aintree this year, and for that matter any other year. That dust a-blowing in the wind may well be someone's beloved being scattered.

It seems Aintree, home of the Grand National, shares the title 'dead centre' of Liverpool with Anfield, home of Liverpool FC. Journalists who use the word 'graveyard' in their Grand National copy may not be using as much licence as you would imagine. Aintree receive about 50 requests a year from the nearest and dearest of the recently deceased whose dying wish was for it to be their last resting place. Top spots include Red Rum's grave, which is opposite the winning post, and the landing side at Becher's. Aintree's Charles Barnett says, 'We have to be a bit careful around Red Rum's grave. Too many ashes tend to kill the grass off.'

A recent request, received by Barnett via email rather than through a séance, was from the son of a man who had just died. The father's dying wish was to be scattered beside Red Rum. According to his son, the man's last words were, 'Suny Bay will win the National.' ▣

THE TROPHY, sponsored by the *Daily Telegraph*, for the season's champion jump jockey will be presented to Tony McCoy today. It is a sterling silver saddle, designed and sculpted by Philip Blacker. Phil rode Royal Mail, who had broken his jaw in the Gold Cup, to win the Whitbread in 1980, which was no doubt testimony to his artistic hands and a considerable feat of training by Stan Mellor.

Living next to his Oxfordshire studio on a pond are Phil's pride and joy, an impressive collection of fancy duck. One day, a well-off owner, who also has one of the most renowned pheasant shoots in the country (we're talking 600 birds plus per day), cast his admiring eye over the duck, en route from his helicopter to see the progress of the life-size bronze he had commissioned. 'And when, Mr Blacker,' he asked, 'do you intend to shoot them?' ▣

THE FOUR-DAY PUNCHESTOWN FESTIVAL drew to a close last night with Charlie Swan riding a brilliantly judged race from the front on Grimes to win the £110,000 Shell Champion Hurdle. Decoupage, returning to hurdles after a spell of chasing, was a good runner-up – for the second year running in the race.

If that was the riding performance of the meeting, then the equine equivalent belonged to Risk of Thunder, who won the La Touche Cup over the banks for the sixth year in a row, prompting his rider, Ken Whelan, to call him the 'bank manager'.

The drive of the meeting belonged to permit-holder Lavinia Taylor and her husband John. They may own Uplands in Lambourn but they still do most of the dirty work themselves. This week the Taylors not only drove Gingembre to Punchestown but, having been up at 5.30 a.m. to feed the horse, Lavinia also led him up in yesterday's David Austin Memorial Novice Chase while John put the saddle on.

The night before they took themselves off for dinner, in the horsebox, to Rathsallagh House, one of Ireland's most wonderful country-house hotels. Obeying a signed instruction to park through the arch round the back of the hotel they proceeded until they became well and truly wedged underneath the arch, unable to go forward or back. Letting some air out of the tyres was only partially successful. The solution? Seven kitchen staff and three guests were summoned to stand in the horse stalls in the back. The combined weight did the trick, and, save the addition of some blue paint, Rathsallagh's arch remains intact. ◘

FORGET BOYZONE OR WESTLIFE. One of the highlights of Sandown's Whitbread meeting was the performance given by Irish band the Saw Doctors in the paddock afterwards while the racecourse dished out free booze.

Earlier in the afternoon John Donnelly, the band's drummer, had been having lunch in the glorious sunshine just outside the VIP tent. Dressed casually in jeans and a silver T-shirt (the Jockey Club's cherished colours?) he felt a bit underdressed to go into the marquee. Instead, while someone fetched him pudding, he struck up conversation with one of the security guards on the door.

'Howa t'ings?' he enquired.

'Could be better,' said the slightly depressed security guard. 'I've got to stay on late tonight because we've a band called the Saw Doctors playing. I wouldn't normally mind, but they're crap.' ◘

THERE WERE, AS YOU CAN IMAGINE, more trainers at Midnight Mass in Lambourn on Christmas Eve than cumulatively at Lingfield for the whole of January. All was going well until a gentleman passed out and hit his head hard on the pew behind. As this was Lambourn, where they are used to jockeys and lads being flattened on a regular basis, he was, while his candles were out, laid down in the aisle, with a kneeler as a pillow.

While the congregation waited for the paramedics, the service continued. The vicar said prayers for the fallen, blessed the down and out and the emergency services, and moved on to the taking of Holy Communion.

On the way down the aisle, former trainer Mark Smyly looked hard at the prostrate body, which had effectively been dolled off, and turned to John Hills.

'Do you think we should pass him on the left or right?' he asked.

'If the vicar's anything like the stewards at Ludlow,' replied Hills, referring to a recent controversy at the Shropshire course, 'he'll give us nineteen days for going the wrong side.' ▣

RICHARD PHILLIPS, THE TRAINER, went home to see his 82-year-old mother recently.

'How's Gee [Armytage]?' she asked fondly, remembering that a long time ago Richard and Gee used to go out with each other.

'She's about to get married,' said Richard.

'To who?' asked his mum.

'To Mark Bradburne,' replied Richard. 'You know, the chap, Lord Atterbury.'

'Oh,' exclaimed his mum. 'Hasn't she done well for herself?' ▣

RICHARD PHILLIPS WAS ENTERTAINING A GUEST on the gallops for a work morning. The guest would have made a good London cabbie because he had an unswerving faith in himself to make informed comment on any subject. He was one of those people who bluffs his way through life as an 'expert'. But Richard soon sussed him. The conversation went roughly like this:

Trainer (as the umpteenth horse passes): 'This one's called Grenfell.'

Guest (confidently): 'Oh yeah, I've heard of that one an' all.'

Trainer (politely but firmly): 'I'm not sure you have actually. It's never run before. It's named after Joyce Grenfell.'

Guest (reminiscing, as if it were yesterday): 'Oh yeah. God [sigh], I backed a few of hers in my time.'

CHARLIE BROOKS THOUGHT ALL HIS CHRISTMASES HAD COME AT ONCE when he received some fan mail recently. 'Dear Charlie Brooks,' it began. 'You're very sexy. I love your legs and bum. I'd like to cuddle and kiss you. Please send a photo.'

The compliments were very well received by Charlie, who has never been known for his legs, which have seen more tendon trouble than Lord Gyllene. But – and as buts go, this is a fairly major one – Charlie was put out to see that it was signed by a Mr Michael. On further investigation, Charlie noted that it had been forwarded by the BBC, who informed him there was an outside possibility they had sent it to the wrong Charlie Brooks. There was, they pointed out, a young girl of the same name who starred in *EastEnders* and who had a very passable chassis.

ALICE PLUNKETT HAS BEEN CELEBRATING becoming the first girl to complete the course at Aintree (1993 Foxhunters) and Badminton (2000) with 'flu'. The Racing Channel presenter now also answers to the name of Elsie. The Richard Hannon-trained two-year-old Elsie Plunkett was meant to be named after her but the owners bottled out when they were unable to contact Alice to obtain permission. Yesterday, at Nottingham, Elsie Plunkett won for the second time and looked Queen Mary material.

'The first time she ran,' says Alice, 'it said in *Racing Post* that she had potential on her breeding so I cut it out and sent it to Mum. When she won it said she was a "typical strong sprinting type", which I take to mean that she has a large backside.'

LESTER PIGGOTT, so the story goes, once rode for a small trainer who mortgaged his house in order to have a huge punt on the race. Conditions – the ground, weight and modest opposition – were ideal for his filly. 'The only thing against her,' he told Piggott in the paddock, 'is the trip. It is 50 yards too far for her, so I want you to hold her up at the back for as long as possible, then hit the front ten yards from the line.'

Piggott promptly went out, made all the running in contrast to instructions and, as the filly ran out of stamina, was passed in the last ten yards to finish second. Piggott dismounted and walked off towards the weighing room in silence. The now homeless trainer was distraught and followed the great jockey, seeking an explanation.

'Well?' he asked, doing his best to hold back the tears.

'Hmm,' mumbled Piggott. 'You were right.'

SINNDAR, who attempts to add the Irish Derby to the Epsom Derby at the Curragh tomorrow, is showing plenty of speed for an endurance horse. A quote (or rather misquote) from his trainer John Oxx in the 'Horses to Note' section of the *Irish Racing Annual* reads, 'He is a very straightforward horse with an excellent temperament and it will be interesting to see how he goes. I expect him to stay 12 miles, and at this stage don't envisage starting him off next season at less than 14 miles.'

WHAT JAWS DID FOR SWIMMING IN THE SEA Graham Thorner may have inadvertently done for charity wheelchair racing.

Graham was taking part in a wheelchair relay in aid of the Inspire Foundation at Tidworth Polo Ground last Sunday in which the baton, a whip, was carried in the mouth, thereby freeing up the hands for the short dash before it was passed over to the next team member. When an over-eager team-mate, keen to get going on his leg, grabbed the whip from Graham, his false teeth were still attached. In one swift movement they were catapulted high into the crowd – not dissimilar to a wayward chip at St Andrews.

Although you'd imagine little difficulty finding a contact lens on a pitch which is about as well manicured as the square at Lord's, let alone a set of four front teeth, the offending gnashers couldn't immediately be found. In something of a panic, and with the toffee pudding now looking a complete non-starter at lunch, Graham eventually discovered them – trodden into the ground. Showing all the grit and determination you'd expect of a former champion jump jockey, but mainly grit, Thorner's smile was fully restored and the toffee pudding consumed.

He lost his original front teeth in one of the first falls he ever had as an amateur, at Fontwell. 'I remember waking up in Chichester Hospital without them,' he recalls. It is alarming to think that archaeologists might find his originals a thousand years hence. Who knows what they might then deduce about twentieth-century man?

Since that fateful Fontwell day his replacements have visited more places, unaccompanied, than the explorer David Hempleman-Adams. Once, when being driven home from the races by Jeff King, he spat out of the window, 'as common jockeys do'. Out with the bath-water, as it were, went the baby. The teeth bounced between cars, off the inside lane and into some cordoned-off roadworks where a steamroller was in action. King was not so much ordered but threatened with death if he failed to reverse up the motorway to retrieve them.

This is reminiscent of the late, great racing journalist Michael Seely, whose teeth fell out in the car park at the races one day. As he went to pick them up Graham Rock, a colleague, drove majestically past in a brand spanking new BMW and ran them over. On seeing him waving his arms and shouting in his mirror, Graham promptly reversed back to Mikey, running over the teeth for a second time. Luckily, the ground in the car park was good to soft and the teeth, by now not so much embedded in the ground as planted like a daffodil bulb six inches down, were delicately scooped up by the great man, cleaned up with his hanky and replaced ready for the day's racing. ▣

HELLO TAYLOR. When John and Lavinia Taylor, who now own Uplands in Lambourn, used to train near Banbury, the extremely practical John spent his spare moments between riding work and transporting their mainly French horses to the races shut up in a barn building a boat.

The result, with Cowes Week just around the corner, is the cleverly named (because it was Taylor-made) *Bespoke*, which finished an encouraging fifth of 34 first time out just off Cork recently, and this despite a design fault on the tiller that makes her somewhat contrary to steer – not unlike some racehorses I've ridden.

Bespoke is no dinghy. She's 30ft long, has a 45ft mast and takes a crew of seven to sail her. On the back of a trailer towed by John's Land Rover she pokes out about 7ft either end, which makes turning a problem. She also rises to a height of 4m, and therein lies another problem.

The last time we spoke about the Taylors, you'll remember, was when they got their horsebox wedged under an arch in Kildare during the Punchestown Festival. Well, isn't it amazing how history repeats itself? To transport *Bespoke* to Fishguard, John had to notify six police forces, and though most boats suffer their worst battering on the high seas it is the high trees, of Lambourn no less, that have so far inflicted the most damage to his ship. The life-line stanchions were ripped off by some branches; until they are repaired, they'll not be much use for life-saving.

As there is now more chance of getting a quad-bike up the River Lambourn than a boat, and as the roads are now out, *Bespoke* is no longer allowed to visit Uplands. Instead she is stabled in Southampton. What is more, with the Taylors buying most of their horses from France, there is now trade going in the opposite direction because the French have chartered *Bespoke* for the Commodores Cup. ▣

ATTENTION ALL SHIPPING. When the River Dee burst its banks recently and spilt over on to Bangor racecourse it left the usual flotsam, jetsam and lagan of north Welsh river-life, but, in what looks like a fairly unfair deal, took with it a complete steeplechase fence and several sets of plastic wings. The whereabouts of the missing fence is causing some concern to Michael Webster, the clerk of the course, and those who have to navigate Liverpool Bay by boat. They already have enough uncharted problems to steer round in the Mersey estuary – like stolen cars. The fact remains, though, that the Dee has done what Tremallt tries and fails to do once a race – completely uproot a fence. ▣

YOU MAY REMEMBER THE DIARY running a story back in June about Roger Charlton having his Subaru Legacy stolen from his yard between first and second lots as he had breakfast. The peculiar thing about it was that the audacious thief left a white pick-up in its place, so the deal was (albeit slightly one-sided) two ways.

The postscript to that story was that the Charlton vehicle was found undamaged five weeks later on a deserted aerodrome in Hampshire, but because the keys had been in it at the time of its disappearance the insurers refused to pay out. In the meantime, the Charltons had bought another car from former jockey (if you count the Newmarket Town Plate as a race) Kevin Williams, so now they have two, one of which will shortly be for sale. Of course, as the thief was eventually caught, the only beneficiary was – and aren't they always? – the car dealer.

Now that you're up to speed on that story, you may well regard today's story as *How to Have Your Car Stolen – Part II*. The setting is picturesque Middleham and the trainer is James Bethell, who (this incident apart) has had a pretty good season from a small yard, doing particularly well with his Clarendon Racing Syndicates. Today he saddles Hunters Tweed in the November Handicap. The ground will be desperate and he feels the four-year-old may be more front-wheel-drive than four-wheel-drive.

Anyway, I digress (how rude of me to talk about racing in this column). To borrow a phrase from *The Bill*, James has had his Land Rover Discovery 'TWOC-ed' (Taken Without Consent). Here's the catch, though: he didn't leave the keys in the vehicle. No. He gave – I repeat, gave – the keys to the thief.

Let me explain. He had a newly arrived lad working for him and was busy with racing, the yearling sales and his move to new premises. So when the lad asked to borrow the Discovery to move from one set of digs to another, the trainer was pleased to oblige. It was the last he saw of either. James stopped the diesel card but it had already been used – in Plymouth. When he rang a contact number for the lad, a woman answered. She was not the least bit surprised, indeed sounded most grateful, when she was told what had happened. 'He was sent to Lincoln prison for stealing my snakes,' she said. 'We've been trying to get rid of him for years. Thanks for giving him the car, though – you've done it for us.'

It turns out that the lad was working under a false name and had tried and failed to get a job with Mark Johnston. Bearing in mind his previous conviction – this may be like seeing a man with a cigarette and lighter outside Parliament and accusing him of the Gunpowder Plot – his original plan may have been to steal Breeders' Cup contender Fruits of Love. It would have made another chapter in that horse's eventful life.

This time, the insurers have coughed up. Reflecting on the incident, James says, 'I should have smelt a rat. He kept saying what a nice vehicle the Discovery was. What really galls me, though, is that I had just paid £100 into his Stable Employment Pension Plan and it can't be returned.' ▩

THE ANNUAL AINTREE COURSE INSPECTION took place a week ago, on 1 April. Ron Barry, the Jockey Club's northern inspector of courses, having walked the course and passed it as fit, phoned his HQ in Portman Square and told them that the start to the National would have to be moved this year because of holes made by badgers digging.

There was a flurry of activity in the racecourse department and a great deal of head-scratching. Only when it got to Simon Claisse, the head of the department, was the April Fools joke sussed. At this point, the Jockey Club tried to call Barry's bluff by telling him that several high-powered meetings had been convened and that the Senior Steward was getting involved. As you'd expect, Big Ron, who twice finished fifth in the National during an illustrious riding career, was unruffled. ▩

A LOT HAS BEEN WRITTEN ABOUT A. P. MCCOY, our popular champ, this week – all of it, without exception, good. Just for some balance, here's what senior weighing-room colleague and great friend Carl Llewellyn – Welsh, so not at all chippy or anything – had to say about him following AP's 1,700th winner, at Uttoxeter. 'He's a miserable, selfish, spoilt, lazy, horrible bastard, a bad loser, very lucky to ride for Martin Pipe but continues to give the rest of us hope because he's useless with women. I bet you don't print that.' ▩

IF YOU HAVE BOOKED A SKIING HOLIDAY in Alpe d'Huez next week, let me be the first to offer you my commiserations. In case you think you've arrived there during a circus midgets convention, Alpe d'Whose, as Steve Drowne is inclined to call it, is the destination for fourteen Flat jockeys.

As well as the Wonderful Steven, the party also includes Messrs Quinn, Rutter, Weaver, O'Neill and Tebbutt, all of whom will be among those taking the shortest route from mountain top to alpine valley and forsaking Southwell for a week. Luke Harvey, who now informs the world of the day ahead's racing on Radio Five, also made the cut after Philip Robinson became a late withdrawal. 'At 5ft 6in I will be the jolly green giant of the party for the first time in my life,' Luke said confidently. 'As I was the last one in, I have to share a room with Alan "Arfur" Daly – that's the downside of it. He wanted to go skiing in the Netherlands but he's been talked out of it.' ▧

PRIDE COMES BEFORE A FALL. When jockey Tom Jenks was in Waterford for a wedding he hopped into a taxi to take him from his hotel to the church.

'You're Tom Jenks, aren't you?' asked the taxi driver.

'That's right, mate,' answered Tom, enormously chuffed because, let's face it, taxi drivers in his home town of Stow-on-the-Wold don't normally recognise him.

'Well,' added the driver, 'you don't get many rides these days, do you?' ▧

BLOODSTOCK AGENT LUKE LILLINGSTON married Tabitha Ross in Dumfries last Saturday. To celebrate the occasion he had a waistcoat made in the red and white racing colours of his maternal grandfather, the 5th Marquis of Abergavenny (colours which have recently been given to Luke, though I believe he has carried them before any horse). Halfway through the reception a friend who knows about these things told him what a lovely touch it was to have had the waistcoat made in his grandparent's colours. 'Thank you,' said Luke. 'Everyone else thinks I've just started supporting Manchester United.' ▧

CHESTER MOUNTS THE BIGGEST SECURITY OPERATION of any racecourse outside Aintree's Grand National meeting, mainly because it is so popular and so close to the town centre. From an eyrie in the old press box, a team of police survey twenty closed-circuit television cameras. So the chances are that anyone picking a pocket or two will have their collar felt by a plain-clothes copper with a cheery 'Smile, you're on Candid Camera.'

By last night – Chester's version of Ladies' Day – the zoom was almost worn out. 'The girls are out in their bingo dresses,' said the avuncular policeman in charge, with a wink. Bingo dresses? 'Yes,' he said. 'Eyes down.' ▩

JEAN-PAUL SARTRE, eat your heart out.

Trainer: 'What are you doing?'

Stable lad: 'Thinking, guv'nor.'

Trainer: 'What are you thinking about?'

Stable lad: 'Just because I'm thinking, it doesn't mean I'm thinking about something.' ▩

MY THANKS TO FRANCOPHILE SIR PETER O'SULLEVAN. Last week we mentioned that Jair du Cochet's jockey Jacques Ricou has a Dalmatian called Twister and a 'caniche' called Mimi, and we pondered what sort of breed a caniche is. Sir Peter says it's a poodle, which explains everything. A poodle owner could never win a Gold Cup. ▩

THREE DAYS IN, fully refreshed after a twelve-hour break between Sandown, the last day of last season, and Ludlow, the first day of the new, and it's the first 'festival' of the season, at Punchestown. It's a good chance to catch up with Irish friends, and I'll be looking up Tony Mullins, son of Paddy and Maureen, and brother of Willie, George, Tom and Sandra. As Maureen is one of eleven children pretty much everyone in Ireland is related to Tony, if not directly by marriage. He now trains and runs Dawn Invasion against Brave Inca today.

As a jockey Tony occasionally had run-ins with his legendary father because they both called it as they saw it. On one of these occasions he was riding in a twenty-runner maiden hurdle at Tipperary. Brendan Sheridan was riding the odds-on shot, Tony was on a 7–4 shot, and after that it was 10–1 the field. For a long way he tracked the odds-on shot but halfway down the back he looked up and realised that the favourite was on empty and two no-hopers had slipped the field. He set off in pursuit, caught one of them, but just failed by the narrowest of margins to catch the other.

When he returned to dismount, his father asked him what he'd been at.

'I was watching the odds-on shot,' explained Tony.

'You're not much of a rider,' said his father. 'You're at your best to ride one. Don't try to ride two.'

It was a salutary lesson, and he never tracked an odds-on shot again. ◼

A YOUNG AMATEUR had ridden out for Ted Smyth one day and asked the trainer at breakfast which race had, in his opinion, been his best. The amateur was expecting the answer to be the Wokingham which he'd recently won, so he was slightly surprised when the trainer, looking up from his *Sporting Life*, replied, 'A six-runner race at Brighton.' Our amateur asked why. 'Two of the runners were useless,' confided Ted, 'two weren't off, and I trained the other two!' ◼

UNLIKE MOST OTHER SPORTS, which rely upon the combatants on the pitch, as much of the colour in racing is provided by the spectators as it is by the competitors. It is therefore with some sadness that I report the passing of a legendary Irish racegoer, Jimmy 'The Buck' Ryan, who died in Fethard, Ireland on 18 October.

Even his slightly irreverent obituary in the local paper said 'he liked a drink or two … before breakfast'. Having twenty years ago struck a deal with the local priest, Jimmy was buried in Fethard's prime plot, opposite the doors of McCarthy's, the famous bar from which he was barred as often as he was allowed in. It is, nevertheless, a measure of Jimmy's character that a portrait of him has been commissioned by McCarthy's and the town has adopted his three-legged Guinness-drinking dog, Kaj, and his geese. Throughout his life he took the view that a job was purely a means to his next drink, so he spent time as a farmer, a fishmonger and a trucker; on building sites, in pubs, in restaurants, on ships, and even in the circus. On one occasion when he promised to deliver a goose to a local family in good time for Christmas lunch, he arrived late on Christmas Eve with the bird still flapping under his arm.

It was, however, his annual trip to Cheltenham around which his year centred. He would stop drinking for a month before so he could spare the cash for the meeting, where he would invariably stay at the Queens Hotel. He never booked a room though. If he was sober enough to make it up the stairs he would kip on a couch on the top landing. The length of his stay was indeterminable. He'd usually make it back in time for Listowel in September, and the bachelor festival in Lisdoonvarna was normally his last stop before returning to Fethard.

Shortly after he was buried, a friend who had missed his funeral, which was attended by publicans from across Britain, turned up at McCarthy's five minutes after closing time. On finding the doors locked he slipped across the road and into the graveyard to say a few prayers beside the spot where Jimmy had been laid to rest. Lo and behold, when he emerged the doors to the bar were wide open as a guest was leaving, so the friend went inside, bought a pint and suggested that Jimmy Ryan be canonised as the patron saint of drinkers.

A. P. MCCOY COULDN'T MAKE AN ENGAGEMENT to open a new function room at the Irish Oak, a pub in Cheltenham's Lower High Street, last Friday so he sent along three jockeys in the fervent hope that their aggregate fame would equal his. The jury, however, is out on whether the combined talents of Mick Fitzgerald, Carl Llewellyn and Mark Bradburne (an Irishman, a Welshman and a Scotsman – sounds like the formula for a bad joke) have the same appeal as one McCoy. So well known is Mark among Cheltenham's Irish, despite two Festival winners, that he spent most of the evening being addressed as Mark Bradbury. ▧

SOFT, SENSITIVE SOUTHERNERS BE WARNED. This is the sort of homespun Yorkshire philosophy we'll all have to get used to when Ascot goes north next summer. Harvey Smith was talking to a former trainer at the sales recently. They were mid-conversation when around the corner appeared larger-than-life bloodstock agent David Minton and his pencil-thin wife Juliet. 'When you see fat shepherd and skinny dog,' commented Harvey in a stage whisper plenty loud enough for the objects of his philosophy to hear, 'you can always tell who does all the effing work.'

IT IS WELL KNOWN that most successful jockeys are driven. In A. P. McCoy's case it's that obsession with winning; in Carl Llewellyn's case it's … well, money, to put it bluntly. He was recently sent the following spoof letter, purporting to be from IMC International but actually from Bindaree's owners Raymond and Caroline Mould.

> Dear Mr Llewellyn,
>
> We act on behalf of a company that manufactures a well-known breakfast cereal. We are currently looking for a familiar face in the sporting world to endorse a new product due to be launched at the beginning of April 2005.
>
> Our attention has been drawn to your photograph in the *Daily Telegraph* and we are most impressed. You are obviously very photogenic with exactly the appeal that we are searching for.
>
> We would be very grateful if you would kindly consider our client's proposition to be the face of our new product (a high-fibre, oat-based cereal to ease constipation). You would be involved in fronting an international advertising campaign to be shown on prime-time television and cinemas worldwide, and in advertisements in popular publications in the UK and abroad.
>
> Our aim, while promoting the product, is to dispel the embarrassment, taboos and myths so commonly associated with constipation; and to educate the general public about the importance of regular healthy bowel movements and how this

can be achieved with our breakfast cereal. We think that you would be perfect for this role: 'Carl Cracks Constipation', 'Llewellyn Loves His Oats', 'Llewellyn Loosens His Movements' etc. The fact that you have been voted 'Rear of the Year' by *Tatler*, achieved worldwide fame winning the Grand National twice, and no doubt have suffered yourself from constipation (along with an extraordinary 93.7 per cent of the population) makes you a very appealing choice for our client.

Although we are not, at this early stage, allowed to release our client's name, we can tell you that the product is wholly based on Welsh-grown oats, and that our client is prepared to offer you a financially very lucrative package.

We would be most interested if you would give this matter serious consideration and contact us at your earliest convenience.

Yours sincerely,
Cassandra B. St Davis

On top of the letter they had printed their own London number. 'He'd rung our Portuguese maid asking to speak to Cassandra four times before ten o'clock on the day he got the letter,' reports Caroline. 'The fourth time she told him that no one called Cassandra lived at the address, only a Mr and Mrs Mould. Even after that he rang once more to make sure.'

Carl unashamedly puts his hands up. 'The letter had me big time,' he admits. 'I was already counting the millions by the time the letter started getting ridiculous about constipation.'

THERE IS ALWAYS SOME PROBLEM, in my experience, with paradise. It's either too wet (Ireland), there are midges (Scotland), there's a war just up the road (the Caucasus Mountains), it's too far from anywhere (Patagonia), or there is a security issue (South Africa). And so it goes on.

It is in the latter's Cape Town that prominent British owner Simon Tindall, a publisher by trade, has recently bought a holiday home. Just to put you in the picture, Simon, 66, is one of our most enthusiastic owners. He owns a point-to-point yard in Sussex and has about a dozen horses in training divided between here and Ireland. Since he has owned this place, however, there have been four or five attempted robberies, one of them, when the television walked out, successful. To combat these intrusions he was contemplating decorating his back fence with some razor wire. The idea is, of course, that the next would-be burglar catches his what-nots on the wire and he returns home, eyes watering and no longer in the market for stallion syndication, to spread the word in a high-pitched voice that robbing Simon is not what it used to be.

So Simon was by the pool contemplating the security alternatives – moats, thorn hedges, barbed wire, broken glass stuck on the wall à la Heath House, Newmarket (Sir Mark Prescott's preferred method of keeping his apprentices within and nobblers without) – when his wife Caroline heard a crash round the back. Emerging was a local with an armful of CDs. Now, an armful of CDs may not weigh you down like a widescreen television or 'white goods' might, but have you ever tried running with a pile of them? They slip and slide and, quite honestly, if you're not a part-time juggler you might just as well be single-handedly carrying the fridge out while trying not to spill the milk in it. So despite the young man's athletic advantage he was handicapped by his booty.

There has been much talk here about whether home owners should be allowed to give burglars one barrel or two. But with little time to contemplate the pros and cons of that argument, or the government health warning attached to tackling intruders, our have-a-go hero – who, let's face it, is not built like a boxer and wouldn't be as quick between the wickets as he once was – saw his window of opportunity. Giving away weight and age – about 45 of each – he had a go (makes you proud to be British, this bit) in a most gentlemanly way. 'What are you doing?' he barked. 'Those aren't yours. Give me them at once. You bugger. Shove off etc.' Almost polite, he was. Indeed he did everything but ask him to square up under Marquis of Queensbury rules. And with CDs airborne he kicked the fellow, hard, in the arse.

The howling burglar, no longer clinging to Simon's music collection but to his own backside, his coccyx now tucked up nicely somewhere within his ribcage, dived into the bushes while Simon summoned a security guard. He was swiftly followed by an armed response unit for their first drive (and I mean 'drive' as the Countryside Alliance would understand it rather than *Top Gear*) of the day. And this is gratitude for you: everyone has told him what a fool he was to tackle the intruder. I say, 'Well done.' ▣

ON THE LAST COUNTRYSIDE MARCH a lady was accosted for wearing a full-length mink coat.

'Do you know how many animals died in order to make that coat?' asked an agitated anti-hunt protester on the side of the road.

'I've no idea,' said the lady, 'but let me ask you this question. Have you any idea how many animals I had to sleep with in order to get this coat?' ▣

IT IS A DANGEROUS JOB BEING A TRAINER. Charlie Mann had his foot broken by a horse that stamped on it a week ago. If you're in a hurry, as Lambourn trainers invariably are, you haven't got time to queue at the doctor's surgery. Instead, you go to the vet.

'You're only the second patient I've ever been able to hold a conversation with,' said the vet as he checked the X-rays.

'And who was the other?' asked the trainer.

'A cockatoo called Jim who came in three weeks ago,' replied the vet.

I wonder which one he got the most sense out of? ◼

IT IS NOT A RARE OCCURRENCE for trainers of jockeys to be caught speeding to the races, but when the opportunist trainer Charlie Mann was given the chance to offer mitigating circumstances, he grasped it in typical Mann fashion by replying that he was late for lunch with the Chief Constable of Thames Valley Police. You or I would applaud the answer. The magistrates thought differently. They gave him an extra point (four instead of three) and doubled his fine. ◼

FLASHING STEEL, in his attempt to make it third time lucky in the Gold Cup, should be coming over for a practice at Cheltenham's next meeting at the end of the month. At the moment he is the only racehorse owned by the former Irish Taoiseach Charlie Haughey, himself a considerable horseman who still, apparently, goes a good clip up Portmarnock beach.

One day, after he had been held up by government business, Haughey was late for a local meet of the Ward Union, which hunts a carted stag to the north-west of Dublin and is increasingly followed by what Bill Clinton once described as 'Dubs'. Mounted on his horse but with not a hound in sight, the Taoiseach came across a local farmer leaning on a gate.

'Could you tell me where the gentlemen went?' Haughey asked.

'The gentlemen,' said the farmer after a moment's contemplation, 'went 40 years ago.' ◼

GAY KINDERSLEY, the former amateur rider and trainer, is forever apologising about his first name. On Wednesday he was at it again when he stood up at a reception given by *The Field* to thank his hosts for their continued support of the National Hunt lady riders' title, won this year by Pip Jones. 'Sorry about my unfortunate Christian name,' he began. 'I was born in 1930 when gay meant happy, clap meant applause and only generals had aid[e]s.'

AT THE HEIGHT OF THEIR FAME, and for some reason unknown to me, the Three Degrees were a gay icon group. On Thursday night they played at Epsom. A few days earlier the course had received a call from someone who wished to have a few more details.

'The concert is after the last race,' said one of Epsom's secretaries.

'Tell me more about your facilities,' added the camp caller.

'Well,' explained our spokeswoman, 'I'd say the Queen's stand is our most impressive feature—'

'Oh I say!' interrupted the caller. 'That's even more interesting than the Three Degrees.'

FATHER SEAN BREEN, the famous tipping priest from Ireland, has been coming to the Festival for as long as he can remember. 'The only thing that's stopped me have been funerals,' he said. 'It's very inconsiderate of people to die just before Cheltenham.'

PETER CURLING HAS COME A LONG WAY SINCE HIS FIRST EXHIBITION, aged 14, in the canteen at Lambourn Engineering, as likely a starting place for one of the world's foremost equine artists as the Old Berks Hunt pantomime would be for an Oscar-winning actor.

Then his work sold for up to £20: now, you could add another three noughts and it's still a good investment.

He likes painting locations he's familiar with and that is evident with his Tipperary landscapes and scenes from Ballydoyle (he's been given the password) and Killeens (Edward O'Grady's establishment). Another string to his bow is his work in Venice. I always wondered if his going there was for a holiday but now I know. His studies of gondoliers in the Cannareggio are every bit as evocative as jockeys at the start of a race. I'm never going to get a job as an art critic, I know, but I can't recommend his work enough.

Apart from being a painter, Peter couldn't be Irish and live in Tipperary without a few horses of his own. One of them is Inca Trail, Best Mate's full-brother but, at the moment, half as good. Trained by Henrietta Knight, he's going novice chasing this season and the best, they hope, is yet to come. He's also had a bit of luck with a good looking but incredibly slow point-to-pointer called Hoch Magandy (a rather poetic Scottish phrase meaning 'sexual intercourse' for the purposes of recreation rather procreation).

Of course, being an artist is not without its moments. A few years ago he was commissioned to do a portrait by the Sultan of Brunei and, at roughly the same time, one of Celtic Swing for Peter Savill's wedding. When he was happy with the results, they were bubble-wrapped up in the studio and the Sultan's was shipped out to Brunei.

The great work of art was duly unwrapped at a ceremony by the Sultan himself. A picture of anticipation, he was delighted, though somewhat mystified, by the end result - a painting of Celtic Swing. Luckily, by this stage, Peter Savill hadn't quite got married, so the paintings could be swapped before he was presented with a portrait of the Sultan. ◙

JIM CULLOTY, who broke his arm at Taunton a month ago, tried everything to get back to ride Best Mate in the King George VI Chase at Kempton on Boxing Day. Nearing the moment when he had to make the agonising decision not to ride the horse, someone asked him what the chances were of his being fit to take the ride.

'It's not looking good,' said Jim.

'Oh well,' replied his questioner, who, thinking of Jim's mental well-being on Boxing Day and thinking it better that he didn't see the race, added the helpful suggestion, 'You'll just have to ring Thomas Cook, then.'

'It's no good,' replied Jim. 'I've tried every bone specialist in the business.' ◙